The Practical
Shakespeare

The Practical Shakespeare

THE PLAYS IN PRACTICE AND ON THE PAGE

Colin Butler

OHIO UNIVERSITY PRESS
ATHENS

Ohio University Press, Athens, Ohio 45701
www.ohio.edu/oupress
© 2005 by Colin Butler

Printed in the United States of America

Ohio University Press books are printed on acid-free paper ⊚ ™

12 11 10 09 08 07 06 05   5 4 3 2 1

Library of Congress Cataloging-in-Publication Data
Butler, Colin.
The practical Shakespeare : the plays in practice and on the page / Colin Butler.
    p. cm.
Includes bibliographical references and index.
ISBN 0-8214-1621-9 (cloth : alk. paper) — ISBN 0-8214-1622-7 (pbk. : alk. paper)
1. Shakespeare, William, 1564-1616—Technique. 2. Shakespeare, William, 1564-1616—
Dramatic production. 3. Theater—Production and direction. 4. Drama—Technique.
I. Title.
  PR2995.B88 2005
  822.3'3—dc22

2004030580

Contents

PREFACE   vii

DE WITT SKETCH OF THE SWAN THEATER   ix

1.   FIRST STEPS: Writing for Performance; Using the Physical Features of the Playhouses; Sound Effects and Music; Writing with Specific Actors in Mind; "The Purpose of Playing"   1

2.   ENTRANCES AND EARLY WORDS   24

3.   EXITS   42

4.   CHARACTERIZATION   60

5.   SCENES NOT SHOWN   81

6.   CONTROLLING THE AUDIENCE'S RESPONSES (I): Places; Times of Day and Night; The Bible   98

7.   CONTROLLING THE AUDIENCE'S RESPONSES (II): Long Plot Lines; Setting Up Situations Early; Risk Management; Two Storms   115

8.   UNTRUTHFUL BEHAVIOR: Telling and Acting Lies in *The Merry Wives of Windsor, Romeo and Juliet, Much Ado about Nothing, All's Well That Ends Well, Measure for Measure, King Lear, Cymbeline,* and *The Winter's Tale*   131

9.   STAGING DECISIVE MOMENTS: The Letter Scene in *Twelfth Night,* The Observation Scene in *Troilus and Cressida,* and Leontes' Denunciation of Hermione to Camillo in *The Winter's Tale*   147

10.   PROLOGUES AND CHORUSES   166

NOTES   183

BIBLIOGRAPHY   191

INDEX   197

Preface

This book provides a comprehensive, plain-English introduction to the way Shakespeare's plays are written. It is designed for students and teachers of English literature and for general playgoers, too. A different aspect of the plays is examined in each of its ten chapters, which are free-standing and which can be consulted individually. For greater convenience, each chapter is subdivided, and each subdivision has its own heading to show its focus of interest. To further improve access, the index at the back of the book lists topics that are discussed as well as names of authors and play titles. There is ample quotation, too, so that readers can understand a point even if they do not know the play. And there are selected cross-references to show the range of Shakespeare's inventiveness.

The way this book is constructed allows it to be used in different ways. For example, a student with an assignment on *A Midsummer Night's Dream* can easily look up how the "hempen home-spuns" make their first entrance; how their understanding of a play differs from Shakespeare's; how Puck is characterized; how Shakespeare gets the plot lines of Titania and Bottom to cross; and why some scenes are not staged but reported. Teachers need precise information, too, but they also have to take a larger view of the plays they are teaching; so, throughout, every significant point made about Shakespeare's playwriting technique is compared with one or more instances besides, and supported by quotation as well. And general playgoers know that, if they have insight into what Shakespeare does in one play, they can follow his other plays much more easily, since he is a very consistent playwright.

The reference text used in this book is the widely available second edition of The Riverside Shakespeare (Boston: Houghton Mifflin, 1997). For the reader's convenience, speakers' names that are abbreviated in Riverside are given in full here; they are followed by a colon, not a period; and all editorial square brackets have been removed.

I have inevitably incurred a large number of intellectual debts while writing this book. Published research into Shakespeare's life and work is copious and, in the notes and bibliography, I have tried to acknowledge the many borrowings I have made. In particular, I am grateful to the various editors of the New Cambridge Shakespeare, the Oxford Shakespeare, and the Arden Shakespeare. Their work has never been far from my elbow, and I have taken full advantage of their scholarship and insights.

More personally, I thank Professor Andrew Gurr, former director of the Renaissance Texts Centre in the University of Reading, England, for reading this book in draft and saving me from a number of pitfalls. He has also very generously answered a number of follow-up questions. Any errors that remain are mine. Further, I thank the master and fellows of St. John's College, Cambridge, England, for their invaluable hospitality while I was first assembling my material; in the University of Utrecht, Holland, Drs J.S.M. Savenije (University Librarian), Drs Klaas van der Hoek (Curator of Manuscripts) and Drs Koert van der Horst (Curator of Manuscripts) for their help with Johannes de Witt's sketch of the Swan theater; Nancy Basmajian, managing editor of Ohio University Press, and her staff, for their lynx-eyed editing and unstinting practical advice; Beth Pratt, production manager of Ohio University Press, and Steve Kress, for the elegant and sensitive design; David Sanders, director of Ohio University Press, for his constant support throughout this project; and Angela J. Butler, whose assistance with the typescript has been indispensable.

De Witt Sketch of the Swan Theater.

Johannes de Witt, a Dutch visitor, was in London in 1596 and wrote about the playhouses he visited to his friend, Arend van Buchell. He included a sketch of the recently opened Swan theater. The original sketch is lost, but van Buchell's copy of it has been preserved. The sketch is the only contemporary picture of the interior of an Elizabethan playhouse available to us.

Conspicuous are the three-tiered enclosure; the platform stage with standing room on three sides; the flanking doors in the tiring-house facade (the screen at the back of the stage, behind which was the tiring-house, or dressing room); the lords' rooms forming a gallery at the back of the stage; the two column-like stage posts supporting the roof over the stage; the hut above the roof of the stage with the playhouse flag flying from it; and the trumpeter, who would signal the beginning of the play. There is no curtain and no scenery, just a bench that can easily be carried on and off. No trapdoor is visible, there is no central opening or arras, and it is not clear whether the sides of the stage are covered, though they normally would be. The light is obviously daylight.

Excavations of the Rose theater show that the London playhouses were not all exactly alike. But the platform stage with the tiring-house facade at the back, flanking doors, a roof or canopy over the stage, and the enclosed shape were recurrent features.

De Witt Sketch of the Swan Theater.

Chapter 1

FIRST STEPS

Writing for Performance; Using the Physical Features of the Playhouses; Sound Effects and Music; Writing with Specific Actors in Mind; "The Purpose of Playing"

I

Differences between writing for reading and writing for performance. Using the two flanking doors at the back of the stage for entrances and exits. Props and the book-keeper. Wall, Moonshine, and some of the pitfalls of literalism in A Midsummer Night's Dream.

Modern editions of *A Midsummer Night's Dream* routinely head up act 1, scene 2, with "*Enter* QUINCE *the carpenter and* SNUG *the joiner and* BOTTOM *the weaver and* FLUTE *the bellows-mender and* SNOUT *the tinker and* STARVELING *the tailor.*" A result of this stage direction—it marks the first entrance of these characters in the play—is that, if you are reading *A Midsummer Night's Dream,* you know before you get to the characters themselves what all their names are and what they do for a living. But Shakespeare did not write his plays to be read, he wrote them to be performed, and writing for performance is very different from writing for reading. If you write for performance, you have to think about what the audience[1] will see even before anyone speaks; what it will hear in addition to the words themselves—for instance, a fanfare or thunder; and in what styles it will hear the dialogue delivered—for instance, in what accents and tones of voice. You also have to think about the order in which you want information given to the audience and whether you want that information imparted directly or indirectly. Entrances can be very complex events, and no two are exactly alike.

As far as Shakespeare was concerned, entrances, like exits, would normally be made through one of two flanking doorways in the tiring-house facade at the back of the stage. One was toward the left-hand side and one was toward the right. In *A Midsummer Night's Dream,* the artisans make their first entrance through one door as Helena is exiting through the other, and, virtually without a break, the stage is now their space. Before they start speaking, they are seen. Although nominally Athenian, they will be wearing the coarse clothes of Elizabethan workingmen. That is why Puck later calls them "hempen home-spuns" (3.1). They may be wearing leather aprons and woolen caps as well: when Shakespeare came to write *Coriolanus,* he had Menenius refer to workingmen as "apron-men" (4.6), and Coriolanus tells of their throwing their caps in the air (1.1). In any printed version of *A Midsummer Night's Dream,* Helena's exit and the artisans' entrance seem to take place one after the other, but, in performance, the audience experiences an overlap, and that automatically leads to comparisons being made. Just the way the artisans look and move contrasts them socially with Helena and her class. It is a contrast that Shakespeare could count on his audiences recognizing and registering instinctively. Elizabethan society was stratified socially; so were playhouse audiences; and so is *A Midsummer Night's Dream.*

Since Quince comes on first, he can be assumed to be the leader, and Shakespeare's audiences might actually know some of the actors coming onstage by sight. Will Kemp(e), for example, played Bottom[2] and was famous for his comic performances. He would generate expectations of humor just by being seen. Shakespeare liked to remind his audiences that they were watching actors at work as they watched his plays. Far from spoiling illusions, these reminders actually increase the audience's involvement and interest. In act 3, scene 3, of *The Merry Wives of Windsor,* for example, Falstaff's page is sent off to tell his master that Mistress Ford is alone, while Mistress Page, intending to surprise Falstaff, goes off to her hiding place. As she does so, Mistress Ford calls out, "Mistress Page, remember you your cue," and Mistress Page replies, "I warrant thee, if I do not act it, hiss me." In terms of the plot, there is no need for these lines. What they do is remind the audience that it is experiencing an art form that, for good as well as for ill, lives through performance. They also encourage it to think that what is about to happen is well worth waiting for.

Shakespeare routinely employs such "actors at work" reminders so deftly that it seems impossible that they could go wrong. But they can, if the thinking behind them is wrong. During the discussion of how *Pyramus and*

Thisby is to be performed, Bottom proposes two such reminders to avoid frightening the ladies (3.1). To offset Pyramus's suicide, he urges Quince to "tell them that I Pyramus am not Pyramus, but Bottom the weaver. This will put them out of fear." And to offset the lion, he says, "Nay; you must name his [Snug's] name, and half his face must be seen through the lion's neck." Like Shakespeare, Bottom understands that drama has power, but Bottom's response to that understanding and Shakespeare's diverge. Shakespeare uses the "actors at work" factor to augment drama's power, since he knows that he can control it. But Bottom, hesitant about drama's power, wants to misuse the "actors at work" factor in order to reduce it. This is rather like removing some of the spark plugs of a Ferrari to make it easier to handle.

When the artisans speak, they use prose, whereas their social superiors speak verse. Quince speaks first, and Shakespeare wants the others to cluster round him so that Bottom can tell them, "Masters, spread yourselves" (1.2). By this means, Shakespeare ensures that the audience will get a good view of them all. Appropriately, Quince is named first as well, and his name, when it is heard, is close enough to "quoins" or "quines" ("wooden wedges") to suggest a carpenter.[3] He might even be carrying a wooden rule: in *Julius Caesar,* Murellus identifies the rule and leather apron as signs of a carpenter's trade (1.1). Just as appropriately, the self-important Bottom is named second, but it is not until line 64 that the audience hears the last name and occupation—Snug the joiner—and, by then, a lot of exposition has been accomplished, including the title of the artisans' play, who its leading characters are, and why it is to be put on.

What Quince says when he first speaks is "Is all our company here?" so it is reasonable to ask where "here" actually is. One editor writes, "This scene is to be imagined as taking place somewhere in the 'town' . . . of Athens, though no scenery or properties need have been used to indicate this in Shakespeare's theatre." Another locates the scene as "Athens. Quince's house."[4] In fact, "here" is not a geographical location but a dramatic concept, and it is intended to contrast with other "here"'s—the ducal palace, various places in the wood—as the play unfolds. Place as a dramatic concept and stages without scenery, like Shakespeare's, obviously go together.

All props would be movable—chairs or benches, for example, that could be brought on and taken off either by the actors or by stagehands. The bookkeeper of Shakespeare's company would have a fair copy of the complete play (hence his title), and, just as in any modern production, props would be noted in it to ensure their readiness to hand. The bookkeeper (always male) would also remind actors of their next entrance.[5] Quince identifies himself to the audience as the bookkeeper as well as the play maker of

Pyramus and Thisby by saying, "In the mean time I will draw a bill of properties, such as our play wants" (1.2). In rehearsal, it also falls to Quince to help out with the cues (3.1; see also 4.1, when Bottom awakes).

As it happens, although it dwells on some of the practicalities of putting on a play, *A Midsummer Night's Dream* is technically less demanding than plays Shakespeare had already written or plays he was to write later (it is in the region of his twelfth). It requires neither balcony nor trapdoor nor (as is explained shortly) a discovery space. In fact, it needs little more by way of physical facilities than does *Pyramus and Thisby* itself, and what they are is made clear when Quince says to his troupe, "[A]nd here's a marvail's convenient place for our rehearsal. This green plot shall be our stage, this hawthorn brake our tiring-house" (3.1). In other words, an open playing area with changing and storage space behind it (the tiring-house) is enough. A rehearsal isn't a performance, of course, but Quince adds, as if it were self-evident, "[A]nd we will do it in action as we will do it before the Duke," implying that what is rehearsed on the "green plot" will transfer directly to a private indoor location for the real thing. And, of course, what will work in private will also work in a playhouse. It is true that there is a wall in *Pyramus and Thisby,* but a prop made by Quince or Snug would do. (There are walls in *Henry VI, Part Two* [4.10], and in *Romeo and Juliet* [2.1], and, in those cases, dialogue alone is enough.) But the wall in *Pyramus and Thisby* is a prime example of how Shakespeare can turn even the most mundane detail into high-quality play making. Because the hempen home-spuns are too literal in their thinking, Snout has to act the part of Wall. This causes a clash between the wall understood literally and the wall understood as part of theater with an actor in the role. Unintended humor is the result. Thisby says that her "cherry lips" have often kissed Wall's "stones" (one meaning of which is "testicles"). She then kisses his/its "hole" (5.1).

Lighting gives rise to a comparable point. For Shakespeare, dialogue alone is enough, for example, "Ill met by moonlight, proud Titania" (2.1). But the hempen home-spuns feel that they need an actor, a bush of thorns, and a lantern. To show that here, too, their thinking is too literal, Shakespeare once more lands them in a muddle of their own making. The dying Pyramus mistakenly says, "Moon, take thy flight" (5.1) instead of "Tongue, take thy flight" (that is, "Tongue, fall silent"), and Starveling, who is playing Moonshine, thinks he is being cued off the stage; so he exits, taking his moonlight with him. This would not plunge the play into darkness, since, whether in a private venue or a playhouse, performance and audience always shared the same light, that is, either candlelight or daylight. However, as Hippolyta realizes, moonlight is still technically needed within *Pyramus and Thisby* if Thisby is to find Pyramus's corpse for the play's big finish. "How chance Moonshine is gone before Thisby comes back and finds her lover?" she asks (5.1). Had words been used for moonlight instead of Starveling, the problem would not have arisen.

II

The arras and the discovery space. The advantage of not using the discovery space in A Midsummer Night's Dream. *Green rushes on stage. The balcony.*

While Shakespeare's minimum requirement might be a playing area accessed from a changing area behind it, his plays, taken together, show that he could make creative use of all the features the various venues of his day offered him. In the public playhouses, these features included a platform stage about five feet off the ground, covered around the sides and surrounded by a standing space or yard; three tiers of seated accommodation forming an enclosure; a fixed screen (the tiring-house facade) across the back of the stage with the tiring-house behind it; a trapdoor in the stage, the trap being accessible from underneath as well; the two flanking doorways (already mentioned) for entrances and exits; possibly a central opening between the two flanking doorways, covered with an arras or a painted curtain; a balcony ("gallery" is the better word) above the tiring-house facade containing "lords' rooms" for the wealthy and providing additional acting space if required; two pillars, or stage posts, supporting a decorated canopy over the stage called the "heavens"; and a hut above the "heavens" from which deities could be lowered and raised by unseen stagehands using winding gear. Right at the top, a flag displayed the insignia of the theater. A trumpet was sounded when a play was about to start. And Shakespeare could count on lively acoustics to ensure the audibility of soliloquies and asides.[6]

However, listing the characteristics of Shakespeare's venues is like listing the instruments in an orchestra: it is not that they are there but how they are employed that matters. So, starting with the arras, here are some of the ways Shakespeare transformed what he had to work with.

An arras (originally a cloth woven in Arras, France) is a tapestry suspended by its upper edge and probably divided. An arras (or a painted curtain) placed over the central opening created a concealed recess that could be used in a number of different ways. First, large props could be kept in it and slid out from it as needed. These might include a couch, as in *Pericles,* or a four-poster bed, as in *Romeo and Juliet* or *Othello* (stage beds were narrower than their real-life counterparts, which were normally the size of a double bed). Large props might also include a throne, or even two: if there are a king and queen in the play, as in *Hamlet* or *Macbeth,* then each has a "chair of state."[7] Second, because the space behind the arras is relatively wide and is connected to the tiring-house, it can be used, in conjunction with the arras, for grand entrances and exits. Third, a closed arras provides an ad hoc place of concealment. In *Much Ado about Nothing,* Borachio, telling how he was surprised by Don Pedro and Claudio while he was perfuming a musty room, says, "I whipt me behind the arras" (1.3). In *Henry IV, Part One,* Falstaff, hunted by the Sheriff, is ordered by Prince Hal, "Go hide thee behind the arras" (2.4). And in *The Merry Wives of Windsor,* when the Falstaff of that play wants to hide from Mistress Page, he declares, "She shall not see me, I will ensconce me behind the arras" (3.3). When used like this, the arras changes from being a neutral stage feature to being a constituent of the plays concerned and a moral indicator, too, since the characters just mentioned have distinct question marks over them. That the arras can have very high dramatic potential is shown in *Hamlet.* Polonius, in Gertrude's closet, "*hides behind the arras*" (3.4). When he makes a noise, Hamlet "*[k]ills Polonius through the arras,*" and only when Hamlet "*[p]arts the arras and discovers Polonius*" does he learn that he has not killed Claudius. "Discovers," by the way, means "reveals" or "uncovers," not "finds," when the arras is involved—hence "discovery space," the root meaning of which becomes obvious if a dash is added ("dis-covery space").

In the past, the discovery space has sometimes been called an "inner stage," but while Shakespeare uses it to extend main-stage action, it is far too cramped and out of sight for full-scale acting to take place inside it; so characters either step into it or step out of it. Stepping out, if properly prepared, can be a major dramatic moment and one that is also open to considerable variation, as a comparison between *The Winter's Tale* and *The Tempest* reveals. In *The Winter's Tale,* an act of stepping out marks the climax of the play. Paulina says, "[P]repare / To see the life as lively mock'd as ever / Still sleep mock'd death" (5.3; "mock'd" means "imitated"). She then "*draws a curtain, and discovers Hermione standing like a statue.*" Leontes, captivated, half orders and half pleads, "Do not draw the curtain" ("draw" now meaning "close," not "open"), and, shortly after, Hermione comes down from her pedestal and comes forward onto the main stage through the parted arras, symbolically reintegrated into life. Thanks to what are called embedded stage directions—that is, stage directions that are contained in the dialogue—there can be no doubt that Hermione comes down from where she is standing and then comes forward. Before Hermione moves, Paulina says, "If you can behold it, / I'll make the statue move indeed, *descend,* / And take you by the hand" (5.3; italics added). Then, when the moment comes for

Hermione to do that, Paulina commands, "'Tis time
more; *approach*" (5.3; italics added).

Embedded stage directions in fact occur througho
and they shed invaluable light on his own thoughts a
of his plays. If, for example, we want to know how
sario" as act 1, scene 5, of *Twelfth Night* becomes incr
is no need to speculate, since, in act 2, scene 2, Viola 1
view of me; indeed so much / That methought her eyes had lost her tongue,
/ For she did speak in starts distractedly." Or if we want an idea of the behavior of the hempen home-spuns in act 3, scene 1, of *A Midsummer Night's
Dream* after Bottom returns transformed into an ass, we can consult Puck's
self-serving account in the next scene. It begins:

> When they him spy,
> As wild geese that the creeping fowler eye,
> Or russet-pated choughs, many in sort
> (Rising and cawing at the gun's report),
> Sever themselves and madly sweep the sky,
> So, at his sight, away his fellows fly[.]

These reported gestures may seem larger than life but, unlike television or
film, the stage generally requires calculated exaggeration if it is to communicate precisely and clearly with its audiences.

With their reunification, Hermione and Leontes reach their dramatic
terminus. Although they live on after *The Winter's Tale* is completed, the play
itself has nothing more to say about them. But when, in act 5, scene 1, of
The Tempest, Prospero "*discovers* FERDINAND *and* MIRANDA *playing at chess,*"
he ushers in a situation that, consistent with the youth and evolving circumstances of the chess players, is inherently open-ended. Prospero has promised to show Alonso "a wonder," but the lines that follow his action are not
quite that ("wrangle" means "quarrel" or "argue"):

> MIRANDA: Sweet lord, you play me false.
> FERDINAND: No, my dearest love,
> I would not for the world.
> MIRANDA: Yes, for a score of kingdoms you should wrangle,
> And I would call it fair play.

Is Ferdinand really cheating? If so, what does that say about the honor he affirms to Prospero in act 4, scene 1? And is Miranda really prepared to endorse

eating for "a score of kingdoms"? Their lines provoke questions more
dily than answers precisely because Miranda and Ferdinand are still characters in the making. When they step out onto the main stage, Alonso
greets them with love and looks forward to their marriage. But *The Tempest*
is set after the fall of man, not before it, so when Miranda naively exclaims,
"How beauteous mankind is! O brave new world / That has such people
in't!" Prospero feels compelled to add, "'Tis new to thee" as a worldly-wise
corrective.

The discovery space's capacity for holding large items can likewise be
turned to dramatic advantage—for example, if Juliet's four-poster bed in
Romeo and Juliet is not manhandled onto the stage for act 4, scene 3, but re-
tained in the discovery space.[8] On this assumption, the arras would be parted
as Juliet and the Nurse enter, and, when Juliet "*falls upon her bed, within the
curtains,*" she would close the bed curtains around herself, the bed itself remaining visible at the back of the stage. This simultaneous use of closed bed
curtains and main stage would express scenically the play's major divisions
at this point. Behind the bed curtains is Juliet, isolated from her family and
committed to her concealed intentions, while, on the main stage, preparations for her imposed wedding to Paris gather pace. When the Nurse "*[d]raws
back the curtains*" in act 4, scene 5, she would reopen the bed curtains and
discover what she believes to be Juliet's corpse. This would reconnect Juliet
with the main stage, providing a focal point for the highly ironic interaction
of subterfuge on the one hand and parental grief on the other that takes
place in front of her before the arras is finally closed. Even if the arras is not
left open but closed at the end of act 4, scene 3, and then reopened for the
beginning of act 4, scene 5, its prominence in the center of the tiring-house
facade would make possible the same message from the stage during act 4,
scene 4, with little, if any, loss of force.

It is possible, though not certain, that the discovery space also housed the
Capulets' tomb in act 5 of *Romeo and Juliet*,[9] thereby connecting it symbolically with Juliet's bed, which would have been moved out of sight in the
meantime. In *Much Ado about Nothing,* the discovery space might likewise
have housed a tomb, namely, the one Hero is supposed to be buried in (5.3).
If it did, there would be two immediate gains. First, a substantial piece of
stage furniture could be kept ready but out of sight until the play required
it. Second, *Much Ado about Nothing* is a comedy; that is, it moves toward a
happy ending. A tomb that was uncovered for the act of penance, then covered up again as the characters leave the stage to wedding talk, would signal
in clear terms that the play's worst moments were over, especially as word
of Hero's innocence is already spreading.

Can it happen that the discovery space is not the ideal option it appears to be? In *A Midsummer Night's Dream,* Titania requires a place to sleep from act 2, scene 2, to act 3, scene 1, when she is awakened by Bottom's singing; and her occupying, then stepping out from, a curtained discovery space seems the obvious solution. But Oberon identifies her actual sleeping place as "a *bank* where the wild thyme blows" (2.1; italics added); so Titania can just as easily sleep to one side of the playing area on a decorated bench. Such an arrangement would be advantageous in private performance. It would also keep the audience mindful of Titania during the involved chain of events that results in Bottom eventually waking her (that chain of events is discussed in chapter 7, section I). And it would allow the audience to witness the full process of Titania waking up and falling in love with Bottom as he sings.

Or she can sleep not on a bench but on a heap of the green rushes routinely used for covering the stage. (Peter Quince's "green plot" [3.1] can refer to the real rushes strewn on the playing area as well as to the notional floor of the wood outside Athens.) Rushes were part of life in Shakespeare's day. They were strewn on domestic floors as well as on playhouse stages, a practice that finds its way into *The Taming of the Shrew* (4.1), *Romeo and Juliet* (1.4), and, more sinisterly, *Cymbeline* (2.2), when Jachimo emerges from the trunk in Imogen's bedchamber with the name of Tarquin on his lips. Rushes were also strewn in the streets if a royal procession were due, as happens in *Henry IV, Part Two,* as act 5, scene 5, opens ("*Enter* STREWERS OF RUSHES"). Even so, sleeping on rushes might sound farfetched, except that, in *Henry IV, Part One,* Glendower, translating for Lady Mortimer, says to Mortimer,

> She bids you on the wanton rushes lay you down,
> And rest your gentle head upon her lap,
> And she will sing the song that pleaseth you,
> And on your eyelids crown the god of sleep.
>
> (3.1)

So Titania's sleeping on rushes, while arguably less practical, is a possibility.

When Shakespeare has Bottom tell his fellow artisans to spread themselves, "spread" doesn't mean in a straight line facing forward, as it would on a proscenium-arch stage. For, with an in-the-round audience, spreading implies depth as well as breadth. The hempen home-spuns would, of course, spread themselves in the horizontal plane. But the vertical plane was at Shakespeare's disposal as well, thanks to the balcony above the stage and the space beneath it through the trapdoor.

In a playhouse, the balcony was reachable through the tiring-house by steps or a ladder out of sight of the audience, and it provided acting space "aloft," or "above." Analysis has shown that Shakespeare places only a very few actors aloft at any one time, that they are relatively static, and that their speeches are brief. This suggests limited space, as would be consistent with temporarily taking over one of the lords' rooms.[10] Even in one of Shakespeare's most laborious scenes—hauling up the dying Antony in *Antony and Cleopatra* (4.15)—only the boys playing Cleopatra, Charmian, Iras, and one or two maids are actually aloft. Exactly how they managed to heave up an adult male from the stage below is open to conjecture, but the text requires it and concedes simultaneously that it is not easy:

> CLEOPATRA: Here's sport indeed! How heavy weighs my lord!
> Our strength is all gone into heaviness,
> That makes the weight. . . .

Shakespeare knew all about playhouse balconies from personal experience: he looked up at them, stood in them, and, like Prospero in *The Tempest* (3.3), looked down from them. Their potential fired his imagination, and their symbolical integration into his plays is seamless. For example, in *Romeo and Juliet,* Juliet comes onstage "*above*" in act 2, scene 2, and Romeo says, "But soft, what light through yonder window breaks? / It is the east, and Juliet is the sun." This is hopeful passion speaking, so Romeo is looking up. But by act 3, scene 5, the tragedy is intensifying, so the scene begins with "ROMEO *and* JULIET *aloft,*" and, when Romeo leaves Juliet, "*He goeth down*" onto the stage in full view of the audience, using the much-mentioned "cords made like a tackled stair" that, in act 2, scene 4, the Nurse had been told to expect from Romeo's man and that may well have been the selfsame rope ladder "with a pair of anchoring hooks" featured in act 3, scene 1, of *The Two Gentlemen of Verona.* Juliet goes down as well, but she does so separately and out of sight through the tiring-house, and, when she reenters for her exchange with Lady Capulet, the stage ceases to be the garden Romeo descended into and is instead an interior room.[11] (Romeo's departure is discussed in chapter 3, section II.)

Nothing stands still in *Romeo and Juliet.* Taken together, these scenes show the balcony being used dynamically to communicate emotional and physical movement in two directions: rising to togetherness and descending to separateness. This is a big advance on the early comedy *The Two Gentlemen of Verona,* in which the balcony is used statically. In that play, Silvia is located "*above at her window*" (4.2), and Proteus is down on the stage. This vertical arrangement symbolizes Silvia's moral superiority over Proteus and her emotional remoteness from him, too. Proteus would certainly like to join Silvia, but Silvia will have none of it and is not going to change her mind. The fixed gap between Silvia "*above*" and Proteus below on the main stage expresses theatrically the fixed moral and relational gap between them.

Since physical elevation and elevated virtue naturally go together, Shakespeare's putting Silvia higher than Proteus is a straightforward piece of theater. But, in *Richard III,* it is with relish for the not-so-straightforward that Shakespeare puts Richard, Duke of Gloucester, aloft, for virtuous is the one thing Richard is not. In act 3, scene 7, Richard needs the backing of the Lord Mayor and citizens, so he is persuaded by Buckingham to adopt an image of piety and play hard to get. Buckingham remains onstage to contrast, in best public relations fashion, "this virtuous prince" (Richard) with Edward, "lulling on a lewd love-bed." Then, "*Enter* RICHARD *of* GLOUCESTER *aloft, between two* BISHOPS." To the audience, though not to the mayor, aldermen, and citizens, the hypocrisy of Buckingham and Richard is blatant. But what really gives this scene its impact is its verticality: Richard's being above the main stage between the bishops implies godliness and the high moral qualities of kingship, which not only Buckingham but every person in the audience knows he lacks.

Richard of Gloucester displays nerve as well as theatricality as he bluffs his way through a high-risk situation in an exposed location. When, with *Richard II,* Shakespeare embarked on his second cycle of history plays—it was eventually to extend through the two *Henry IV* plays to *Henry V*—he again found expressive use for the balcony, but the theatrical figure occupying it this time is so weak that he will shortly lose his crown. Richard II's appearance with Carlisle, Aumerle, Scroop and Salisbury "*on the walls*" of Flint Castle (3.3)—that is, on the balcony—is the prelude to royal disgrace. Following his exclamation, "Down court! down king!," Richard and his entourage descend to the aptly-named base court. The symbolism of Richard's moving from high to low is obvious and is meant to be so. An exchange between Bullingbrook and Northumberland gives him a certain amount of time to make his way down, but it is brief enough to suggest that a dramatic pause is intended before Richard comes onto the main stage, to be greeted with mock subservience by Bullingbrook.

It is possible that Richard comes onto the main stage through one of the flanking doors,[12] but the balcony can be used in conjunction with the central opening as well. In *Henry V,* Henry begins act 3, scene 3, by taking up his position "*before the gates*" of Harflew (Harfleur) after "*some* CITIZENS *on the walls*" have taken up theirs. That is, Henry and his train are onstage looking toward the central opening (the arras would be closed) and the balcony above, where the citizens are.[13] There is a temporariness and a tension in this visual arrangement, since, normally, a king should be aloft and the citizens below. However, Henry's threat of force majeure is followed by the governor's capitulation and, when Henry orders, "Open your gates," the arras is drawn apart. The governor and, possibly, the citizens having already left the balcony, the victorious Henry enters the gates of Harfleur with Exeter, exiting the stage through the central opening while a flourish rings out. In this scene, the balcony and the central opening are combined to provide an impressive visual and aural demonstration of power politics. (The Chorus's introduction to this scene is discussed in chapter 10, section III.)

III

The trapdoor. The stage posts as places of concealment. The painted "heavens" and the descents of deities. Contemporary allusions. The Globe's flag.

As mentioned in section II of this chapter, the vertical plane of the Shakespearean stage extends downward as well as upward if the space beneath the stage is used; and the total playing area can be construed theologically if the trapdoor is understood to represent the mouth of hell, for then human affairs can be situated onstage between the "heavens" above and hell below. For example, there is a spirit-raising scene in *Henry VI, Part Two* (1.4), in which a circle is formed and "*the Spirit riseth*" through the trapdoor; and when the command is given, "Descend to darkness and the burning lake!" the Spirit exits the way it entered ("*Exit Spirit sinking down again*"). In a note to "*the Spirit riseth,*" Michael Hattaway writes, "The circle may very well have been marked out by a circle of lighted candles" and adds, "Spirits customarily entered through the stage trap."[14]

The *Henry VI* plays were written very early in Shakespeare's career and did much to establish him as a rising star. *Macbeth,* on the other hand, was written when his career was some three-quarters over and he was a made man. Yet when Macbeth seeks out the Weïrd Sisters (4.1), Shakespeare happily returns to connecting evil entities with the trapdoor. After the Third Apparition leaves the stage through the trapdoor, the Witches' cauldron is evidently removed the same way, since Macbeth asks, "Why sinks that cauldron?" The theatrical effectiveness of the trap's use here is well calculated. It is the forces of evil that make the cauldron sink and Macbeth who has to ask why. This shows where the balance of control lies. A balance of control is not, of course, the same thing as a balance of power. The forces of evil do not make Macbeth do anything, but their weasel words nudge him toward conclusions that will be his downfall. One is that he should kill Macduff in order to "make assurance double sure" (leading on, when he learns that

Macduff has fled to England, to the resolve to murder his family); the other is that he will die a natural death.

The most famous uses of the trap, however, probably occur in *Hamlet*. First, the ghost of Hamlet's father must exit through the trapdoor as "[t]he glow-worm shows the matin to be near," since it (the Ghost) calls out "Swear" from various places under the stage (1.5). The Ghost seems to think that it is in purgatory. Nevertheless, as it exits, Hamlet exclaims, "And shall I couple hell?" Very probably, Hamlet's mind has moved on to the punishment that he would incur himself, were he to avenge his father's murder. (The point is returned to toward the end of the next paragraph.)

Second, the open trap serves as Ophelia's grave (5.1) and, as such, it accumulates a multiplicity of meanings as the scene progresses. Initially, it is associated with Ophelia's suspect death by drowning. Then, after Hamlet and Horatio enter, the first skull thrown up reminds Hamlet of Cain, "that did the first murder!"—a condemnatory link with Claudius, who has murdered his brother. The most famous skull in English literature—that of Yorick, the king's jester—is subsequently handed up, and it evokes the gruesomeness and mystery of death as well as Hamlet's anger with Gertrude. Love, bereavement, anger, and revenge come together as Hamlet and Laertes fight in the trap. Andrew Gurr and Mariko Ichikawa write of this development, "To the symbol-conscious Elizabethan audience . . . jumping into the trap . . . confirmed Hamlet's readiness to enter hell like Laertes in pursuit of his revenge. Revengers paid the price of damnation for the blood they drew."[15] Eventually, the trapdoor is closed over Ophelia, the stage is cleared for the next scene, and Claudius's dissembling "This grave shall have a living monument" remains with the audience as an earnest of death and evil deeds to come.

To either side of the trapdoor and toward the front corners of the stage were the stage posts, the two heavy timbers that supported the stage's roof or canopy. They were painted to look like marble in the Swan, and probably in other theaters, too, and they added to the arras or to specially constructed mobile props as alternative hiding places for characters. Characters "concealing" themselves behind stage posts remain in full view of the audience, and that has two consequences. The first is that the audience has to be told what they are supposed to be up to. In *A Midsummer Night's Dream,* Oberon declares, "I am invisible, / And I will overhear their conference" as Demetrius enters, followed by Helena (2.1); and *Much Ado about Nothing* has Benedick exclaim, "Hah! the Prince and Monsieur Love. I will hide me in the arbor," as he retreats behind a stage post (2.3). When, in the same play, Beatrice's turn to hide comes, Ursula states that she is "couched in the woodbine coverture" (3.1; to "couch" means to "hide," usually with a stooping action); and in *Hamlet,* Hamlet and Horatio conceal themselves behind a stage post with the words "Couch we a while and mark" as Ophelia's funeral procession approaches (5.1; to "mark" is to "observe"). The second consequence is that the reactions of the eavesdroppers can be fully incorporated into the main onstage situation. Beatrice is unlikely to remain impassive as Hero says of her, "Disdain and scorn ride sparkling in her eyes"; Benedick delivers asides to the audience from his hiding place; and Hamlet's behavior will prepare the audience for his leap into Ophelia's grave to fight with Laertes.

As for the canopy the stage posts support, its first function was to protect the actors and their valuable costumes from rain.[16] Shakespeare may have been inspired by this mundane function when writing act 3, scene 3, of *Much Ado about Nothing.* Just before Dogberry and Verges exit, the Second Watchman says, "Let us go sit here upon the church-bench." The line implies moving to a new position. The Second Watchman is given asides to speak, so that new position must be to one side of the stage, and it could well be between the stage post on that side of the stage and the tiring-house facade, so that, when Borachio and Conrade are ordered to stand where they are, they can be cut off from the flanking doors. Since the Watch's initial position is on a bench and therefore fixed, Borachio and Conrade need to be maneuvered near them to be overheard, *Much Ado about Nothing* being a play in which stage space is fully exploited—a little earlier, Beatrice has entered act 3, scene 1, "like a lapwing," and Hero and Ursula are intended to "trace this alley up and down" after her entrance. Borachio and Conrade enter with enough energy to carry them to the stage's perimeter, either to the front or to the side opposite the Watch, and Borachio is given the line "Stand thee close then under this penthouse, for it drizzles rain" (he may even hold his hand out over the edge of the stage as he says it). This is enough to get them to move near the Watch, which is on its feet by the time it senses that treason is likely, if not before, but which is kept where it is by the Second Watchman's "yet stand close" (the phrase means here "keep absolutely still" or "don't move yet"). When the play is read, Shakespeare's contrivance is obvious, since weather is not an issue anywhere else in the play. But, as Shakespeare knew, such artifice goes unnoticed during performance.

The underside of the canopy was painted with celestial designs, creating the opportunity for easily understood symbolism. In *Hamlet,* the canopy suggests the heaven the sinful Claudius prevents himself from reaching. Setting up the sword fight that will end the play, Claudius exclaims:

> Give me the cups,
> And let the kettle to the trumpet speak,
> The trumpet to the cannoneer without,

The cannons to the heavens, the heaven to earth,
"Now the King drinks to Hamlet." . . .

(5.2)

As he utters these lines, Claudius may well be meant to raise his hand to the
painted "heavens," then lower it, so that it points to the trapdoor. Such a gesture would be a fitting one for him to make. The audience knows of his
wicked intent, and the sense of a character firmly on the road to perdition
has already been instilled by Claudius himself in act 3, scene 3, after he has
tried in vain to pray: "My words fly up, my thoughts remain below: / Words
without thoughts never to heaven go."

Outside the Christian frame of reference, winding gear above the "heavens" permitted antique deities to descend and rise again. This form of vertical symbolism can be spectacular. In *Cymbeline*, Jupiter "*descends in thunder and
lightning, sitting upon an eagle: he throws a thunderbolt*" (5.4). His assurance that
"[y]our low-laid son our godhead will uplift" gains instant credibility from
this display; and his parting words, "Mount, eagle, to my palace crystalline,"
are the sound cue for him to be cranked up again by a stagehand or stagehands overhead. Not all so-called theophanies—that is, divine appearances—
need be so rambunctious, however. If, as is frequently assumed, Diana (*Pericles,* 5.1) and Juno (*The Tempest,* 4.1) descend from above, they do so with music
and decorum. Alternatively, they may appear on the balcony first, then enter
through a flanking door or the central opening. Expressing divine superiority would then be a further use of the balcony. Andrew Gurr and Mariko
Ichikawa are confident that Juno was lowered and raised again but that, in *As
You Like It,* Hymen enters through the Globe's central opening (5.4).[17]

The Tempest supplies one of the better-known examples of an external
event finding its way into a Shakespeare play, namely, the running aground
in 1609 of the *Sea Adventure* (more usually called the *Sea Venture*) on the
island of Bermuda (known as the Isle of Devils), together with the unexpected reappearance of its complement in 1610. For, far from being diverted
from the outside world by attending a play, Shakespeare's audiences are repeatedly reminded of it. They might be reminded of something big, like
the Gunpowder Plot (*Macbeth*), or of something more everyday, like bowls
in *Cymbeline,* brothels in *Measure for Measure,* or "westward-ho!"—the
Thames watermen's cry—in *Twelfth Night.* Near the Globe, there were four
flour mills. In *Coriolanus,* Shakespeare uses them to unite contemporary
London and the classical world (the play opens with the price of grain an
issue):[18]

AUFIDIUS: I am attended at the cypress grove. I pray you
('Tis south the city mills) bring me word thither

How the world goes, that to the pace of it
I may spur on my journey.

(1.10)

In 1599, the newly opened Globe was itself an object of attention and prompted a number of allusions. *As You Like It,* possibly the Globe's inaugural play, appears to make direct reference to the new playhouse's motto. It was *totus mundus agit histrionem* (roughly, "everyone is a player"), and it is paraphrased in Jaques's "All the world's a stage, / And all the men and women merely players" (2.7). And *Hamlet,* in addition to having Claudius point to the "heavens," has the Prince stand beneath the freshly painted canopy and speak of "this majestical roof fretted with golden fire" (2.2).[19]

Above the Globe, in the fresh air above the smell of garlicky breath, there flew a flag depicting Hercules (Heracles) carrying the globe of the world on his shoulders, and not even this escapes Shakespeare's ingenuity, as *Hamlet* and, possibly, *Much Ado about Nothing* show. Hamlet declares that Claudius no more resembles his late father than he (Hamlet) does Hercules (1.2), and he also resolves to remember his father for as long as "memory holds a seat / In this distracted globe" (1.5). Rosencrantz states that the "little eyases" carry away "Hercules and his load too" (2.2), meaning that child actors are proving more successful than adult ones; and Hamlet leaves act 5, scene 1, with the words "Let Hercules himself do what he may." These allusions to the flag compare Hercules, the achiever, and Hamlet, the nonachiever. *Much Ado about Nothing* is thought to have been written late in 1598, and Shakespeare may well have had the Globe in mind, since the play contains four references to Hercules. The Globe's flag would have lent special emphasis to two of these. First, Benedick excoriates Beatrice as someone who "would have made Hercules have turn'd spit" (2.1). "Spit," here, is the rotating kitchen implement used for roasting meat. When Hercules was enslaved to Omphale, Queen of Lydia, he was required to dress as a woman and do women's work. Benedick reveals his awe of Beatrice's shrewishness by suggesting that Beatrice would have gone even further and made Hercules a kitchen hand.[20] Second, Don Pedro boastfully proposes to undertake "one of Hercules' labors" (2.1). However, Hercules' capacity for getting things right highlights Don Pedro's capacity for getting things wrong.

IV

Sound effects, songs, and instrumental music.

Shakespeare enriched his plays by adding a whole range of sounds to the spoken word, including cannon. Claudius's "the cannoneer without" (5.2) suggests a gunner behind the theater needing a sound cue from the stage via kettle drum and trumpet, and comparable cuing appears to occur in *Henry VI, Part One,* where a stage direction for Talbot reads "*Winds his horn. Drums strike up; a peal of ordinance*" (2.3). "Winds" means "blows," and the ordnance, again, could well be behind the theater and out of sight. That, at any rate, is where the distinguished illustrator C. Walter Hodges locates Shakespeare's cannon, though, more recently, in *Rebuilding Shakespeare's Globe,* Paul Cox (the book's artist) depicts a gallery jutting out from the "heavens" above the stage with a cannon in place there.[21] Wherever cannon were situated, however, Shakespeare was aware that they and other acoustic supplements can extend the physical limits of the stage significantly. For example, *Antony and Cleopatra* requires "*the noise of a sea-fight*" (3.10), that is, a sound scene to round out the words of the actors. Sounds can also trigger the disclosure of important emotions. Near the opening of *Hamlet,* Hamlet, Horatio, and Marcellus are waiting for the Ghost to appear. Since they are up on the guard platform, they are well away from Claudius. Then "*[a] flourish of trumpets, and two pieces goes off within*" (1.4)—and immediately, Hamlet is reconnected with his stepfather. His explanation to Horatio of what is happening reveals his burning resentment of Claudius:

> The King doth wake to-night and takes his rouse,
> Keeps wassail, and the swagg'ring up-spring reels;
> And as he drains his draughts of Rhenish down,
> The kettle-drum and trumpet thus bray out
> The triumph of his pledge.
>
> (1.4)

The finesse with which Shakespeare employed cannon should not be obscured by their most sensational intervention, namely, the burning down of the Globe on June 29, 1613, during a performance, possibly the premiere, of *Henry VIII.* (The precise moment is usually identified with the stage direction "*Drum and trumpet; chambers discharg'd*" in act 1, scene 4.) This is how Sir Henry Wotton (who had not been there) described the event in a letter to his nephew, Sir Edmund Bacon, three days later:

> Now, King *Henry* making a Masque at the Cardinal *Wolsey's* house, and certain Chambers being shot off at his entry, some of the paper, or other stuff wherewith one of them was stopped, did light on the thatch, where being thought at first but an idle smoak, and their eyes more attentive to the show, it kindled inwardly, and ran round like a train, consuming within less than an hour the whole house to the

very grounds. . . . [O]nly one man had his breeches set on fire, that would perhaps have broyled him, if he had not by the benefit of a provident wit put it out with bottle Ale.[22]

"Chambers" are small cannon—Falstaff speaks of venturing "upon the charg'd chambers" in *Henry IV, Part Two* (2.4)—and multiple firing shows Shakespeare's alertness to what was due to stage royalty. The thatch was a cost-cutting substitute for tiles. In retrospect, the fire looks like the end of an era. As Andrew Gurr puts it, "[Shakespeare's] will seems to indicate that some time before he died he had given up his shares in the Globe and the Blackfriars theaters, and also his rooms in the Blackfriars gatehouse. If so, the burning of the Globe may have marked his final withdrawal from the city which had seen his greatest triumphs."[23]

It is easy to overlook, even when reading Shakespeare aloud, the extent to which he exploits what might be called the rhetoric of sound; yet his plays routinely require firecrackers, trumpets, drums, and clashing swords as well as cannon, and they must have provided a highly diversified experience. Repeatedly, he also uses music in an integrated way, both with and without words. Three songs, standing for many more, show this well. First, one of the themes of *As You Like It* is man's inhumanity to man. The song "Blow, blow, thou winter wind, / Thou art not so unkind / As man's ingratitude" (2.7) gives that theme expression at the moment when, with contrasting generosity, Duke Senior welcomes Orlando and the exhausted Adam. Second, the carpe diem strand of *Twelfth Night* is well communicated by Feste's song "O mistress mine," since it is sung at a late hour for the death-marked Sir Toby (2.3). Third, in act 2, scene 3, of *Cymbeline,* all Imogen wants, having been separated from her husband, is to be left alone. Instead, she is subjected to a serenade that, in itself, is a delightful aubade—"Hark, hark, the lark at heaven's gate sings." But Imogen is being harassed, as is brought out by what Cloten says to the musicians before they play and sing: "If you can penetrate her with your fingering, so; we'll try with tongue too." These three examples alone show Shakespeare using songs to emphasize a line of thought (*Twelfth Night*) and to generate dramatic contrast (*As You Like It* and *Cymbeline*).

Shakespeare also makes full use of music without words, and, again, a handful of examples must stand for many. As *Twelfth Night* opens, music famously accompanies the lovesick Orsino, but it is quickly disturbed by him, communicating his own disturbed state from the outset of the play. In *Pericles* and in *The Winter's Tale,* music is used for atmospheric effect. In *Pericles,* as Cerimon sets about reviving the apparently dead Thaisa, he calls for "rough and woeful music" (3.2; "rough" means "harsh" or "discordant," that is, of the sort to revivify Thaisa. Some editions associate this music with a viol); and in *The Winter's Tale,* when Hermione is revived from suspended animation, Paulina commands, "Music! awake her! strike!" (5.3). Less solemnly, *Much Ado about Nothing,* which has already deployed a masked ball in act 2, scene 1, to emphasize deception, brings the play's double love theme to a successful conclusion with a harmonious dance onstage. Benedick calls out, "Strike up, pipers," and the dance takes place before the characters exit.[24]

V

Players' names and appearances. Boys as women. "The purpose of playing."

Given today's globalized theater industry, a modern playwright's relationship with the performers of his or her plays can be remote to nonexistent. Shakespeare, on the other hand, was used to working as part of a team, and it is still possible to link certain parts to certain names. In addition to Bottom in *A Midsummer Night's Dream,* Will Kemp, who was also renowned for his jigs, played Launce in *The Two Gentlemen of Verona,* probably Costard in *Love's Labor's Lost,* Peter in *Romeo and Juliet,* and the original Dogberry in *Much Ado about Nothing.* Robert Armin took this last role over following Kemp's departure in 1599 and also played Touchstone in *As You Like It,* Feste in *Twelfth Night* (Armin could sing as well as act), and the Fool in *King Lear.* Richard Burbage, Shakespeare's star, played Richard III, Romeo (in 1596, when he was about twenty-eight, opposite Master Robert Goffe's Juliet), Hamlet, Othello, Lear, and "all the other leading roles in Shakespeare's plays." Thomas Pope may have played Falstaff, and Shakespeare himself is traditionally associated with playing older parts, notably Adam in *As You Like It.* As to working in combination, Will Kemp as Bottom was paired with Richard Cowley as Quince in *A Midsummer Night's Dream,* and the double act was repeated in *Much Ado about Nothing,* with Cowley playing Verges to Kemp's Dogberry.[25]

Listing names from the past generates more the illusion of closeness to bygone days than the real thing, though that is perhaps less the case when a part is linked to physical appearance. The relative heights of Kemp and Cowley probably explain Leonato's remark to Dogberry about Verges: "Indeed, neighbor, he comes too short of you" (*Much Ado about Nothing,* 3.5), and this discrepancy feeds neatly into characterization, since both Bottom and Dogberry are overbearing, while Quince and Verges have to assert themselves. As to whether, in absolute terms, Kemp was tall or Cowley short, an answer, albeit not a conclusive one, seems to lurk in Quince's prologue to

Pyramus and Thisby, in which Pyramus (Bottom) is referred to as "sweet youth and tall" (5.1).

Shakespeare also wrote for an outstandingly thin actor, John Sincler (or Sincklo). In *The Comedy of Errors,* Sincler is Dr Pinch:

> a hungry lean-fac'd villain,
> A mere anatomy, . . .
> . . . .
> A needy, hollow-ey'd, sharp-looking wretch,
> A living dead man. . . .
>
> (5.1)

With accompanying gestures and emphases on key words, such to-the-life description must have been a rich source of laughter. Sincler is also associated with the First Keeper in *Henry VI, Part Three* (3.1; a "keeper" is a gamekeeper); the Tailor in act 4, scene 3, of *The Taming of the Shrew* (tailors were proverbially thin); Robert Faulconbridge in *King John;* Starveling (another tailor) in *A Midsummer Night's Dream;* and the Apothecary in *Romeo and Juliet,* of whom Romeo says, "Famine is in thy cheeks, / Need and oppression starveth in thy eyes" (5.1). In *Henry IV, Part Two,* Sincler probably played Simon Shadow, whom Falstaff describes as a "half-fac'd fellow. . . . He presents no mark to the enemy" (3.2); and, toward the end of the same play, Doll Tearsheet calls the skinny Beadle (Sincler again) a "thin man in a censer" and a "filthy famish'd correctioner" (5.4; a "censer" was a pan for burning perfumes, often ornamented with figures in low relief). Whether Shakespeare was writing a comedy, a tragedy, or a history play, Sincler's emaciated appearance repeatedly drew vivid, crowd-pleasing lines from him.[26]

That boys played female parts in Shakespeare's day is common knowledge. They were taken on as apprentices and treated as protégés of the company. It may be said in passing that the post-Shakespearean practice of using female actresses in their twenties and beyond can put quite a few years on his Juliets, Hermias, Helenas, and Heros as originally conceived. When, in *Cymbeline,* Belarius finds the disguised Imogen, he puts down a marker for modern casting directors by exclaiming, "Behold divineness / No elder than a boy!" (3.6).

Boy actors were bewigged, costumed, and coached in the movements of women to make them look like the real thing. In the induction to *The Taming of the Shrew,* the Lord gives the order, "Sirrah, go you to Barthol'mew my page, / And see him dress'd in all suits like a lady," concluding: "I know the boy will well usurp the grace, / Voice, gait, and action of a gentlewoman."

"Usurp" means to appropriate what does not belong to you by right—here, by right of nature. And "gentlewoman" means very precisely, in the social understanding of Shakespeare's day, a lady of rank and breeding, to be differentiated in accent and deportment from, say, the Hostess in the second Henriad. With Bartholomew's gift for mimicry, only tears might have to be forced—according to the induction, with an onion held in a napkin.

Amazing as it may seem nowadays, boy actors could carry off all of Shakespeare's female parts with complete conviction. For example, in a 1610 Oxford performance of *Othello,* Desdemona was said to plead her case effectively and, once dead, to "[entreat] the pity of the spectators by her very countenance."[27] But, of course, everybody knew that his female figures were boys dressed up, and Shakespeare repeatedly exploits the fact. For example, in *Antony and Cleopatra,* when Cleopatra foresees herself being travestied in Rome, she naturally imagines that a boy will play her: "[A]nd I shall see / Some squeaking Cleopatra boy my greatness / I' th' posture of a whore" (5.2). If an actress speaks these lines, they don't make much sense. Only a boy actor known to be such can really make their combination of wit, pride, and pathos work onstage.

However well they are feminized, however, boy actors cannot hide their individual build and appearance, and Shakespeare has uses for these, too. In *The Merry Wives of Windsor,* Slender's ridiculousness is enhanced by his almost marrying not just any boy dressed up but "a great lubberly boy" (5.5). Conversely, the original Maria in *Twelfth Night* was obviously small enough to provoke a laugh when Viola says, "Some mollification for your giant, sweet lady" (1.5) and another when Sir Toby says, "Good night, Penthesilea" (2.3; Penthesilea was the warrior queen of the Amazons). And Shakespeare's first Viola must have looked just as Malvolio describes him/her: "Not yet old enough for a man, nor young enough for a boy. . . . 'Tis with him in standing water, between boy and man" (1.5). Essential to the joke is that Malvolio is describing a boy playing a young woman disguised as a young man.

Like adults, boys can be paired, and Shakespeare apparently had for a time two talented youngsters, one tall, one small, to write parts for. They played Helena and Hermia in *A Midsummer Night's Dream,* in which Helena calls Hermia a "puppet" and Hermia calls Helena a "painted maypole" (3.2). The short boy must have been dark as well, since Lysander speaks of "Ethiop" and "tawny Tartar" (3.2). The same pair is assumed to have played Rosalind and Celia in *As You Like It,* and Beatrice and Hero in *Much Ado about Nothing.*[28] In *As You Like It,* Rosalind describes herself as "more than common tall" (1.3), and, in *Much Ado about Nothing,* Hero is described by Benedick first as "too low for a high praise, too brown for a fair praise, and too little for a great praise" (1.1), then as "Leonato's short daughter" (1.1). In context, Benedick's words are amusing anyway, but Shakespeare doesn't stop there. He has Benedick speak of Beatrice much more equivocally than he does of Hero and so uses one boy actor's personal appearance—the short, dark one's—to allow Benedick to hint at his real feelings about the character played by the other boy.

Perhaps not surprisingly, it was rumored during Shakespeare's day that boy actors were adult actors' catamites:[29] So is there a homoerotic element to Shakespeare's plays? Anyone who has seen boys acting female roles will know that some can wear what women's clothes they like and still look like boys, while others become more ambivalent in their wigs and dresses. Some of that ambivalence is arguably present in *Twelfth Night*. For example, Orsino says to Cesario/Viola,

> Diana's lip
> Is not more smooth and rubious; thy small pipe
> Is as the maiden's organ, shrill and sound,
> And all is semblative a woman's part.
>
> (1.4)

The surface point is that Orsino is so infatuated with Olivia that he cannot, despite some very obvious clues, detect that there is a woman right in front of him who is as lovesick as he is. But an undertone of affection on Orsino's part for Cesario, as distinct from Viola, can be contended as well—or conceivably for the boy actor—as if Shakespeare wanted to acknowledge proscribed passions, too. One way or another, the boy-girl-boy complex (which is added to by Malvolio's description of Viola/Cesario in the following scene) must surely have cut across conventional gender boundaries.

In the last analysis, however, that remains speculative. What is not speculative is that, in the course of time, boys grow up and their voices break. For an acting company, breaking or broken voices can create difficulties—hence Orsino's compliment to the boy actor playing Viola/Cesario that his voice is still "sound." Small wonder, then, that, when Hamlet greets the newly arrived players in Elsinore and notices that the boy actor has grown, he expresses apprehension: "Pray God your voice, like a piece of uncurrent gold, be not crack'd within the ring" (2.2), that is, is not becoming unsuitable for women's parts. But even such a difficulty can be turned into successful theater. In *A Midsummer Night's Dream*, Peter Quince wants Flute to play Thisby, but Flute replies, perhaps with resentment, perhaps with a touch of pride, "Nay, faith; let not me play a woman; I have a beard coming" (1.2). A beard coming implies that the actor's voice is breaking or broken. And in

Cymbeline, when Arviragus (Cadwal) and Guiderius (Polydore) are preparing to honor what they think is the body of Fidele, the original Arviragus was obviously in dire straits, since he is given the line, "And let us, Polydore, though now our voices / Have got the mannish crack, sing him to th' ground." But, evidently, his fellow actor was even worse off, since he replies:

> Cadwal,
> I cannot sing. I'll weep, and word it with thee;
> For notes of sorrow out of tune are worse
> Than priests and fanes that lie.
>
> (4.2)

Indeed they are, so in the end both agree to speak the dirge, even though it was obviously intended to be sung.[30] In the case of Arviragus and Guiderius, Shakespeare was writing for two male adolescents playing their own sex, not the opposite one. For all that, their lines evidence once more his resourcefulness in integrating the features of real actors as well as of real venues in the construction of his plays.

Finally, since a play's performance is the raison d'être of everything else about it, it remains to be asked how Shakespeare understood, in Hamlet's phrase, "the purpose of playing." Hamlet, as a character in a play, is not necessarily Shakespeare's spokesman, but what he says about acting is crucial:

> Suit the action to the word, the word to the action, with this special observance, that you o'erstep not the modesty of nature: for any thing so o'erdone is from the purpose of playing, whose end . . . was and is, to hold as 'twere the mirror up to nature: to show virtue her feature, scorn her own image, and the very age and body of the time his form and pressure. (3.2)

At the heart of these lines are axiomatic interests in human nature and human affairs, and in ways of speaking and acting appropriate to their representation. It is often said that the lines are a criticism of Will Kemp's ad-libbing and playing for laughs, but that restricts them unnecessarily, since they can be applied to Shakespeare's plays in general. And, in part, they have a precedent, too. In *The Taming of the Shrew,* which was written at some time between 1590 and 1594, the Lord congratulates the First Player on having played a part "aptly fitted and naturally perform'd" (induction). In performance, the line is soon left behind. But it is there in the script, and it indicates that, very early in his career, Shakespeare was already drawn to the idea of putting human nature onstage in precise and truthful ways.

Chapter 2

ENTRANCES AND EARLY WORDS

I

Who, where, and what.

Shakespeare's entrances are exposed affairs. Characters become visible as soon as they leave the tiring-house, and, given that the platform stage in front of them could be some twenty-five feet deep and forty-four feet wide, they could have quite a distance to traverse before reaching their first speaking positions.[1] In such circumstances, whether entrances open a play or take place later, they require play making of a very high order. "DUKE: Escalus. / ESCALUS: My lord." So begins *Measure for Measure*. The scene is probably intended to be played standing rather than seated—it is relatively short, transitional in character, and rather too informal for heavy furniture to be moved on and off the stage. The Duke may also have already divested himself of his robes of office, since, using the past tense, he says that he has "Lent [Angelo] our terror, dress'd him with our love."[2] Nevertheless, everything about his entrance would mark him out as an authority figure. Being a duke, he would be preceded by members of his household, including, possibly, Escalus. Modern editions of the play routinely include "LORDS" in the stage direction to act 1, scene 1, and some add "ATTENDANTS" as well. Both lords and attendants would position themselves so as to assert the Duke's preeminence visually, and they would wait for him to speak. When he does, he does so imperiously.

Escalus is a subordinate. He doesn't speak until he is addressed by name, and his answer shows respect for someone placed above him. Although he is not called "Old Escalus" until line 45, his age is already visible, since, out of deference, he keeps his hat in his hands in the presence of the Duke, whereas the Duke is wearing his. Old age and wisdom traditionally go together, so the question arises as soon as Escalus is seen whether he will be as wise as he looks—and, by the end of the play, the answer will be "Not quite." When the Duke goes on to address Escalus at length, his words highlight the latter's experience and skill in government. This is intended to contrast with the Duke's first speech to Angelo.

Angelo is not onstage yet and has to be sent for. This simple device gives his entrance prominence. It also communicates his name, which combines the sound of a heavenly angel with the suggestion of a false coin (an "angel" *without* the "o" was a gold coin).[3] Before Angelo enters, the Duke asks, using a ducal plural when he speaks of himself, "What figure of us think you he will bear?" This continues the coin imagery (a "figure" is a "likeness") and, being a question, it raises doubts about how Angelo will conduct himself as the Duke's likeness in office, that is, as his deputy. These doubts are increased by the Duke's ambiguous "[W]e have with special soul / Elected him our absence to supply" and by Escalus's answer, which begins, "If any in Vienna be of worth." It seems an endorsement, but it isn't quite.

When Angelo enters at the back of the stage, the Duke identifies him for the audience's benefit with "Look where he comes." Angelo may already be wearing the robes of office the Duke speaks of having lent him. If so, Angelo rather anticipates Macbeth's asking Rosse and Angus, "[W]hy do you dress me / In borrowed robes?" (*Macbeth*, 1.3). Angelo's first lines, hinting at his hypocrisy to come, are sugared: "Always obedient to your Grace's will, / I come to know your pleasure." The Duke's reply begins, "There is a kind of character in thy life." These words suggest that Angelo's commission will test his morality as well as his technical competence. Angelo is also instructed to be mindful of "[m]ortality and mercy" and "[s]o to enforce or qualify the laws / As to your soul seems good." That is, he has to decide whether to apply the law absolutely or conditionally, and the hint is that, as he applies the law to others, so it will be applied to him. This hint is in keeping with the play's title, which derives from St. Matthew's Gospel 7:1. In the Geneva Bible, the verse reads, "Judge not, that ye be not judged. For with what judgement ye judge, ye shal be judged, and with what measure ye mette, it shal be measured to you againe"; and the gloss in the margin comments, "for hypocrites hide their owne fautes, and seke not to amende them, but are curious to reprove other mens." (Those of Shakespeare's contemporaries who owned their own Bible probably owned a Geneva Bible, but it was the Bishops' Bible that was read out in church. Shakespeare, who may have owned a Geneva Bible himself, inclines now to one, now to the other. All biblical quotations in this book are taken from the Geneva Bible.[4])

Measure for Measure's opening scene is just over eighty lines long, yet within its brief compass, the play's shape is already becoming discernible, thanks to the differentiated entrances of three of its principal characters. First, Escalus and Angelo are to be tested, each in his own way. Second, the law and its application are to be placed under scrutiny. Third, while the Duke's purpose or purposes have yet to be clarified, his intention to give his suspect deputy full powers and monitor the results is now known.

What's in a name? Angelo's is given early and it doesn't quite ring true, but the Duke's, while given as "Vincentio" in the 1623 First Folio cast list, is never said on stage: the Duke's powers are more important to the play, so his authority and designs are prioritized instead. *Measure for Measure* is not the only play in which a name is held back. In *All's Well That Ends Well,* the King of France, another authority figure, goes unnamed throughout the play. In *Hamlet,* Claudius is named in the stage direction to act 1, scene 2, but never in the dialogue; so, for the entire play, the audience sees a central character who is never referred to by name, Shakespeare preferring provocative appellations like "the King," "uncle," and "brother." And *Twelfth Night* has a name held back. Viola asks, as she enters the play, "What country, friends, is this?" (1.2), and the Sea Captain replies, "This is Illyria, lady." His deferential "lady" is more subtle than it seems: it enables Shakespeare to withhold Viola's name until act 5, when her rites of passage are complete and Sebastian addresses her with "'Thrice welcome, drowned Viola!'" (5.1).

Shakespeare does not normally hold back names, however, and, when he wants them known, he can move fast, as Escalus's case shows. "Happy be Theseus, our renowned Duke!" exclaims Egeus as he enters *A Midsummer Night's Dream* with Hermia, Lysander, and Demetrius (1.1); and Theseus helpfully replies, "Thanks, good Egeus." Then, as soon as Egeus has identified "my child, my daughter Hermia" by word and, presumably, by gesture, he gives the successive commands "Stand forth, Demetrius" and "Stand forth, Lysander," adding essential information about their relationships to Hermia as the two characters do as they are told. Once Lysander has used Helena's first entrance to name her—"Look, here comes Helena," he says—the whole quartet of lovers is known by name and appearance, and much of their situation is known as well. Shakespeare's procedure here is not far from a roll call, and that is what Peter Quince actually uses to get his troupe of actors named out loud during their first appearance. "Answer as I call you" (1.2), he says, and they eventually do, excepting Snug the joiner, who, being named last, has no need to call out, "Here, Peter Quince."

Because of their focusing effect, place names are as important as characters' names, and entrance lines are one way of getting them heard. Lucentio's "Tranio, since for the great desire I had / To see fair Padua, nursery of

arts" (1.1) locates *The Taming of the Shrew,* and Leonato's "I learn in this letter that Don Pedro of Arragon comes this night to Messina" (1.1) locates
Much Ado about Nothing, especially as the Messenger adds, "He is very near
by this, he was not three leagues off when I left him" (1.1). The Sea Captain's placing of *Twelfth Night* in Illyria has just been quoted.

When Egeus, Hermia, Lysander, and Demetrius first come on in *A Midsummer Night's Dream,* they demonstrate how entrances can be used to clarify situations quickly—a must for a dramatist with a live audience to catch
and retain. So what does Shakespeare actually do? In *A Midsummer Night's
Dream,* knowing that questions naturally attract answers, he has Theseus ask
Egeus, "What's the news with thee?" and Egeus, by way of reply, can then
launch straight into the Hermia-Lysander-Demetrius imbroglio. Many years
later, in *Cymbeline,* Shakespeare happily reverted to the same technique. The
Second Gentleman asks, "But what's the matter?" (1.1), and the First Gentleman has all the cue he needs to start explaining. Leading questions need-
n't even take place on stage. When Orlando opens *As You Like It,* he seems
to be responding to a question put by Adam just before the two of them
make their first entrance. It doesn't matter that Adam gets told what he must
know already. The audience doesn't know it, and that is what counts.

Questions are not Shakespeare's only means of getting things explained.
The Comedy of Errors uses a command. The Duke of Ephesus orders Egeon
of Syracusa to "say in brief the cause / Why thou departedst from thy na-
tive home" (1.1), and Egeon, obedient to the Duke's command if not to his
"in brief," embarks on a long, static account of his plight. *Love's Labor's Lost*
uses a solemn reminder. The play opens with the King of Navarre remind-
ing Berowne, Dumaine, and Longaville that they have sworn to spend three
years with him in stillness and contemplation, and it makes sense for him to
do that, since the three are about to confirm their oaths by signing a written agreement. Modern audiences may regard lengthy expository statements
as artificial and cumbersome and so may be grateful that arresting opening
lines are also part of Shakespeare's repertoire. For example, there is the
Countess's "In delivering my son from me, I bury a second husband" (*All's
Well That Ends Well*); Flavius's "Hence! home, you idle creatures, get you
home!" (*Julius Caesar*); and the Ship-Master's "Boatswain!" (*The Tempest*).
Each of these lines leads swiftly into the thick of things.

II

Entrances and characterization.

As with situations, so with characters: entrances can clarify them quickly. The
uncertain note sounded when Angelo enters *Measure for Measure* is exactly

right for a play to which deferred character revelation is central, but other types of play require certainty from the start. Philo opens *Antony and Cleopatra* with "Nay, but this dotage of our general's / O'erflows the measure" (1.1) and, in a couple of lines, he sets Antony up for his tragedy. Immoderation and selfishness bellow out of Sir Toby Belch's late-night "What a plague means my niece to take the death of her brother thus? I am sure care's an enemy to life" (*Twelfth Night,* 1.3). And Coriolanus's "What's the matter, you dissentious rogues, / That rubbing the poor itch of your opinion / Make yourselves scabs?" advertises his divisive arrogance as soon as he opens his mouth (*Coriolanus,* 1.1). These three instant characterizations are achieved in two different ways. In *Antony and Cleopatra,* Shakespeare uses explicit statement—a lesser character commenting on a greater one—whereas in *Twelfth Night* and *Coriolanus,* he combines situation and dialogue to elicit the right inferences from the audience.

Other ways of using entrance lines to achieve instant characterization include a character explaining himself; one character characterizing another without being aware that he is doing so; and one character knowingly characterizing another. This is Richard of Gloucester explaining himself at the beginning of *Richard III:*

> Now is the winter of our discontent
> Made glorious summer by this son of York;
> . . . .
> Grim-visag'd War hath smooth'd his wrinkled front;
> And now, in stead of mounting barbed steeds
> To fright the souls of fearful adversaries,
> He capers nimbly in a lady's chamber
> To the lascivious pleasing of a lute.
> But I, that am not shap'd for sportive tricks,
> Nor made to court an amorous looking-glass;
> I, that am rudely stamp'd, and want love's majesty
> To strut before a wanton ambling nymph;
> I, that am curtail'd of this fair proportion,
> Cheated of feature by dissembling nature,
> Deform'd, unfinish'd, sent before my time
> Into this breathing world, scarce half made up,
> And that so lamely and unfashionable
> That dogs bark at me as I halt by them—
> Why, I, in this weak piping time of peace,
> Have no delight to pass away the time,
> Unless to see my shadow in the sun

And descant on mine own deformity.
And therefore, since I cannot prove a lover
To entertain these fair well-spoken days,
I am determined to prove a villain
And hate the idle pleasures of these days.

Elizabethan audiences *expected* Richard to be wicked: to them, he was the king who murdered his way to the throne; so *Richard III* (a major success for Shakespeare and Richard Burbage) was written with the grain of popular sentiment. Andrew Gurr quotes from the 1597 quarto edition of the play— "Containing his treacherous Plots against his brother Clarence: the pittiefull murther of his innocent nephewes: his tyranicall usurpation: with the whole course of his detested life, and most deserved death"—and comments that "[w]hoever wrote that had seen the play in performance and registered the emotions appropriate to the main incidents in the plot."[5] Some in Shakespeare's audiences might also have seen *Henry VI, Part Three,* which immediately precedes *Richard III* in the four history plays known as the first Henriad and which portrays Richard as a monster in the making. But whatever preconceptions individual members of the audience brought with them, it is unlikely that anyone was fully prepared for the electrifying combination of blatancy and vehemence with which *Richard III* opens.

Shakespeare wants Richard deplored, but, even more, he wants him understood. Richard's entrance speech is, therefore, a self-analytical soliloquy. Richard, essentially a loner with a lot of self-hatred in him, inclines to "I"-centered turns of phrase laced with sexual jealousy, compensatory violence, and morbid ambition. No one is needed to identify him as he enters "*solus*" and limps out onto the stage, biding his time until he sees fit to speak. He was known to be hunchbacked and lame, and Burbage would certainly have played to these characteristics, given the presence in the dialogue of "lamely," "I halt," and "see my shadow in the sun." Richard has the whole platform stage to himself—originally, it may have been the Theatre's outdoor stage[6]— and he dominates his surrounding audience for forty lines of lucid rhetoric before Clarence and Brakenbury come on. He gives no sign of expecting sympathy: his tone is by turns defiant and assertive, and the nature he displays is as deformed as is, in his opinion, the physique it is connected with. Richard is not always this confident in the play. But, whenever he is onstage subsequently, regardless of where he positions himself, the eye instinctively follows him as a force to be reckoned with.

When it comes to one character characterizing another without knowing that he is doing so, *Much Ado about Nothing* shows how subtly this may be done. As Don Pedro makes his first entrance, he asks, "Good Signior

Leonato, are you come to meet your trouble?" (1.1), and everything hangs on how the word "trouble" is responded to. If it is ignored, the question will have been no more than a prince's banter; but if it is picked up, the word will become part of the play's buildup. In fact, it is picked up not once but twice by Leonato, and it may well be that the original Leonato gave the word special emphasis as he spoke it: "Never came *trouble* to my house in the likeness of your Grace, for *trouble* being gone, comfort should remain" (1.1; italics added). The word sticks, and, from this exchange on, Don Pedro, who has already been ominously associated with "this night," is a marked man, even though that is not Leonato's intention.

Nevertheless, it might be thought that, for all that it is repeated and possibly given special emphasis, the word "trouble" is still too fleeting a part of the dialogue to have the same effect on an audience that it is likely to have on a reader. Yet Shakespeare frequently introduces small forward-looking details into the flow of his plays, and they overwhelmingly suggest good stagecraft, not quirkiness. A case in point occurs during the opening of *The Merry Wives of Windsor,* when Parson Evans speaks of "Anne Page, which is daughter to Master George Page," and Slender breaks in with "She has brown hair, and speaks small like a woman" (1.1; "small" means "high-pitched" or "piping"). Slender's foolishness is self-evident, as it is meant to be, and "speaks small like a woman" is presumably also a joking reference to the fact that Anne Page is being played by a boy. But the word "brown" is functional as well as descriptive since, thanks to it, the audience can now identify Anne Page as soon as it sees her. That happens some 140 lines later, when she comes on carrying wine. The plot does not seem to require this particular entrance—she says nothing, and her father tells her to leave straight away, which she does—but Shakespeare seems to be investing heavily in first impressions here. On the reasonable assumption that some of Anne Page's hair is showing, she is recognizable on sight, and her first entrance takes place between Slender's being foolish and Page's giving an order—that is, she is presented to the audience as a marriageable daughter sandwiched between an unattractive matrimonial prospect and a father accustomed to being obeyed. That oppressive situation bears directly on everything she says and does thereafter. There is no way of knowing how the first Anne Page was meant to make her exit, but some kind of body language emphasizing her situation seems certain.

When two main characters come onstage together and one knowingly characterizes the other, what is said can shed light on both of them. Act 1, scene 2, of *Henry IV, Part One,* has Falstaff entering both the play and the history of English theater with the question "Now, Hal, what time of day is it, lad?" and the answer he gets from Prince Hal, who enters the play with him, fixes Falstaff in a handful of lines. This double entrance is crafted the way it is for three reasons. First, as a major new character in the play, Falstaff needs instant definition. Second, as a clown, he is a novelty in a Shakespeare history play, so instant definition is even more necessary. Third, the audience needs to see early and clearly that the crown prince is in an unworthy relationship, if the conception of Prince Hal as prodigal son is to come across as the play unfolds. Falstaff's asking after the time is a sure giveaway of disorderliness, and Hal's rejoinder immediately presents the once-slim old knight as self-indulgent, unruly, and irresponsible:

> Thou art so fat-witted with drinking of old sack, and unbuttoning thee after supper, and sleeping upon benches after noon, that thou hast forgotten to demand that truly which thou wouldest truly know. What a devil hast thou to do with the time of the day? unless hours were cups of sack, and minutes capons, and clocks the tongues of bawds, and dials the signs of leaping-houses, and the blessed sun himself a fair hot wench in flame-color'd taffata; I see no reason why thou shouldst be so superfluous to demand the time of the day.

The original Falstaff's physical appearance and Hal's words presumably complemented each other.

In contrast, Hal makes *his* first entrance in the play with part of *his* characterization—the negative part—already established. Some in the audience might already have seen *Richard II,* and, if so, they might recall Bullingbrook's lament in that play about his dissolute and desperate son, in whom he yet sees "some sparks of better hope" (5.3); others might well know from elsewhere the story of the wild prince who became Henry V; but Shakespeare could not absolutely rely on foreknowledge. So, when Prince Hal enters *Henry IV, Part One,* his father has just said that "riot and dishonor" stain his son's brow (1.1). With those words still fresh in the audience's memory, the crown prince's "dishonor" is then corroborated by Falstaff's familiar way of addressing him as they come on stage together. On the other hand, Hal's first lines to Falstaff are conspicuously chiding, and that chiding indicates that theirs is a relationship on notice. Hal may enter the play speaking prose, but the verse of royal responsibility is not far off. Clear-sighted and judgmental, he will, before the scene is out, be soliloquizing about his intended "reformation," which he expects to look all the better for his antecedent faults. If this reformation is to be achieved, irresponsibility as symbolized by Falstaff must eventually be rejected. This happens at the end of *Henry IV, Part*

Two, and the obituary of the Prince Hal–Falstaff relationship is finally pronounced by Fluellen in *Henry V:* "[S]o also Harry Monmouth, being in his right wits and his good judgments, turn'd away the fat knight with the great belly doublet" (4.7). That turning away is already prefigured in the first entrance of the crown prince and Falstaff in *Henry IV, Part One.*

III

Dogberry and Friar Francis as new characters entering Much Ado about Nothing *late. Known characters returning after an exit: Malvolio* (Twelfth Night), *Prince Hal* (Henry IV, Part One), *and Bertram, Count of Rossillion* (All's Well That Ends Well).

Shakespeare tends to introduce his major characters early on, but in *Much Ado about Nothing, Twelfth Night, Othello, Pericles,* and *The Winter's Tale,* important new characters are introduced well after the play has begun. In *Much Ado about Nothing,* this happens not once but twice. The first latecomer is Dogberry, constable of the Watch (3.3). When Don John offers to prove Hero's infidelity to Don Pedro and Claudio, watchfulness is called for, since Don John is a known villain. But watchfulness is precisely what Don Pedro lacks, though he is unaware of this, and Dogberry, too, is anything but watchful (his "vigitant" is the verbal equivalent of his bungling in general). Like Don Pedro, who is a prince, Dogberry is an authority figure and— again like Don Pedro—Dogberry is proud; and both are incapable of resolving difficult situations unaided. In other words, the constable's characterization is effectively a critique of the prince's, and the judgment invited on them both is that they are asses. When Dogberry enters the play, he brings the Watch with him, and its lowly members turn out to be more suited to their responsibilities than their betters. As Borachio will put it, "What your wisdoms could not discover, these shallow fools have brought to light" (5.1).

The second latecomer is Friar Francis (4.1). He becomes necessary when Don Pedro, Claudio, and Leonato all fail Hero in the church. The Friar's authority derives not from rank or office but from his knowledge that bereavement can intensify love and from his persuasion that deception is right if its end is right. No character already in the play is capable of introducing these new considerations. It is true that the Friar does not put matters right single-handedly. But his timely intervention keeps the plot going when it would otherwise seize up, and it also makes the play more substantial than it otherwise would be.

When characters return to the stage after they have been on before, they normally do so as more or less known quantities; so the question of who they are recedes behind that of what they will say and do next. This opens up options for Shakespeare regarding *how* he returns his characters to the stage. One option is to write his characters straight back into the action. That will be discussed shortly. Another is to use the physical depth of the stage to bring characters out of the tiring-house and then, in full view of the audience, keep them at a distance from other characters already onstage instead of having them engage with them straight away. Two contrasting moments from *Coriolanus* and *All's Well That Ends Well* show the dramatic enhancement that can be achieved with this second sort of entrance.

In act 2, scene 3, of *Coriolanus,* the people have to decide whether or not to support Coriolanus's consulship. It is a delicate moment. The Third Citizen, knowing Coriolanus, says, "If he would incline to the people, there was never a worthier man"; and, as he says these words, Coriolanus, wearing a gown of humility, enters with Menenius. The two remain apart while the Third Citizen explains that Coriolanus is to be approached in ones, twos, or threes and that he is to ask for the support of each citizen separately ("He's to make his requests by particulars"). Then the citizens exit. Thanks to Coriolanus's war record and the Third Citizen's biased words, all Coriolanus now has to do is what any politician has to do at election time, namely, be nice to the electorate. But the physical gap between Coriolanus and the people marks a psychological as well as a social one. As Coriolanus and Menenius move into their first speaking positions, it becomes immediately clear that, gown of humility or no, Coriolanus's pride is likely to ruin everything:

> MENENIUS: O sir, you are not right. Have you not known
> The worthiest men have done't?
> CORIOLANUS: What must I say?
> "I pray, sir"—Plague upon't! I cannot bring
> My tongue to such a pace. . . .

In the event, there is enough goodwill in the people to see Coriolanus through, but the inevitable is only postponed, for Coriolanus's contemptuous disposition makes it possible for Sicinius and Brutus to turn the people against him afterward. Their opportunism secures a victory for their short-sighted factionalism, but the price is Rome's security, and Coriolanus, unwilling to close the gap between himself and the people that was represented symbolically when he came onstage in the gown of humility, is, and is seen to be, principally at fault.

Whereas *Coriolanus* concerns matters of state, *All's Well That Ends Well* concerns matters of the heart. In act 1, scene 3, Helena, who secretly yearns for Bertram, is sent for by his mother, the Countess of Rossillion, who has learned that Helena loves her son. After Helena first appears at the back of the stage, the Countess gets nine uninterrupted lines before Helena speaks, and the Countess's ninth line—it is, "Her eye is sick on't; I observe her now"—has two meanings, a physical and an emotional one. The physical meaning is that, while the Countess has been speaking, Helena has made her way from one of the flanking doors in the tiring-house facade to a position that is close enough for the Countess to read her features in detail. The emotional meaning derives from the fact that, as the widowed Countess speaks her lines, personal memories surface in her that enable her to understand and justify Helena's love for someone above her station. Consequently, the Countess's "I observe her now" also means "I understand her now and sympathize with her as well." This is the Countess's speech in full ("sick on't" means "sick with love"):

> Even so it was with me when I was young.
> If ever we are nature's, these are ours. This thorn
> Doth to our rose of youth rightly belong;
> Our blood to us, this to our blood is born.
> It is the show and seal of nature's truth,
> Where love's strong passion is impress'd in youth.
> By our remembrances of days foregone,
> Such were our faults, or then we thought them none.
> Her eye is sick on't; I observe her now.

"These" in the second line refers to the sufferings love brings, and the Countess's meaning is that, while she and Helena are divided by birth, they are united as women who know what it means to be young and in love. J. L. Styan comments, "In performance [the word 'these'] is a cue for the Countess to indicate, and Helena to display, her amorous sufferings. The boy actor playing Helena has the difficulties of his part eased as he wanders the length of the platform [stage] with downcast eyes."[7]

The Countess's words are a widow's words, and, while widows were and are not necessarily elderly—certainly not in Shakespeare's time, when women married young and bore children as soon as possible—*All's Well That Ends Well* is one of those plays by Shakespeare in which characters of comparatively advanced years come across as understood from within. Much is made of the ways Shakespeare writes for the different social strata in his audiences, but his differentiation by age and maturity is just as astute. The Countess speaks directly to those who can themselves recall young love after the passage of years and the changes they bring. Her words can be compared with the reunion of Leontes and his wrinkled Hermione at the end of *The Winter's Tale,* a scene that, to this day, can move an audience to tears. George Bernard Shaw thought that the Countess's part was "the most beautiful old woman's part ever written."[8] Sometimes Shakespeare's touch is so light that it is easy to miss what he is doing. Act 1, scene 1, of *The Winter's Tale* has Camillo say of Mamillius, "[I]t is a gallant child; one that, indeed, physics the subject, makes old hearts fresh. They that went on crutches ere he was born desire yet their life to see him a man." Older members of the audience, es- pecially grandparents perhaps, will attach deep personal meaning to the phrases "makes old hearts fresh" and "desire yet their life to see him a man."

Entrances that bring known or partly known characters *straight* back into the action can facilitate plot development, make a moral point, or develop a characterization already under way. Each of these can be achieved *plausi- bly* because, as noted above, known characters bring known characteristics with them. Shakespeare, while not predictable in the pejorative sense, is a great exploiter of consistency.

Facilitating Plot Development (In act 2, scene 3, of Twelfth Night, *Malvolio reenters to reprove Sir Toby, Sir Andrew, and Feste for being noisy late at night.)* Malvolio, the steward in *Twelfth Night,* is a gentleman whose formal respon- sibilities include maintaining good order in Olivia's household. Additionally, he likes to pass himself off as a puritan, that is, as morally precise. So, he is hostile to Feste, the clown, and, if Sir Toby and Sir Andrew are excessive in self-indulgence, he is excessive in reproving them. In fact, consistent with his name, he does "nothing but reprove" (1.5), and this understandably builds up resentment. On the other hand, because they are knights, Sir Toby and Sir Andrew are Malvolio's social superiors, and Sir Toby is Olivia's uncle as well; so conflicts of status and Malvolio are never far apart, either. Then there is Maria, Olivia's gentlewoman. While somewhat more responsible than her mistress's houseguests, Maria wants Sir Toby to marry her. So, if and when things come to a head between the knight and Malvolio, she will take sides against the steward anyway. But, more than that, in the course of act 2, scene 3, Malvolio threatens to report her to Olivia for abetting the noisemaking, and that gives her a specific incentive to act against him.

In act 2, scene 3, then, Sir Toby, Sir Andrew, and Feste are carousing at a late hour, when Malvolio reenters with reproval once more on his lips. He is right to seek to quell "this uncivil rule," but his language is insolent and his censoriousness has been heard too often before. So, Malvolio's action provokes reaction, and Maria, duly threatened with being reported, under- takes to gain revenge by making Malvolio a laughingstock ("a common recreation"). Although not immediately obvious, this is plot development of a very high order, for, thanks to Malvolio's return *in the form Shakespeare gives it,* the play can now progress seamlessly to Maria's forged letter, Malvolio's confinement in a dark room, and his humiliation when, in act 5, he claims that Olivia has done him "[n]otorious wrong."

Making a Moral Point (In act 3, scene 3, of Henry IV, Part One, *Hal reenters ready to do his duty as crown prince, but Falstaff greets him with a cowardly joke.)* Part of the greatness of Malvolio's return in *Twelfth Night* lies in the skill with which Shakespeare makes it look as if it simply had to happen. He does this by having Maria cue it in advance. "If my lady have not call'd up her steward Malvolio and bid him turn you out of doors, never trust me," she says, and, within a dozen noisy lines, Malvolio bursts in with, "My masters, are you mad? Or what are you?" But on other occasions, Shakespeare prefers to create the illusion of coincidence. In act 3 of *Henry IV, Part One,* the need is to show that Prince Hal is developing beyond Falstaff. The Percys have rebelled, and Prince Hal is offstage acknowledging his royal responsibilities to his father. Meanwhile, Falstaff is symbolically still in Eastcheap, claiming that a seal ring worth forty marks has been stolen from him. The Hostess's reminder that, according to Hal, the ring was copper causes Falstaff to exclaim, brandishing his stick: "'Sblood, an he were here, I would cudgel him like a dog if he would say so" (3.3). The stage direction then reads: "*Enter the* PRINCE *marching, with* PETO, *and Falstaff meets him playing upon his truncheon like a fife.*" In other words, Falstaff stops brandishing his stick and puts it to his mouth as soon as he sees Hal coming onto the stage. Hal's "coincidental" return at a time of national crisis juxtaposes two morally divergent modes of behavior: Hal shows that he is ready for duty and Falstaff buries his subversive cowardice in a joke. It is a key confrontation, and it has precise echoes in the two plays that follow *Henry IV, Part One.* At the end of *Henry IV, Part Two,* Hal's rejection of Falstaff includes the words "I know thee not, old man, fall to thy prayers. / How ill white hairs becomes a fool and jester!" (5.5). And in *Henry V,* Fluellen's obituary of the Falstaff–Prince Hal relationship disapprovingly recalls Falstaff as having been "full of jests, and gipes, and knaveries" (4.7; "gipes" means gibes).

Developing a Characterization Already Under Way (In act 5, scene 3, of All's Well That Ends Well, *the possibility is examined whether Bertram, Count of Rossillion, can be made to love his wife.)* There are characters in Shakespeare who have to be broken and remade before they can proceed along the path of virtue. Master Ford is one of these (*The Merry Wives of Windsor*). So are Claudio (*Much Ado about Nothing*) and Leontes (*The Winter's Tale*). They hurt themselves by rejecting the women closest to them, but they find happiness once they see the error of their ways. Although *The Merry Wives of Windsor* arguably predates both the other plays and Claudio is only betrothed, Master Ford can fairly speak for the other two characters as well as for himself. In his moment of change, his lines acquire a gaunt and haunting poetry:

> Pardon me, wife, henceforth do what thou wilt.
> I rather will suspect the sun with cold
> Than thee with wantonness. Now doth thy honor stand,
> In him that was of late an heretic,
> As firm as faith.
>
> (4.4)

In *The Merry Wives of Windsor* and *Much Ado about Nothing,* as in *The Winter's Tale,* the woman's love is constant while the man's is temporarily contaminated. But what if that basic situation were to be made more challenging for the audience to accept? What if the woman's love is constant but the man has never loved her in the first place? Can *that* man be broken and remade so that his feelings are changed? Can he be *traumatized* into love? These questions are central to *All's Well That Ends Well,* and, when Bertram makes his last entrance (5.3), they await answers.

As far as Bertram is concerned on his return to Rossillion, breaking and remaking are the last things likely to happen to him. He has come back from the wars with the military reputation he has craved; the King is proposing a new beginning; and, for that matter, the play is nearly over. Yet Shakespeare's intention, precisely at this late point, is to confront Bertram with his past misdeeds and, in so doing, to test the possibility of his being traumatized into becoming a family man. Bertram enters act 5, scene 3, looking distinctly proud of himself—Lafew's "He looks well on't" makes this clear. His first words—"My high-repented blames, / Dear sovereign, pardon to me"— exude the cocksure insincerity of a man who thinks that he has gotten away with some very bad behavior. But then the breaking starts, and, well before it is over, Bertram is so distressed that the King says straight out, "You boggle shrewdly, every feather starts you." Finally, when Helena presents herself to him as if from the grave, Bertram exclaims, "Both, both. O, pardon!" meaning that, for the first time in the play, he accepts her as a wife in fact as well as in name.

But is Bertram really a runaway who has been broken and remade into a loving husband in the play's last act? Or is he, ambushed by adverse circumstances, speaking in the heat of the moment? Given Bertram's characterization in the body of the play, whether he could really be made to love against his will is doubtful; but, given the circumstances in which Helena returns to him, it is just possible. Both interpretations have their merits, and the play refuses to choose between them. In fact, Bertram's traumatization is deliberately put in so late that not even a clue can be given as to how things will turn out. Instead, the play ends with an emphatic "if," leaving the audience to reach what conclusions it can: "KING: All yet seems well, and if it end so meet, / The bitter past, more welcome is the sweet." *All's Well That Ends Well* is a comedy of sorts, but built into it is a profound mistrust of oversimplification. In it, Shakespeare shows that he was determined not to let his art falsify life with a glib happy ending.

IV

Necessity and likelihood in Othello. *Lear returns to die onstage.*

To pass from *All's Well That Ends Well* to *Othello* is to pass from a self-questioning comedy to a very pure form of tragedy.[9] Although it disregards the unities of place and time, *Othello* is a coherent whole, not a collection of episodes; it contains the fearsome (that is, a sense of misfortune in the making) and, in Desdemona's murder, the piteous (actual misfortune which is manifestly undeserved); Othello is not a villain, but he is capable of committing a tragic error; and, too late, he acquires tragic insight, that is, he undergoes a change of state from ignorance to knowledge.

Section III of this chapter emphasizes that, when characters return to the stage once a play is under way, what is already known about them engenders a sense of what they may go on to do. The coherence of *Othello* is directly attributable to Shakespeare's handling of this combination—called "necessity" and "likelihood" in the analysis of tragedy Aristotle makes in his *Poetics*. "Necessity" means that if you stop the play at any significant point and look back, everything seems inevitably to lead up to that point; and "likelihood" means that, by the time that stoppage point is reached, the potential for further developments is already discernible. Othello's return to the stage in act 3, scene 4, provides a very clear example of how necessity and likelihood can work in a play. By the conclusion of act 3, scene 3, Othello has been brought by Iago to the point at which he is determined to kill Desdemona, and he leaves the stage with the menacing line "I will withdraw / To furnish me with some swift means of death / For the fair devil." Act 3, scene 4, opens with Desdemona fretting about the loss of Othello's handkerchief but also denying to Emilia that Othello is jealous. Suddenly, Emilia says, "Look where he comes," and the audience knows that the stressed black figure returning to the stage has murder on his mind.

The necessity of Othello's condition when he exits at the end of act 3, scene 3, is readily apparent, since Iago's machinations to that point in the play have taken place in full view of the audience; and, when Othello returns, he has likelihood written all over him. But likelihood crucially leaves a gap between intending and doing. That is, while Othello is potentially lethal when he returns, the audience knows that the situation is still retrievable, if only Othello could see what is really happening or, indeed, if only he would yield to the pressure contained in his description of Desdemona as a "*fair* devil" (italics added), instead of resisting it. This sense of "if only" is inseparable from the experience of *Othello*. As the play unfolds, "if only" generates tension, exasperation, even anger in the audience. And when Othello finally makes things irretrievable by murdering Desdemona, "if only" colors the way he is judged. Othello's foolishness, his capacity for extreme violence ("I will chop her into messes" [4.1]; "messes" are "small pieces"), and his self-righteousness all make a strong case for condemnation. On the other hand, his belated grief and remorse make qualified compassion possible. Both lines of thought have their validity, and neither entirely cancels the other. And, of course, there is more to *Othello* than Othello. His tragic misdeed throws a retrospective light onto the love, trust, and decency that are distributed through the play as well as onto the malice and gullibility that bring him down. That is why many audiences come away from *Othello* with, among other things, an immense sense of waste. Generally speaking, the more destructive the play becomes, the more what is damaged or destroyed appears valuable.

Death in *Othello* is premature and deplorable—and that includes Brabantio's death from grief (it is reported by Gratiano in act 5, scene 2). Death as life's natural terminus is omitted because it would not be consistent with the plot's disturbed nature. However, if death as life's natural terminus *can* be integrated into a play, then a different and arguably even greater profundity can be achieved. This happens in *King Lear* when, in the concluding scene (5.3), Lear returns to the stage to die.

Lear has grown old before he has grown wise, and his unwisdom leads him not to see, until it is too late, two things among others: that to surrender his crown is to surrender his power; and that Cordelia can love him and a husband, too. When Lear makes his last entrance with the dead Cordelia in his arms, the audience can already see from this dreadful parody of a loving embrace what his original folly has made possible: a loss that, in its finality as in its timing, is too painful for him to bear. When Lear speaks, he pours out a grief that few audiences can be indifferent to, whatever judgments they may simultaneously entertain about the speaker; and drama seems to

reach an outer limit in the sense that, while grief can be expressed in a thousand different ways, Lear's can never be exceeded:

> Howl, howl, howl! O, you are men of stones!
> Had I your tongues and eyes, I'd use them so
> That heaven's vault should crack. She's gone for ever!
> I know when one is dead, and when one lives;
> She's dead as earth.

But there is more to this scene than grief. There is, visibly, Lear's age, too.
Lear is not old in the simple and stagy way that Adam is old in *As You Like
It*. He is old in the mingled way of a strong, authoritative personality expe-
riencing a weakening of the powers that have made him what he has been.
He is learning what it means to be finite:

> LEAR: I kill'd the slave that was a-hanging thee.
> GENTLEMAN: 'Tis true, my lords, he did.
> LEAR: Did I not, fellow?
> I have seen the day, with my good biting falchion
> I would have made them skip. I am old now,
> And these same crosses spoil me. Who are you?
> Mine eyes are not o' th' best; I'll tell you straight.

Lear's mixed condition issues in correspondingly mixed dialogue. He recalls
the days when he was strong enough to use a "falchion" (a "sword"), and he
is proud of the fact that he has, at his age, still been able to kill Cordelia's
murderer. But then, in an old man's way, he admits to being wearied by
"crosses" (that is, "contrarieties"); and his sight is failing. "Who are you?" is
addressed to Kent, and "I'll tell you straight" means "I'll make out who you
are straight away."

Death, the necessity within, occurs at exactly the right dramatic moment.
Lear dies in helplessness and in hope, and both signify:

> Why should a dog, a horse, a rat, have life,
> And thou no breath at all? Thou'lt come no more,
> Never, never, never, never, never.
> Pray you undo this button. Thank you, sir.
> Do you see this? Look on her! Look her lips,
> Look there, look there! *He dies.*

Is the button Lear's or Cordelia's? Many commentators, assuming a return of *hysterica passio* (2.4), say Lear's; but there is an arguable lack of hysteria to these lines that strengthens the case for the button being Cordelia's. Either way, Lear's helplessness is apparent. It is an ex-king's helplessness, which heightens its poignancy, but helplessness is not confined to kings. In the nature of things, it can befall anyone; so Lear, dying, is a powerful universal symbol. Lear's surge of hope that Cordelia is not really dead, uttered in the context of his own dying, communicates the tenderness of love. But it also communicates love's ever-present closeness to grief. Love, like everything human, falls within the compass of the finite, and a loved one is always there to be lost. To the ever-loyal Kent, Lear's death signals his own—"My master calls me, I must not say no"—but to Edgar it signals a new beginning offstage. It also elicits from him a formulation of one of Shakespeare's fundamental dramatic insights: that while being is common to everyone, its experience varies from individual to individual. Initially, Edgar's concluding couplet can sound a little trite. But there is no obvious limit to the reflections it can generate: "The oldest hath borne most; we that are young / Shall never see so much, nor live so long."

Chapter 3

EXITS

I

Perfunctory and skillful exits. Catering to performance practicalities.

Characters in a play cannot just walk off the stage without a reason, so writing them off is as necessary as writing them on. "When you have spoken your speech," Peter Quince instructs Bottom in act 3, scene 1, of *A Midsummer Night's Dream*, "enter into that brake." Quince knows that exiting correctly is an important part of performing correctly, and what he means by his instruction to Bottom is that when Bottom, as Pyramus, reaches "But hark; a voice! Stay thou but here a while, / And by and by I will to thee appear," he is to interpret these lines as an implied exit cue and comply with it. Similarly, during the actual performance of *Pyramus and Thisby* in act 5, scene 1, Pyramus and Thisby exit from either side of the wall to meet at "Ninny's tomb," Pyramus's enscripted cue being "Wilt thou at Ninny's tomb meet me *straightway?*" and Thisby's being "'Tide life, 'tide death, I come *without delay*" (italics added). Their departure is rightly recognized by Wall as an implied exit cue for himself, so he leaves the stage as well. In fact, he marks the finality of his exit with an unshared rhyming couplet: "Thus have I, Wall, my part discharged so; / And being done, thus Wall away doth go." It is not entirely clear whether the couplet's author is Quince or Wall, though it is probably Quince, given the verse. Either way, a true talent for the stage is on display, even if the couplet falls short of greatness.

Although Shakespeare's exits are not as gauche as Wall's, he is not above perfunctory ones when it suits him. *A Midsummer Night's Dream* opens with

Hermia attaching herself to Lysander in defiance of her father's wishes and Theseus's disapproval. It beggars belief, therefore, that Hermia and Lysander should subsequently be left alone together, but precisely that is what Shakespeare needs so that the lovers can detail their elopement onstage and then tell Helena what they intend to do. So he summarily writes off the others by having Theseus allege unspecified "business / Against our nuptial" and the need for private discussion with Demetrius and Egeus. And that solves that.

Such unvarnished expediency is rare in Shakespeare, however. Most of his exits are masterly, and many (as actors and producers well know) have more to them than is apparent at first sight. Both sorts occur in *Much Ado about Nothing.* First, I will discuss a masterly exit, then one that is not as obvious as it may seem when it is read.

In act 3, scene 2, Benedick is teased by Don Pedro and Claudio for having had his beard shaved off and for being in love after all he has said about marriage. The scene plays so naturally that any ulterior motive for the teasing escapes notice. But Shakespeare wants Leonato and Benedick offstage when Don John arrives to assert Hero's infidelity so that he (Shakespeare) can exploit their unprepared reactions in act 4, scene 1, when Hero is rejected by Claudio. So, at precisely the right moment, he makes Benedick lose his temper and lead Leonato off to talk with him about marriage in understandable privacy. "Old signior," says Benedick, "walk aside with me, I have studied eight or nine wise words to speak to you, which these hobbyhorses must not hear" (3.2). The way is then clear for Don John to enter a brief five lines later in the circumstances Shakespeare requires.

As an example of the second sort of exit, following Hero's rejection and collapse in act 4, scene 1, Shakespeare has to get Don John, Don Pedro, and Claudio off the stage, since Friar Francis's exploitation of her apparent death is obviously a nonstarter if they know that it is a trick. So, when Hero drops to the ground, Don John is made to declare, "Come, let us go. These things, come thus to light, / Smother her spirits up," and all three exit.

On the face of it, their exit appears forced. Hero's collapse is unexpected— it was Leonato who was supposed to be killed, not Hero (2.2), and while Don John is callous enough for anything, that surely cannot be the case with Don Pedro and Claudio. However, it is important to note, first of all, that the exit lines just quoted *are* Don John's, not Claudio's or Don Pedro's, even though Don John is Don Pedro's inferior and his prisoner. That is to say, it is evil that takes the initiative in this unforeseen situation, which is in line with the ascendancy it has already established in the play. Second, Don John uses the imperative phrase "Come, let us go," which suggests that the other two are not yet moving or, if they are, that they are moving toward Hero.

In other words, if Borachio's plot to "misuse the Prince," "vex Claudio," and "undo Hero" (2.2) is not to go awry under the impact of Hero's collapse, Don John has to intervene before Claudio and, possibly, Don Pedro may want to backtrack. So he whisks them off then and there, denigrating Hero as he does so to make sure that they continue to see her as he wants them to. "*Exeunt Don Pedro, Don John, and Claudio*" therefore really means that Don John exits but that Don Pedro and Claudio are removed. Being understood that way, Don John's exit with Don Pedro and Claudio, while providing Shakespeare with the departures he needs, loses much of its forced appearance. It shows the predominance of evil, and it also shows how weak Don Pedro and Claudio are in relation to Don John at this point in the play.

If exits service practicalities of plot, they also service practicalities of staging—for example, costume changes. In act 4, scene 1, of *A Midsummer Night's Dream,* Theseus and his entourage come upon Lysander, Hermia, Demetrius, and Helena while out hunting. Theseus takes young love's side against Egeus, the upshot is two more weddings, and everyone involved will need a change of clothes for the celebrations in act 5 (including the actor playing Egeus, if, as is likely, he is doubling as Philostrate). So, Shakespeare writes the hunters off the stage first: "THESEUS: Away with us to Athens. Three and three, / We'll hold a feast in great solemnity. / Come, Hippolyta." Obedience then sees the lovers off: "LYSANDER: And he did bid us follow to the temple. / DEMETRIUS: Why then, we are awake. Let's follow him, / And by the way let's recount our dreams." Bottom, waking up, holds the stage by launching into a twenty-line soliloquy about his dream before taking himself off to Athens. All of this enables the couples to bedizen themselves in the tiring-house before they come on again in act 5 in the same order as they had exited (Philostrate enters in the retinue of Theseus and Hippolyta, from which Egeus is fittingly absent). And the three couples' staggered and talkative return gives the hempen home-spuns the time they need offstage to prepare themselves for *Pyramus and Thisby.* Ready for them in the tiring-house are clean linen for Thisby, strings for their false beards, and new ribbons for their pumps (light shoes)—all itemized by Bottom in his exit speech at the end of act 4, scene 2, which concludes with the stage-clearing lines "No more words. Away, go, away!"

What works in one play will work in another. During act 3 of *Much Ado about Nothing,* Ursula enters to inform Hero that her bridegroom and his companions have come to fetch her to church, whereupon Hero exits with the stage-clearing line, "Help to dress me, good coz, good Meg, good Ursula" (3.4). While Dogberry and Verges take part in the intervening scene with Leonato (3.5), Hero gets herself ready in the tiring-house. Leonato, summoned to the wedding by a messenger, then exits to join the bridal party waiting out of sight to make its processional entrance (4.1); but he leaves Dogberry and Verges holding the stage as they drink the wine he has offered them. That generates more valuable seconds offstage for Leonato to take up his position. Unlike Hero at the end of act 3, scene 4, he may be largely or fully costumed by the time of his exit, since he says, "I'll wait upon them, I am ready" as he leaves the stage with the messenger (3.5). In both these comedies, the timing needs to be precise. By comparison, in *Henry IV, Part One,* the king has from the end of act 3, scene 2, to the beginning of act 5, scene 1, to change from his "easy robes of peace" into the "ungentle steel" of his armor. But the point remains: if a change of costume is called for, the actors concerned have to be plausibly removed from the stage and their absences covered while they ready themselves for their next entrance.

Macbeth shows that such a mundane practicality can be used for high dramatic effect. After Duncan's murder, Macbeth's hand is, or hands are, covered in blood, as are Lady Macbeth's. It would be pig's blood in reality,[1] so some straightforward cleaning up is needed. Shakespeare makes this need part of his plot. To avoid detection, the Macbeths must remove any sign of guilt before anyone else comes onstage, so an exit long enough for both of them to wash and for Macbeth to change into his nightgown is required. It is precipitated by Macduff's knocking outside (he will say after he enters that he has come by prearrangement to fetch Duncan). The knocking is carefully phased and, to make everything go smoothly, Shakespeare has Lady Macbeth explicitly link the second burst with exiting to wash and the third burst with an offstage change of costume ("watchers" means "people who have not yet gone to bed"):

> My hands are of your color; but I shame
> To wear a heart so white. (*Knock.*) I hear a knocking
> At the south entry. Retire we to our chamber.
> A little water clears us of this deed;
> How easy is it then! Your constancy
> Hath left you unattended. (*Knock.*) Hark, more knocking.
> Get on your night-gown, lest occasion call us
> And show us to be watchers.
>
> (2.2)

To provide maximum time offstage, Shakespeare gives the Porter a soliloquy that rivals Bottom's in length. It is twenty-one lines long and associates the Macbeths' castle with hell—and then comes his garrulous exchange with Macduff as well. All this gives Macbeth some forty-two lines to wash himself and put on his nightgown before reentering to Macduff's "Our knocking has awak'd him; here he comes" (2.3). Lady Macbeth gets even longer, namely, eighty lines, and her cleaned-up reentrance is made to look like a response to the alarm being sounded on the bell. By these means, high drama and lowly ablutions are perfectly synchronized.

II

Romeo parts from Juliet. Laertes leaves Elsinore.

It is easy to think of entrances as being positive, since they add to what is there, and of exits as being negative, since they subtract. But *Macbeth* is not Shakespeare's only play to show that, if managed imaginatively, exits can be as positive as entrances. For example, in a sequence of exits spread over the first two acts of *The Two Gentlemen of Verona,* Valentine sets off for love in Milan, Proteus then follows on the road to treachery, and Julia departs third, the sad truth about Proteus waiting for her in Milan. For the characters concerned, each of these exits is a departure into the unknown and each, in its own way, encourages a rising sense of expectation in the audience as the play's complications establish themselves.

Technically more ambitious and dramatically more portentous than the exits in *The Two Gentlemen of Verona* are Romeo's departure from Juliet in act 3, scene 5, of *Romeo and Juliet* and Laertes' from Ophelia and Polonius in act 1, scene 3, of *Hamlet.* Romeo's exit contributes directly to the play's gathering sense of doom, and Laertes' exit, initially less troubled than Romeo's, is nevertheless essential to *Hamlet's* tragic ending.

Romeo, banished for killing Tybalt, has secretly spent his wedding night in Juliet's room, but, with dawn approaching, he must leave. As Romeo puts it, "I must be gone and live, or stay and die." In such circumstances, only a paradox will do. To heighten the poignancy, Shakespeare initially has Romeo willing to leave and Juliet wanting him to stay; then, as Romeo changes his mind, Juliet's solicitude prevails over her love, and their attitudes become reversed. The scene is a tour de force of "harsh discords": love compels separation, the lark displaces the nightingale, and the lightening of day brings a darkening of woes. Unlike the lovers, Shakespeare knows two things at this point: that they will never again enjoy each other's company in this life; and that a frustrated communication will be their downfall. Consequently, with acute irony, he makes Juliet demand incessant news, and he has Romeo promise to "omit no opportunity" to send his greetings; and he writes expressions of foreboding into Juliet's lines, though only he, at this juncture, knows that they will be fulfilled, and how. One such line, spoken by Juliet as she follows Romeo's descent down the rope ladder, explicitly combines the physical verticality of the situation with the play's recurrent death imagery: "Methinks I see thee now, thou art so low, / As one dead in the bottom of a tomb." The first line of this quotation is a regular iambic pentameter, and it emphasizes the word "lów." The second line, while ostensibly also an iambic pentameter, in fact reverses the pattern of unstressed and stressed syllables in the second foot to emphasize the word "déad" ("As óne / déad in / the bót / tom óf / a tómb"). "Lów" and "tómb" come close to rhyming in an ominous way as well.

. It is worth adding that Friar Lawrence's verbal lead into this scene explicitly connects Romeo with disguise. In act 3, scene 3, he tells Romeo, "Either be gone before the watch be set, / Or by the break of day disguis'd from hence"—and it is now break of day. In her Oxford Shakespeare edition of *Romeo and Juliet,* Jill L. Levenson remarks, "The play never establishes whether Romeo flees in disguise" (p. 282, note to 3.3.167), but disguise in Shakespeare is a routine symbol for things not being as they should be, and here it would emphasize that, at this point in the play, Romeo has all but lost his civic identity. Shakespeare's source—Arthur Brooke's *The Tragicall Historye of Romeus and Juliet*—attires Romeo "like a merchant vent[u]rer, from top even to the toe," but Friar Lawrence's verbal lead is not so specific: the general prospect of disguise is enough on its own to underline Romeo's estranged situation. However, if he needs to, Shakespeare can always increase the precision of his verbal leading. In act 2, scene 1, of *Julius Caesar,* for example, Lucius informs Brutus before they come onstage that the men accompanying Cassius have "their hats . . . pluck'd about their ears, / And half their faces buried in their cloaks." In other words, they look exactly like conspirators, and by having Lucius bring them into his presence knowing that they look like that, Brutus symbolically aligns himself with their enterprise even before they enter.

In *Hamlet,* Laertes' departure for Paris also generates an exit that is heavy with consequences, though this time none of the characters involved has reason to suppose this. Polonius will be dead and Ophelia mad when Laertes returns in act 4, scene 5, and the ignorance brought about by an absence lasting some three acts is as important to Shakespeare as Laertes' youthful passion, since, deprived of direct knowledge, Laertes is given to brooding and is susceptible to the whisperings of, in Claudius's words, "buzzers [who] infect his ear / With pestilent speeches of his father's death" (4.5). Not knowing the true circumstances of Polonius's death, Laertes wrongly suspects Claudius when he bursts back into the play. But he is no match for the wily Claudius, who, with studied calmness, is already beginning to win him round when Ophelia enters. As soon as Laertes sees her, the impact of her madness overwhelms him, and this makes him easy meat for Claudius. In short, without Laertes' early exit and delayed return, *Hamlet* could not end as it does, with its restatement of the play's revenge theme, the poisoned rapier, and the deaths of Claudius, Gertrude, Laertes himself, and Hamlet.

III

Exits resulting from commands.

Valentine, Julia, Romeo (despite his unwillingness), and Laertes all leave the stage voluntarily in response to the circumstances of the moment. However, perhaps predictably, many of Shakespeare's exits result from commands—on the face of it, a humdrum device, but one that he sees to be rich in dramatic possibility. Two commands in *A Midsummer Night's Dream* show this well. First, the Second Fairy's "Hence, away! now all is well. / One aloof stand sentinel" (2.2) ironically exposes Titania to Oberon's ill will and adds a useful dash of aggression, too, if the fairy standing "aloof"—that is, at a distance—is physically disposed of by an attendant of Oberon's, as happens in some productions. Second, Titania's "Fairies, be gone, and be all ways away" (4.1) obtains for her privacy with the assified Bottom, which she would normally find unthinkable—at least, she believes it does, not knowing that Oberon is watching "*unseen.*" This assumed privacy makes intensified interaction with Bottom possible. As the embedded stage directions disclose, this intensified interaction is at once comic, grotesque, erotic, and passionate:

> TITANIA: So doth the woodbine the sweet honeysuckle
> Gently entwist; the female ivy so
> Enrings the barky fingers of the elm.
> O, how I love thee! how I dote on thee!
> > *They sleep.*

What if a command is *not* given in the context of an exit, even though one obviously should be? This happens in act 3, scene 3, of *The Merry Wives of Windsor,* and the result sheds a bright light on Master Ford's character as it is at that point in the play. Shakespeare likes to keep his audiences fully informed as a matter of course, so, with John and Robert's first exit pending, he has Mistress Ford run over with them what they are to do. They are to go into the brew-house to wait until called, and then their second exit will be to take the buck-basket on their shoulders "without any pause or staggering" and hurry it offstage to Datchet-mead and "the muddy ditch close by the Thames side." A different flanking door would be used for each of these exits to foster the notion that the virtual space behind the tiring-house facade is divided as well as extended. John and Robert are then ordered off, as is Robin, Falstaff's page. With Mistress Page in hiding, the stage becomes a trap for Falstaff. But it is a trap for Ford, too.

Fearing Ford's return, Falstaff hides himself in the buck-basket, and, as arranged, John and Robert are ordered to carry both it and him off the stage. As they prepare to exit, Ford bursts in with Page, Caius, and Evans. Ford is master of the house, yet he is not even master of himself at this moment, as is shown by what follows. A man more in possession of himself would countermand the exit instruction given to John and Robert, order the basket to be put down, and have its contents investigated. But Ford is so distracted by the association of buck with cuckold that his judgment fails him, and John and Robert carry Falstaff off the stage, just as they have been told to. By means of the exits ordered by Mistress Ford and of the omission by Ford of the one command that would really make the difference, Shakespeare accomplishes three things. He prevents his play from coming to a halt, which it would do if Falstaff were discovered by Ford at this point; he paves the way for Falstaff's next punishment; and he demonstrates comically the personal disarray and defective judgment jealousy can cause.

Since drama is an active art, one way of increasing the *expulsive* force of commands is to add anger. Anger and exits form a natural pair: anger arises when something or someone has become insufferable, and insufferableness readily leads to a casting out. In act 1, scene 3, of *Henry IV, Part One,* Henry commands Worcester:

> Worcester, get thee gone, for I do see
> Danger and disobedience in thine eye.
> O, sir, your presence is too bold and peremptory,
> And majesty might never yet endure
> The moody frontier of a servant brow.

Henry has four reasons to be angry. First, in the play's opening scene, Westmerland has told Henry that Worcester is "[m]alevolent to you in all aspects." Second, Worcester has just openly reminded Henry that he is a usurper and that the Percys have helped him. Third, "in thine eye" suggests that Worcester has accompanied his words with an ocular challenge. To look a monarch in the eye was a breach of protocol. That is why Lear, clinging to the remnants of his authority, exclaims to Oswald, "Do you bandy looks with me, you rascal?" (*King Lear,* 1.4) and strikes him (which he should not do).[2]

The fourth reason—it is the one that determines the character of Henry's own eventual exit—is that Henry is determined to demonstrate that he is in charge. Having taken the crown from Richard II by outfacing him, he is resolute that no one will in turn force the crown from him or call into question his "majesty," that is, his claim to legitimacy, even by a look. When Henry opens this scene, he says that he intends to be "mighty" and "fear'd," since to be otherwise would be to forfeit respect, and that would be dangerous. His strong line with Worcester is a product of this intention. So is his strong line with Hotspur, whom he orders, "Send me your prisoners with the speediest means, / Or you shall hear in such a kind from me / As will displease you." And so is his exit. The stage direction simply reads, "*Exit King with Blunt and Train,*" but Henry's is, demonstratively, a *royal* exit. Having instructed Hotspur what to do, Henry leaves at a time of his own choosing, in good order and in accordance with protocol. That is, he exits as someone insisting on his majesty being accepted without question.

The good order of Henry's exit is crucial. It is not neutral; it is a show of authority on Henry's part, and Henry, ever alert to public relations, is a showman to his fingertips. Conversely, a disorderly exit would show a lack of authority. This happens in the "solemn supper" scene in act 3, scene 4, of *Macbeth,* and it provides such an instructive contrast to Henry's show of legitimacy that it repays a small digression. Anger is present in the "solemn supper" scene, too, but it is directed *at* the king by his wife, not *by* the king at another or at others. What really powers the exit command is anxiety.

The scene opens as if all were well. Macbeth explicitly says, as Rosse and Lennox enter with the lords and attendants, "You know your own degrees, sit down." Observing protocol, the queen "keeps her state," that is, remains seated on her throne, but Macbeth, feigning affability in order to mislead, permits himself to "mingle with society" in unkingly fashion. However, during the scene, he is—or thinks he is—twice confronted by Banquo's ghost, and his guilty behavior threatens to give the game away. Finally, Rosse asks what it is precisely that Macbeth claims to have seen. That is the question that must on no account be answered, so the queen cuts in with, "I pray you speak not. He grows worse and worse, / Question enrages him." Then she orders the guests to leave without more ado, attendants and all. Her words form an antithetical pair with those the king used to open the scene. The queen's words are: "At once, good night. / Stand not upon the order of your going, / But go at once." The guests' abandoning their order of precedence as they depart symbolizes Macbeth's inability to assert and sustain the legitimacy he has claimed for himself by murdering Duncan. So does the fact that they exit not at his command but at the queen's.

Lest anger appear to be the prerogative of suspect characters, it should be remembered that angry commands can also have a cleansing effect. A spectacular example of this occurs in *Twelfth Night*. It is clear from act 1, scene 3, onward that, at some point, Olivia will have to be firm with Sir Toby, if temperance and moderation are to return to her household. Her watershed act of assertion occurs in act 4, scene 1, when Sir Toby draws his sword on Sebastian (whom Olivia believes to be Cesario), and Olivia, in a crisis of concern, pours out her pent-up emotions:

> Will it be ever thus? Ungracious wretch,
> Fit for the mountains and the barbarous caves,
> Where manners ne'er were preached! Out of my sight!
> Be not offended, dear Cesario.
> Rudesby, be gone!

Sir Toby exits immediately. He never recovers from this verbal drubbing, and, following a couple of brief returns, he is written out of the play along with Sir Andrew and Maria. Olivia's flush of anger makes her decisive. Without it, Shakespeare would have had to devise an entirely different way to remove misrule from the play, and it is not easy to see how he could have done this.

IV

Exits and emotions. Meanings of "human" as applied to Macbeth. Outstanding exits in Henry IV, Part One, Julius Caesar, *and* The Winter's Tale *("Exit pursued by a bear" [3.3]).*

It should be clear by now that the character of exits changes in accordance with the emotions and issues that form their contexts. Shakespeare's range in this regard is very wide, as the merest glance reveals:

There is a *horrifying clash of associations* in *Titus Andronicus* as Titus and Lavinia, his raped and mutilated daughter, exit to prepare the heads of Chiron and Demetrius as pies for their mother, Tamora. Titus has the knife and Lavinia has the basin for the blood:

> TITUS: Hark, villains, I will grind your bones to dust,
> And with your blood and it I'll make a paste,
> And of the paste a coffin I will rear,

And make two pasties of your shameful heads,
And bid that strumpet, your unhallowed dam,
Like to the earth swallow her own increase.
. . . .
He cuts their throats.
So now bring them in, for I'll play the cook,
And see them ready against their mother comes.
Exeunt bearing the dead bodies.

(5.2)

Malvolio's impotent *resentment* as he storms out of *Twelfth Night* is well known, but just as negative is the leave-taking *hatred* of Timon of Athens in the play of that name: "And grant, as Timon grows, his hate may grow / To the whole race of mankind, high and low! / Amen" (4.1).

Shylock's last lines in *The Merchant of Venice* express the *desolation* of a broken man: "I pray you give me leave to go from hence, / I am not well" (4.1).

All's Well That Ends Well includes the *poignancy* of Helena begging a kiss from the infuriated Bertram:

BERTRAM:　　　　　　　　　　　　What would you have?
HELENA: Something, and scarce so much; nothing indeed.
I would not tell you what I would, my lord.
Faith, yes:
Strangers and foes do sunder, and not kiss.
BERTRAM: I pray you stay not, but in haste to horse.

(2.5)

And *Henry V* contains one of the most *patriotic* exits in English literature, namely, "Cry, 'God for Harry, England, and Saint George!'" (3.1).

Vengefulness, extreme self-pity, a sense of defeat, importunate love, and military motivation: Shakespeare obviously never intended his exits to be isolated and compared in this way but, even so, putting them into a list brings out clearly how they repeatedly contribute to sharply drawn human situations.

However, "human" is a word that requires further defining, since it can be used honorifically to mean having a moral sense and being therefore better than any animal, or it can be used anthropologically to mean having at least some of the defining qualities of being a human being, not excluding the bad ones. A question-begging case is that of the murderer. Can a murderer be human? And, if so, in what sense or senses? In act 2, scene 1, of *Macbeth*, Macbeth steels himself to murder Duncan, who is asleep. It is a moment Shakespeare has prepared very carefully. Macbeth has made his scruples clear; his wife has pressured him into acquiescence by challenging his manhood; and, immediately before his soliloquy, Macbeth has ordered his servant, "Go bid thy mistress, when my drink is ready, / She strike upon the bell." Shakespeare wants Macbeth completely alone onstage.

During his soliloquy, Macbeth comes face to face with the moral enormity of what he is about to do. As he reflects, however, he realizes that he is interposing words between himself and the deed: the longer he reflects, the more likely he is to backtrack. So the situation is exactly poised. But, just as he starts to waver, the bell rings, and this acoustical reminder of his wife makes him submit to her will once more. Consequently, he exits with murderous intent, but at the same time exuding reluctance, craven obedience, and an acute sense of guilt: "I go, and it is done; the bell invites me. / Hear it not, Duncan, for it is a knell, / That summons thee to heaven or to hell." Macbeth's exit shows him to be human in both senses of the word. Since he has a sense of right and wrong, he is better than any animal; but since he is capable of murder, he has something of the worst of human nature in him as well.

Macbeth is one of those Shakespearean characters whose successive exits amount to a countdown, since they will not outlive the play they are in; and whether their deaths are original to Shakespeare or determined by his source material, they are nothing if not varied. For example, Macbeth's queen dies ignominiously to an offstage cry of women (*Macbeth,* 5.5); Clarence is finished off in a malmsey-butt (*Richard III,* 1.4); and Arthur jumps to his death from his prison (*King John,* 4.3)—no mean feat in practice, since the boy actor playing Arthur has to jump from the balcony onto the open stage without hurting himself.[3] In principle, Shakespeare is indifferent to whether his characters die on- or offstage, as long as their deaths and, as necessary, the removal of their bodies have dramatic worth. This is demonstrated by three last exits that are outstanding even by Shakespeare's standards: those of Hotspur (*Henry IV, Part One*), Julius Caesar (*Julius Caesar*), and Antigonus (*The Winter's Tale*).

Act 5, scene 4, of *Henry IV, Part One,* includes Hotspur, dead, on Falstaff's back. It is an astonishing image, but it makes complete sense. Hotspur, the honor-greedy rebel, and Falstaff, the undutiful coward, belong together as enemies of the state as it now is under Henry IV, and their grotesque conjunction shows their common baseness. When Falstaff finally carries Hotspur off the stage, it is in the service of a lie: Falstaff is claiming his reward for having "killed" him. Hotspur exits, therefore, with his dignity comprehensively negated, as befits a rebel. Prince Hal, now reformed, refers to him as "luggage" (5.4).

Julius Caesar's last exit (3.2) is also colored by Shakespeare's abhorrence of political instability and civil war. Brutus, the rationalist, has organized the murder of Caesar in order, as he sees it, to curtail Caesar's emerging tendency toward tyranny. It is a well-intentioned and patriotic act of violence, and Brutus might well be able to persuade the Romans that he has acted for the best, except that Antony intervenes. Antony's motivation is personal and vengeful, and he is prepared to instigate civil war to achieve his ends. The polarization between Brutus and Antony is symbolized by the ambiguity of Caesar's body: it is either the remains of a forestalled tyrant or, as Antony believes, the remains of "the noblest man / That ever lived in the tide of times" (3.1). It is supremely important who finally bears the body offstage and in conjunction with what words since, if Antony prevails, so will demagogy.

Antony obtains permission to produce Caesar's body in the marketplace in order, as he beguilingly puts it, to deliver a funeral oration for his friend (3.1). Brutus's rational prose—without the body present—is convincing until Antony, speaking verse and having brought the body onstage, successfully works on the crowd's emotions, turning it into a destructive mob. It is this mob that bears Caesar's body off, intending to burn down the houses of the men they call traitors; and Antony, satisfied to see the force he has unleashed, follows up with "Now let it work. Mischief, thou art afoot, / Take thou what course thou wilt!"

Like the carrying off of the bodies of Hotspur and Julius Caesar, the bear's fatal pursuit of Antigonus in act 3, scene 3, of *The Winter's Tale* is a precise symbol as well as a powerful one. As the act draws to a close, Shakespeare wants to show that he is redirecting his tragicomedy toward new beginnings and new life. Antigonus, unlike Paulina, his wife, is unable to rise above Leontes' jealousy, so there is an element of personal punishment in his death. But Shakespeare also needs to keep Leontes alive for the happy ending in act 5, so Antigonus dies as a scapegoat, too. He is killed by a bear to symbolize what a bestial emotion like jealousy is capable of; and the audience, well used to bears, would draw the obvious conclusion that, in a better state of affairs, the man would control the bear, not be its victim. To emphasize the purgative nature of Antigonus's final exit, it is followed by the introduction of new characters into the play (the Shepherd and his son). It is also followed by the discovery of Perdita (alive) and by the Shepherd's key line "thou met'st with things dying, I with things new-born." As the newcomers leave the stage, the Shepherd's son announces his intention to bury what remains of Antigonus. The play can now wind its way toward reconciliation, part of which will be the replacement of Antigonus as Paulina's husband by Camillo, the healer.

V

Prospero's question-raising exit from The Tempest.

As Antigonus's departure alone shows, one explanation for Shakespeare's exits working as well as they do is that, even when their form is extraordinary, their whys and wherefores are perfectly straightforward. But Prospero's last exit from *The Tempest* (5.1) is a well-known exception, and there are two reasons why this should be.

One is the persistent belief that *The Tempest* expresses Shakespeare's wish to retire from playhouse life. S. Schoenbaum traces this belief back to 1838, when a minor man of letters, Thomas Campbell, wrote, "Here Shakspeare [*sic*] himself is Prospero, or rather the superior genius who commands both Prospero and Ariel. But the time was approaching when the potent sorcerer was to break his staff, and to bury it fathoms in the ocean—Deeper than did ever plummet sound. That staff has never been, and never will be, recovered."[4] Never mind that Prospero actually proposes to bury his staff in the earth, not the ocean. If Prospero "is" Shakespeare, it looks as if *The Tempest* contains the exit to end all exits, namely, that of the dramatist himself.

But is *The Tempest* as autobiographical as all that? Shakespeare returned to Stratford to live in 1610; *The Tempest* is likely to have been written there late that year;[5] Prospero speaks of retiring to Milan (5.1); and he asks to be released from "this bare island" (epilogue), that is, from the stage. Furthermore, some of the play's most famous lines are valedictory in character:

> But this rough magic
> I here abjure; and when I have requir'd
> Some heavenly music (which even now I do)
> To work mine end upon their senses that
> This airy charm is for, I'll break my staff,
> Bury it certain fadoms in the earth,
> And deeper than did ever plummet sound
> I'll drown my book.
>
> (5.1)

Consequently, it is easy to assume a personal adieu in *The Tempest,* especially since, in act 4, scene 1, Prospero seems to envisage holus-bolus the end of playwriting, of the Globe theater, and of life itself:

> Our revels now are ended. These our actors
> (As I foretold you) were all spirits, and

Are melted into air, into thin air,
And like the baseless fabric of this vision,
The cloud-capp'd tow'rs, the gorgeous palaces,
The solemn temples, the great globe itself,
Yea, all which it inherit, shall dissolve,
And like this insubstantial pageant faded
Leave not a rack behind. We are such stuff
As dreams are made on; and our little life
Is rounded with a sleep.

Yet such lines belong to specific contexts in the play, and it is a matter of historical fact that Shakespeare, far from breaking his staff and drowning his book after *The Tempest,* went on to author or coauthor *The Two Noble Kinsmen,* the now lost *Cardenio,* and *Henry VIII.* And there is also the fact that *The Tempest,* which was written for the Blackfriars theater, shows relish for writing for indoor performance.[6] So it is unwise to see Prospero's leave-taking as Shakespeare's.

But the sheer tenacity of the belief that it *is* Shakespeare's leave-taking reveals an important point about the way Shakespeare writes, namely, that he writes paradigmatically. Paradigms are patterns or exemplars. They are precise in their details, but, when it comes to interpretation, they are not necessarily confined to a single meaning. When, in *A Midsummer Night's Dream,* Bottom asks Quince, "What is Pyramus? a lover, or a tyrant?" (1.2), what he wants is a paradigm, but one with a single clear meaning, to help him understand his part. On the other hand, when a modern interpretation of a character, or of a whole play, is billed, say, as a Hamlet or a *Coriolanus* "for our time," it means that there are patterns in the original characterization or original whole play that can be assimilated to later situations Shakespeare could not have fully envisaged. Writing paradigmatically is, therefore, strong in two ways, but it also has a disadvantage. It is strong in that it fosters intelligibility and makes for adaptability over time. But when it comes to ascertaining the author's original intention, paradigms are not always helpful, since they have it within them to assume a life of their own.

The second reason why Prospero's last exit is problematic is that it occurs neither when, nor in the manner that, it might be expected to. It might reasonably be expected to take place at the end of act 5, when Prospero releases Ariel with the words, "Be free, and fare thou well!" But, while the other characters leave the stage at that point, Prospero remains to deliver an epilogue. And what makes *that* unusual is that, as the stage direction "*Spoken by* PROSPERO" makes clear, he addresses the audience directly as if the play were over, while remaining in character as if it were still running.[7] It goes without saying that Prospero's epilogue is a skillful essay in milking applause at the end of a live performance. But the fact that Prospero remains in character invites the conjecture that Shakespeare did not want his audience to think of *The Tempest* as over and done with when it reached its last line. He seems rather to have wanted it to persist in the audience's memory as an experience to be reflected on. Perhaps Alonso is indirectly hinting at this when he says to Prospero, as if the latter has a real life to report: "I long / To hear the story of your life, *which must / Take the ear strangely*" (5.1; italics added).

In fact, of course, Alonso and Prospero are two characters talking to each other within a play, so Prospero has no reportable real life as such. But Prospero, speaking his epilogue at the play's outer edge, seems to be implying that, while *The Tempest* is a work of fiction, its effectiveness is comparable to that of lived events. That would be a large claim on Shakespeare's part, but it is a defensible one, and it is consistent, too, with Hamlet's articulation of "the purpose of playing" as "holding as 'twere the mirror up to nature" (*Hamlet*, 3.2. "The purpose of playing" is discussed in chapter 1, section V).

VI

Aborted exits.

No examination of Shakespeare's exits is complete without consideration of aborted exits, that is, of exits that are intended but that are then prevented for one reason or another. Inconspicuous in performance, aborted exits are technically indispensable, since they keep characters plausibly onstage when their presence there is essential. In act 1 of *Henry IV, Part One,* if the enraged Hotspur does actually exit to pursue Henry, as he threatens to do, then he will not be present and susceptibly "drunk with choler" (1.3) when Worcester returns. So Shakespeare gives Northumberland the restraining line "Stay, and pause a while. / Here comes your uncle," and it is enough to ensure that Hotspur is onstage when he is in the right frame of mind to welcome Worcester's treason. In act 2 of *A Midsummer Night's Dream,* Oberon's "Tarry, rash wanton!" (2.1) keeps Titania available for the important big quarrel between them. And in act 4 of *The Merchant of Venice,* Portia's "Tarry, Jew" (4.1) compels Shylock to hear out the consequences of the law now that it is no longer his ally. However, one of Shakespeare's most skillful and least obvious aborted exits occurs in the last act of *Much Ado about Nothing.*

When act 5 opens near Leonato's house, Leonato is convinced that Hero is "belied," but he has no evidence to support that conviction. Consequently, he has nothing with which to rebut Don Pedro when the latter asserts: "My heart is sorry for your daughter's death; / But on my honor she was charg'd with nothing / But what was true, and very full of proof."

Leonato, in an impotent rage, exits with Antonio at this point, and Don Pedro and Claudio, who have come onstage eager to separate themselves from Leonato, ought therefore to exit, too. But, having expediently removed Leonato and Antonio by means of a perfunctory one-liner—Leonato's "Come, brother, away!"—Shakespeare needs to keep Don Pedro and Claudio onstage till Borachio and Conrade arrive with Dogberry from the prison, so that they can be shamed by Borachio, who has the solid evidence Leonato lacks. Once that is done, Leonato, having been independently briefed by the Sexton offstage, can reenter with Antonio to confront Don Pedro and Claudio from a position of strength.

Shakespeare initially delays the exit of Don Pedro and Claudio by having Benedick enter by one door as Leonato and Antonio leave by the other, but, of itself, that would achieve little: Don Pedro and Claudio have been looking for Benedick anyway, so they could now all leave the stage together. This is where the duel with Claudio, handily promised by Benedick to Beatrice in act 4, scene 1, comes into its own. Shakespeare never intends for this duel to take place, but, simply because Benedick has agreed to it, he (Benedick) needs to go through the process of challenging Claudio and, while he is at it, to separate himself from Don Pedro as well. So, what with Don Pedro and Claudio's preliminary banter with Benedick plus Benedick's challenge and words of separation to Don Pedro, some eighty-four lines elapse before Benedick exits—and on his own, as his estranged situation requires. Again, there is nothing to stop Don Pedro and Claudio from exiting, too, but instead they are kept right where they are, this time by reviewing, as anyone might, what Benedick has just said. Consequently, they are still onstage when Dogberry and the Watch make their crucial entrance with Borachio and Conrade, who are tied up on the Sexton's orders (4.2). Even then, Don Pedro and Claudio could still remember their hurry and leave, since it is Leonato Dogberry wants to see, not them. But Don Pedro recognizes Dogberry's prisoners, and Claudio naturally wants him to ask what they have done; thus, Don Pedro and Claudio are brought to their moment of truth. Shamed by what they learn from Borachio, they then have to face Leonato. When their deftly delayed exit does finally occur, their pride is replaced by insight and regret, and, as part of the play's movement toward reconciliation, they agree to rejoin Leonato the following morning.

Shakespeare's virtuoso handling of Don Pedro's and Claudio's aborted exit prompts a postscript about exits in general. When Shakespeare's soliloquies, characterizations, or verse are discussed, testimonies to his greatness routinely pour forth, but when the word "exits" is uttered, conversation comes to a halt. Yet open a collected edition of his plays at virtually any page, and "*Exit*" (or "*Exeunt*") leaps to the eye. In other words, exits are so numerous and so integral to the plays in which they occur that there is no alternative to taking them seriously. Their quality may dip here and there, though the reader is more likely to spot that than the playgoer. In their variety and ingenuity, however, they add up to one of the great glories of Shakespeare's stagecraft.

Chapter 4

CHARACTERIZATION

I

From abstractions to individual characters. Why individual characters and whole plays make sense. Characterization and the mediation of issues.

Act 5 of *A Midsummer Night's Dream* begins with an exchange between male and female ways of thinking. Hippolyta is intrigued by what the lovers have been saying about the previous night, but Theseus will have none of it:

> Lovers and madmen have such seething brains,
> Such shaping fantasies, that apprehend
> More than cool reason ever comprehends.
> The lunatic, the lover, and the poet
> Are of imagination all compact.
> One sees more devils than vast hell can hold;
> That is the madman. The lover, all as frantic,
> Sees Helen's beauty in a brow of Egypt.
> The poet's eye, in a fine frenzy rolling,
> Doth glance from heaven to earth, from earth to heaven;
> And as imagination bodies forth
> The forms of things unknown, the poet's pen
> Turns them to shapes, and gives to aery nothing
> A local habitation and a name.
> Such tricks hath strong imagination,

That if it would but apprehend some joy,
It comprehends some bringer of that joy;
Or in the night, imagining some fear,
How easy is a bush suppos'd a bear!

Theseus's target is the imagination. In his view, what the lunatic sees is self-evidently untrue; the lover sees beauty where it does not exist ("Egypt" implies swarthy and offends against Elizabethan notions of beauty); and "aery nothing" is all that lies behind the poet's creations. In all three cases, "cool reason" has the upper hand, and the imagination is discredited.

Hippolyta is less certain. She, too, distances herself from "fancy's images," but, at the same time, she feels intuitively that she has been listening to something significant, so, for want of better, she inclines to words like "strange" and "admirable" (meaning "to be wondered at"). What she cannot know is that the play that she is in, *A Midsummer Night's Dream,* completes her case and accommodates Theseus's, too. In dismissing poets, Theseus dismisses playwrights. But the playwright of the play in which Theseus does his dismissing—Shakespeare himself—knew that writing a play combines the imagination (including the strange and the admirable) *with* cool reason. *A Midsummer Night's Dream,* a play that is simultaneously imaginative and reasoned, is his proof.

Theseus may be dismissive, but his tracing of a process from initial inspiration to specific formulations betrays an insider's knowledge of playwriting. He speaks of "joy" generating "some bringer of that joy" and of "fear" generating some bringer of that fear, and the movement from abstract to concrete he describes is a linchpin of the art. Sir Philip Sidney (1554–1586) highlights the same movement in *A Defence of Poetry,* which was written in 1581(?), circulated in manuscript, and published in 1595. It was, therefore, broadly contemporaneous with *A Midsummer Night's Dream,* which is usually dated 1595/1596. Certain philosophers, says Sidney, called anger "a short madness," but if you really want to know what madness is, then what you need is "Ajax on a stage, killing or whipping sheep and oxen, thinking them the army of Greeks, with their chieftains Agamemnon and Menelaus."[1] Sidney and Shakespeare are often compared with each other, since their positions, while not identical, can be close. However, a major difference between them lies in their respective attitudes to the unities of place, time, and action, that is, the placing of theoretical restrictions on where a play is to be located, how much time it is supposed to take place in, and by how much its plot can proliferate. Sidney favored these restrictions, but Shakespeare was more interested in unifying his plays by means of character and theme and therefore felt free to disregard them.[2]

Theseus's bear is anonymous, as is the one which pursues Antigonus out of *A Winter's Tale,* but the bear-baiting enthusiasts of Shakespeare's England were not above favoring a bear with a proper name—hence Slender's reference in *The Merry Wives of Windsor* to "Sackerson" (1.1), which was a real live Bankside bear. Names are functional. For a start, they establish a relationship between the name's owner and those who know the name. That is why Claudius's *not* being named anywhere in the dialogue of *Hamlet* is so effective. It emphasizes the fact that, because of his guilty secret, Claudius is not properly knowable to those around him: he is a king of surfaces and stealth. Giving characters a name also imparts to them the twin illusions of individuality and autonomy, and locating them in a particular place—"a local habitation"—reinforces those illusions. For example, anyone visiting Datchet, near Windsor (England), may find the temptation to look for the site where Falstaff was thrown into the Thames hard to resist. Even when names are unusual—like Guiderius in *Cymbeline*—and even when the "local habitation" might give pause—Bohemia in *The Winter's Tale* is notoriously set on the coast—no one takes exception as long as the characters themselves and the plays they are in make sense.

But why—to take characters first—*should* they make sense? Part of the answer is that Shakespeare normally constructs characters in such a way that the big abstractions they personalize are clearly apparent in them. Jealousy is recognizable in Othello, ambition in Lady Macbeth, and cowardice in Falstaff. This easy recognizability is what makes the vast majority of his characters seem transparent. The fact that initial characteristics can be modified during the course of a play does not affect the basic principle. In Lady Macbeth, guilt supersedes ambition, and, as she sleepwalks in act 5, scene 1, she makes new sense in terms of her new dominant characteristic. In Leontes (*The Winter's Tale*), jealousy yields to love, and his characterization modulates accordingly. But there is no loss of clarity in either character. As for characters who are open to more than one interpretation, that phenomenon arises because they contain more than one significant characteristic. For example, in *Henry IV, Part One,* Prince Hal shows opportunism *and* duty. The essential difficulty is not that the characterization of such characters is blurred but that it is not possible to reduce their characteristics to a single denominator.

As to the plays as a whole making sense, Shakespeare understands exceptionally well how individual characteristics interact with one another, and this understanding informs both the construction of his casts of characters and the way he mediates issues. Ordinary experience teaches that human characteristics like love, jealousy, honor, or greed all have their own distinctive shape, feel, and drive—their grammar, so to speak—and Shakespeare turns this grammar to his advantage. For example, ambition can work on moral weakness in such a way that a Lady Macbeth may credibly pressure her hero husband into murder, and the repercussions arising from "the deed" involve the remainder of *Macbeth*'s cast in accordance with the characteristics they are given. By this means, the play becomes a total statement, and the Doctor is as much part of the whole as Banquo, Macduff, or the Weïrd Sisters. Shakespeare does not normally foist behavior on his characters arbitrarily. He makes their behavior consistent with the characteristics he gives them and with the characteristics of those around them.

When it comes to mediating issues, Shakespeare's way of working is both to express them and to imply their evaluation by means of his characters' interaction. One of Shakespeare's great "issue" plays is *Coriolanus*. It is "about" civic duty, factionalism, and the security of the state, and Coriolanus, the tribunes, Aufidius, and the rest of the cast are so characterized and deployed that these abstractions are, literally, enacted before the eyes of the audience in such a way that they can be understood and assessed, too. Coriolanus is proud and reluctant to compromise, the tribunes are opportunistic but shortsighted, Aufidius is predatory, and so on. As these and the other characters in the play act and react, the play's issues are moved along as well. This seamless duality explains why it is that a play like *Coriolanus* makes sense in either psychological or in "issue" terms, yet it seems mutilated unless both domains are ultimately interpreted together.

It was Shakespeare's success in presenting human characteristics onstage that prompted Samuel Johnson famously to declare, "Nothing can please many, and please long, but just representations of general nature" ("just" means "accurate" and "general" means "human").[3] To the eighteenth-century Johnson, the customs and conventions of Shakespeare's day were remote and rebarbative. Yet the plays lived on, not least in London's Drury Lane theater, and Johnson argues that this is because the human traits they communicate are not confined to a single time but are permanent. In a striking phrase, he claims that those traits and, therefore, the plays that express them have "the stability of truth" ("stability" means "invariability").[4] It is a convincing argument. Who has not known a latter-day Romeo, shut up in his room, isolated from his parents, and lovesick? Or an Antony, over the hill and enslaved to a love he would be better off without?

II

Self-knowing characters, especially evildoers. Complementary characterization. Why some evil characters change and others do not.

Important to Shakespeare's characterization is self-knowledge. Some characters have it from the outset, others come to it later on. From a dramatist's point of view, there are advantages to both sorts. Characters who know themselves early can, like Richard III, explain themselves to the audience before things really get under way, while characters who do not know themselves can undergo a process of self-discovery. One group from which self-knowledge is inseparable is Shakespeare's evil characters, the reason being that evil is a moral concept, so evil characters have to be, or have to become, self-knowing; otherwise they would not be evil.

Consistent with his practice of personalizing abstractions, Shakespeare likes to conceive evil in terms of perpetrators and either actual or potential victims. Macbeth needs time to discover the full extent of his evil, but when he yields to it by murdering Duncan and arranging for the murders of Banquo, Fleance, and Macduff's family, he does so knowingly, his acts are voluntary, and his victims do not deserve what befalls them. In *Measure for Measure,* Angelo needs time, too, but, once he falls, it is only thanks to others that he sins less than he wants to.

Knowing oneself to be evil, proposing to inflict damage, and then doing precisely that connects such otherwise disparate villains as Aaron the Moor (*Titus Andronicus*), Don John (*Much Ado about Nothing*), Iago (*Othello*), and Edmund (*King Lear*). This is Aaron explaining himself with an evildoer's natural self-centeredness. Symbolically, the actor playing him would be blacked up for the part:[5]

> Even now I curse the day—and yet I think
> Few come within the compass of my curse—
> Wherein I did not some notorious ill:
> As kill a man, or else devise his death,
> Ravish a maid, or plot the way to do it,
> Accuse some innocent, and forswear myself,
> Set deadly enmity between two friends,
> Make poor men's cattle break their necks,
> Set fire on barns and haystalks in the night,
> And bid the owners quench them with their tears.
>
> (5.1)

This is Don John, the self-styled "plain-dealing villain" (1.3), speaking of Claudio (the blasphemy is intentional on Shakespeare's part): "If I can cross him any way, I bless myself every way" (1.3). This is Iago, the white villain, speaking of Othello, the black victim:

> The Moor is of a free and open nature,
> That thinks men honest that but seem to be so,

And will as tenderly be led by th' nose
As asses are.
I have't. It is engend'red. Hell and night
Must bring this monstrous birth to the world's light.

(1.3)

And this is Edmund:

A credulous father and a brother noble,
Whose nature is so far from doing harms
That he suspects none; on whose foolish honesty
My practices ride easy. I see the business.
Let me, if not by birth, have lands by wit:

(1.2)

It is Edmund, too, who spells out that evil characters are evil by choice, not out of necessity. They are entirely responsible for what they do:

This is the excellent foppery of the world, that when we are sick in fortune—often the surfeits of our own behavior—we make guilty of our disasters the sun, the moon, and stars, as if we were villains on necessity, fools by heavenly compulsion, . . . and all that we are evil in, by a divine thrusting on. (1.2)

Shakespeare knew that an individual's psyche is a lock that can be opened if the right psychological key can be found. Don John, guided by Borachio, attacks Claudio through his jealousy and Don Pedro through his pride; Iago attacks Othello through his naïveté and jealousy; and, just as he says he will, Edmund exploits his father's credulity and his brother's "foolish honesty." This lock-and-key complementarity has two advantages. First, it removes in principle the need for any external means of doing damage. Don John thinks fleetingly of poison (1.3), but such crudeness is at variance with the whole analytical thrust of Shakespeare's plays, so the thought comes and goes as a passing expression of spite. Building vulnerability into characters and exposing them to those wanting to take advantage of it makes for much more illuminating theater. Second, if complementarity is restricted in application, a play can be made to divide. This happens in *The Merry Wives of Windsor*. Shakespeare wants to keep Master Page out of the "Ford/Brook" episode that dominates the earlier part of the play, so, when Pistol works on Ford's jealousy, Ford is taken in, but, when Nym tries the same thing on Page, Page is unreceptive. This leaves him free to be outwitted by his daughter and Fenton in the latter part of the play.

Why do some evil characters change while others do not? Aaron is con-
demned to death, Iago is seized, and Don John is recaptured, all without re-
penting. That is, they represent Shakespeare's view of evil as being as permanent as the devil, and the refusal of Aaron and Iago to repent also allows
Shakespeare to put the dramatically attractive phenomenon of defiance on
stage. Iago's last lines in *Othello* are good theater because they are enigmatic,
but Aaron's, which now follow, are good theater because they are straight-
forwardly outrageous.

> Ten thousand worse than ever yet I did
> Would I perform if I might have my will.
> If one good deed in all my life I did,
> I do repent it from my very soul.
>
> (5.3)

If repentance occurs in a character, there have to be convincing reasons
for it. Edmund shows this clearly. Given the preponderance of his behavior
in *King Lear,* he might well be expected to remain evil to the end. Yet, defeated and facing death, he is moved by Edgar's account of Gloucester's death
(5.3), and, shortly afterward, he says, "I pant for life. Some good I mean to do,
/ Despite of mine own nature" (5.3). It is possible that Shakespeare wanted
to show that Edmund is not entirely without human susceptibility. What is
certain is that Shakespeare saw that he could intensify the play's ending by
having Edmund reveal, but too late, that he has arranged for Cordelia to be
put to death. In short, Edmund's repentance arguably makes sense, given the
extreme nature of its circumstances. At the same time, however, it is difficult
to exempt it entirely from suspicion of authorial manipulation.

In *Much Ado about Nothing,* Borachio's repentance is much more obviously governed by expediency. Borachio is one of the play's evil trio, along
with Conrade and Don John, but although the three form a unit, their roles
are differentiated. Conrade, who is scarcely characterized at all, functions
principally as—from Shakespeare's point of view—a handy listener: villains
can scarcely impart confidences to good characters, so, either soliloquies or
other villains are required if the audience is to be privy to their secrets. So,
first, Don John tells Conrade (and the audience) how resentful he is (1.3),
and second, Borachio tells Conrade (and the Watch, which is listening in)
how Don John has deceived Don Pedro and Claudio (3.3). Thereafter, Conrade plays the captured villain, in which role he provokes one of Dogberry's
best speeches ("Dost thou not suspect my place?" [4.2]). Conrade's surliness
serves the play best if it remains intact until he is led out of the play in act

5, so repentance is not really an option for him. Don John is a more active character than Conrade, but since he represents evil as a permanent threat to others, repentance is not for him, either. However, Borachio, while initially close to Don John, is not characterized as absolutely as his master, and he can therefore repent when he hears of Hero's alleged death, on the grounds that his plan was not intended to go so far in her case. In real life, it is doubtful whether such a rogue as Borachio would soften as he does, but comedies permit a certain license, Shakespeare needed someone in the know to rebut Don Pedro and Claudio, and a remorseful Borachio fits the bill. Unusually for Shakespeare, Borachio's moment of remorse has no dialogue. Shakespeare must have intended that it be signaled by gesture when the Sexton says, "Hero . . . upon the grief of this suddenly died" (4.2).

While Edmund, Aaron, Don John, Iago, and Borachio all exhibit self-knowledge, there are other characters in Shakespeare, like Othello or Don Pedro, whose self-knowledge is largely or entirely absent. And there is a small but dramatically potent third group consisting of characters with a latent inner self with which they are unexpectedly confronted. In addition to Angelo (*Measure for Measure*), it includes Proteus (*The Two Gentlemen of Verona*) and Cressida (*Troilus and Cressida*).

III
Characters with a latent inner self: Proteus, Angelo, and Cressida.

Many, if not most, human beings have a potential inner self that they may be entirely unaware of unless some unusual combination of pressure and opportunity provokes it. This can happen during a shipwreck, or in a fire, when people who never thought they had it in them turn out to be heroes. Sometimes, however, the passage from latent to patent can bring disgrace. And sometimes, too, the combination of pressure and opportunity can be sexual in character. In *The Two Gentlemen of Verona*, Proteus's father, by an action that Shakespeare makes a chance one to avoid all hint of scheming on Proteus's part, sends his reluctant son to the ducal court in Milan. "Proteus" means "changeable," and, when he arrives, his unexpected love for Silvia is, in contrast with his love for Julia, immediate and powerful:

> Even as one heat another heat expels,
> Or as one nail by strength drives out another,
> So the remembrance of my former love
> Is by a newer object quite forgotten.

> (2.4)

The same sort of thing happens in *Romeo and Juliet* and *A Midsummer Night's Dream:* Romeo and Lysander—the latter under the influence of Oberon's magic—also undergo sudden and extreme redirections of passion. But in the case of Proteus, moral decline is entailed, and that is what Shakespeare chooses to explore. Once Proteus succumbs, principled restraint is swept away, isolation and deviousness follow, and Proteus, to his own surprise, acquires a new "Mr. Hyde" personality to try out:

> I will forget that Julia is alive,
> Rememb'ring that my love to her is dead;
> And Valentine I'll hold an enemy,
> Aiming at Silvia as a sweeter friend.
> I cannot now prove constant to myself,
> Without some treachery us'd to Valentine.
>
> (2.6)

By characterizing Proteus as he does, Shakespeare automatically raises the double question of whether he should be reclaimed from his delinquent ways and, if so, how. Shakespeare opts for reclamation on condition of repentance. That decided, he ensures that Proteus does nothing irrevocable and steers the play toward a happy-ish, if rather unconvincing, ending. But Proteus's characterization is too powerful for such a bland rounding off. Its real moment of validity comes earlier in the final scene, when Proteus, in view (unknown to him) of Valentine and Julia, attempts to rape Silvia. On the page, the episode has little impact, but on stage it is electric, not because of Proteus's intended violence but because he is suddenly made aware that his shameful hidden self is known to others who know him. The first key word is "Ruffian!" It is shouted out by Valentine and tells Proteus that he is seen by his friend. The second is "Valentine!" and it is shouted out by Proteus. No additional words are necessary, only an ensuing dramatic silence, during which a character stripped of any saving pretence stands exposed to every watching eye. It is a moment tailor-made for an open playing area and a surrounding audience.

Measure for Measure, too, makes patent what is latent in a character by means of pressure and opportunity, but the later play is altogether more elaborate, and Angelo is more fully constructed as a character than Proteus. Angelo's pretended puritanism is linked to his sexuality, which is initially too repressed to be insistent. Lucio says that Angelo is one "whose blood / Is very snow-broth; one who never feels / The wanton stings and motions of the sense" (1.4), and Angelo, having been stirred by Isabella, confirms this by saying of himself, "Ever till now, / When men were fond, I smil'd and wond'red how" (2.2). It is true that Angelo has been betrothed to Mariana. But Angelo's relationship with her, while it is dishonorable as far as Angelo is concerned, is not presented by Shakespeare as a specifically sexual one.

The reason for delaying Angelo's sexual awakening is to derive maximum dramatic capital from it when it happens. Sexuality is a natural drive, but, because of its power and its potential for far-reaching consequences, organized society sees no choice but to moralize it; and Angelo, who is characterized as a moral being, automatically thinks in, and judges himself in, moral terms. Before his sexual awakening, he pontificates with complete sincerity, "'Tis one thing to be tempted, Escalus, / Another thing to fall" (2.1). Afterward, he subjects himself to a moralist's condemnation:

> O fie, fie, fie!
> What dost thou? or what art thou, Angelo?
> Dost thou desire her foully for those things
> That make her good? . . .
>
> (2.2)

As with Proteus, once restraint is gone, Angelo falls fast and far, and, once fallen, he, too, has to redefine himself in light of what he discovers about himself. As the character within the character emerges, Angelo becomes a full-blown hypocrite, a lecher, a misuser of office, a would-be judicial murderer, and a liar, determined both to have his way and not to be called to account if he can help it. Since, like Proteus, Angelo sins more in intent than in fact, the opportunity exists for repentance and reclamation. But it is an enigmatic ending that awaits the found-out deputy:

> DUKE: By this Lord Angelo perceives he's safe;
> Methinks I see a quick'ning in his eye.
> Well, Angelo, your evil quits you well.
> Look that you love your wife; her worth worth yours.
>
> (5.1)

The play is much closer here to *All's Well That Ends Well* than to *The Two Gentlemen of Verona,* and, like that other so-called problem play, it leaves the audience with unanswered questions to think about. Will Angelo love Mariana as required? Will Mariana be happy? Is Angelo really punished in full measure? Is marriage to Mariana not a punishment in itself? In fact, Angelo might be said to get off lightly, since one meaning of the Duke's "Well, Angelo, your evil quits you well" (5.1) is "your evil is well rewarded."[6]

As the examples in the previous paragraph show, there is a tendency for questions prompted by the ending of *Measure for Measure* to be personal in nature, and with that tendency goes the feeling that, if the right *personal* answers can be found, then the problems the play sets will be solved. But, leaving aside the fact that characters in a play are not real people, it needs to be asked whether personal questions are adequate in principle to Angelo's characterization, or whether, while valid, they are too narrow in scope.

The adequacy of personal questions and answers arises as an issue because Angelo, as the Duke's deputy, is an officeholder, and the word "office" runs through *Measure for Measure* like a red thread. The Duke says, "I have on Angelo impos'd the office" (1.3); Escalus speaks of Elbow's "readiness in the office" (2.1); the Provost tells Pompey that the executioner "in his office lacks a helper" (4.2); the Provost also speaks of being thought by Angelo to be "remiss in mine office" (4.2); and the Duke discharges the Provost from his office (5.1). The social structure of *Measure for Measure*'s Vienna is prominently developed, and it is clear from the way the word "office" is used in the play that it implies authority and responsibility in combination.

An important part of Angelo's characterization is to show not just how low a single individual can fall but how dangerous an officeholder can become once the power and authority of his office is annexed to personal interest. As deputy, Angelo is part of civilized society, but he regresses to a sub-civilized condition under the influence of his appetite. His lust aroused, he tries to force Isabella to comply with his wishes, and, when Isabella, thinking in social terms, threatens to "tell the world aloud / What man thou art" (2.4), his response shows how divergent office and officeholder have become:

> Who will believe thee, Isabel?
> My unsoil'd name, th' austereness of my life,
> My vouch against you, and my place i' th' state,
> Will so your accusation overweigh,
> That you shall stifle in your own report,
> And smell of calumny. I have begun,
> And now I give my sensual race the rein.
> Fit thy consent to my sharp appetite,
> Lay by all nicety and prolixious blushes
> That banish what they sue for. Redeem thy brother
> By yielding up thy body to my will,
> Or else he must not only die the death,
> But thy unkindness shall his death draw out
> To ling'ring sufferance. Answer me to-morrow,

Or by the affection that now guides me most,
I'll prove a tyrant to him. As for you,
Say what you can: my false o'erweighs your true.

(2.4)

This is political as well as sexual language, and its culmination in the word "tyrant" is not gratuitous. Shakespeare deplores tyranny as the supersession of just rule by oppression (Macbeth is a tyrant, and Julius Caesar appears to have the makings of one). He also deplores, in his predemocratic way, any failure of those set above others to live up to their responsibilities (the big reason why Coriolanus is open to censure once he leaves the battlefield). Both considerations converge in Angelo, the irresponsible deputy. That is why, while it is legitimate up to a point to understand Angelo's characterization in personalized terms, it is also unduly restrictive. The social component of his characterization matters too.

When, in *Troilus and Cressida,* Shakespeare was characterizing Cressida, he drew on the received perception of her as female infidelity incarnate. That is to say, any audience would *expect* Cressida to move away from Troilus before the play was out, so Shakespeare's task—and opportunity—was to make that move as interesting and credible as possible. To do that, he set out to explore the personality that lay behind the cliché, "'[a]s false as Cressid'" (3.2), and he used a three-part structure: (1) from the beginning of the play to Cressida's two declarations of love for Troilus when she learns that she is to be separated from him (4.2 and 4.4); (2) Cressida's transfer from Troilus to Diomedes and the kissing scene (4.4 and 4.5); and (3) the observation scene, in which Cressida opts for Diomedes (5.2). The observation scene is discussed below in chapter 9, section II. However, Cressida's character starts to disclose itself well before that scene takes place.

In the first part of Shakespeare's three-part structure, the precariousness of Cressida's situation is emphasized. A young woman in a man's world, she is the daughter of a traitor in the dubious care of an uncle whose personal authority is minimal; and while Troilus wants her, he does not offer marriage. Cressida is witty and attracted to Troilus, but she knows that her chief source of power is to "hold off" (1.2) for as long as possible in order to remain wantable. This makes her calculating and given to playing hard to get. Nevertheless, when Cressida learns that she is to go to the Greeks, she declares, "But the strong base and building of my love / Is as the very centre of the earth, / Drawing all things to it" (4.2), and again, "My love admits no qualifying dross, / No more my grief, in such a precious loss" (4.4). These declarations sound conclusive, but their apparent absoluteness invites testing to see whether all is as it seems to be. That testing begins when Cressida is brought into Diomedes' proximity.

Understanding Cressida's characterization at the time of her handover and subsequently depends considerably on understanding how her part was originally meant to be played, and it is not always easy to recover Shakespeare's intentions from the text. But there are indications. Toward the end of act 4, scene 4, just before Cressida is handed over, Diomedes engages with Troilus in a competition of male assertiveness. Diomedes comes across as sexually blatant, but it is not clear how Cressida reacts to him since, during his verbal contest with Troilus, she is given nothing to say. Yet some favorable reaction is probable, and not just to the flattery that overlays the contempt in Diomedes' "To her own worth / She shall be priz'd." (It would be enlightening to know whether the original Cressida was expected to react revealingly to Diomedes' "The lustre in your eye, heaven in your cheek, / Pleads your fair usage, and to Diomed / You shall be mistress, and command him wholly.") In an embedded stage direction, Shakespeare has Troilus take Cressida's hand as they exit with Diomedes: "Lady, give me your hand, and as we walk, / *To our own selves* bend we our needful talk" (italics added). These lines hint that some sort of interpersonal chemistry is already under way between Cressida and Diomedes, and that Troilus senses it. That hint may well be strengthened by Paris's "Hark, Hector's trumpet!" as Cressida leaves the stage. "Strumpet" is easily heard in "Hector's trumpet" and is just as easily detached from Hector and attached to the departing Cressida. The question arises, of course, whether "strumpet" is a deliberate aural pun by Shakespeare or just coincidence. However, in act 4, scene 5, following Ulysses' character assassination of Cressida, the cry goes up, "The Troyans' trumpet," and, again, "strumpet" sounds through. So, in view of the repetition and of the context of each "strumpet," a deliberate aural pun seems to be the case.

The kissing scene (4.5) seems to signal something, too. When Diomedes enters with Cressida, his sexuality is insisted on: in Ulysses' metaphor, "He rises on the toe." But how Cressida enters is unspecified, unless Agamemnon's description of her as "Calchas' daughter" is intended to say in so many words that she is a female with a capacity for betrayal. The kissing itself can be interpreted as a presumptuous assault on a disadvantaged female who defends herself with her wit. But when it is over, Nestor's verdict is "A woman of quick sense," to which Ulysses adds, "[H]er wanton spirits look out / At every joint and motive of her body." Nestor may be referring to Cressida's wit, but what has Ulysses seen? Does Cressida really reveal wantonness while she is being kissed?

That is possible, but it could also be that Ulysses is referring to the way Cressida interacts with Diomedes as they exchange a private word before they exit together. Diomedes says, "Lady, a word. I'll bring you to your fa-ther." On the page, Diomedes' second sentence looks as if it follows straight on from his first, but the far greater likelihood is that there is a hiatus be-tween them at the period, during which Diomedes and Cressida put their heads together while Ulysses watches them and then provides a commen-tary. Here if not before, Shakespeare seems definitely to be thinking ahead to the observation scene (which also has Diomedes and Cressida putting their heads together). There is no great need for them to exchange a private word onstage before exiting after the kissing, unless Shakespeare wants the audience to be in no doubt both that intimacy is developing and that Ulysses is aware of it. And if that is indeed what Shakespeare wants, Ulysses' lines be-ginning "Fie, fie upon her! / There's language in her eye, her cheek, her lip" amount to retroactive stage directions with a clear message: under the influ-ence of Diomedes, a new Cressida is emerging fast, and the strong base and building of her love for Troilus are no longer what they seemed to be.[7]

IV

Hearing a play. Characters revealing themselves by the way they sound as they speak. The importance of small details.

Hearing is a highly discriminating sense, capable of distinguishing a wide range of tones and undertones, and Shakespeare's characterization depends as much on hearing as on seeing, for it seems that his audiences were more used to assimilating a play through their ears as well as their eyes than today's audiences are. In *The Taming of the Shrew,* the Lord says to the players, "There is a lord will hear you play to-night" and, almost immediately afterward, "(For yet his honor never heard a play)" (induction). Nor is this isolated usage. In *A Midsummer Night's Dream,* Philostrate tries to dissuade Theseus from choosing *Pyramus and Thisby,* but Theseus insists by saying, "I will hear that play" (5.1); the Prologue to *Henry V* invites the audience, "Gently to hear, kindly to judge, our play"; Hamlet asks Polonius, "How now, my lord? Will the King hear this piece of work?" (3.2); and, in the same scene, the Prologue says to his royal audience, "For us, and for our tragedy, / Here stooping to your clemency, / We beg your hearing patiently." Quantity makes the case: hearing is a high-priority sense for Shakespeare.

Act 1, scene 1, of *King Lear* provides an excellent example of characteri-zation by means of what is heard. Each of Lear's daughters is asked in turn to say which one loves him most. Goneril responds first:

> Sir, I love you more than words can wield the matter,
> Dearer than eyesight, space, and liberty,

Beyond what can be valued, rich or rare,
No less than life, with grace, health, beauty, honor.

But what the attentive ear hears, thanks to the hollow sound of these lines, is that Goneril loves her father *less* "than words can wield the matter." And, when Regan responds, not only does her stilted English transmit her insincerity, it transmits her anxiety to upstage her sister, too:

I am made of that self metal as my sister,
And prize me at her worth. In my true heart
I find she names my very deed of love;
Only she comes too short, that I profess
Myself an enemy to all other joys
Which the most precious square of sense possesses,
And find I am alone felicitate
In your dear Highness' love.

In contrast, Cordelia initially chooses to "[l]ove, and be silent." Then, when pushed by Lear to "mend [her] speech a little," she delivers lines that, as much by sound as by content, communicate maturity, tenderness, and respect, together with well-judged censure of her sisters:

Happily, when I shall wed,
That lord whose hand must take my plight shall carry
Half my love with him, half my care and duty.
Sure I shall never marry like my sisters,
To love my father all.

To hear Goneril, Regan, and Cordelia speak virtually one after the other is to be exposed to distinguishing characteristics in the sisters that will be valid for the rest of the play.

However, not all of Shakespeare's dialogue is so subtle. This is Constance in *King John:*

Death, death. O amiable lovely death!
Thou odiferous stench! sound rottenness!
Arise forth from the couch of lasting night,
Thou hate and terror to prosperity,
And I will kiss thy detestable bones,
And put my eyeballs in thy vaulty brows,

And ring these fingers with thy household worms,
And stop this gap of breath with fulsome dust,
And be a carrion monster like thyself.

$$(3.4)^8$$

There is a primitive, block-busting power to this speech, but it is as unnuanced as its speaker, for Constance's characterization consists of anger, resentment, and little else. In fact, Queen Elinor calls her an "unadvised scold" (2.1; "unadvised" means "rash" or "thoughtless"), and neither Constance's characterization nor her verse develops beyond that.

Antony and Cleopatra provides a polar opposite. In act 2, scene 5, a messenger enters to tell Cleopatra that Antony is married to Octavia, and Cleopatra's response is immediate:

CLEOPATRA: The most infectious pestilence upon thee!
Strikes him down.
MESSENGER: Good madam, patience.
CLEOPATRA: What say you? *Strikes him.*
                        Hence,
Horrible villain, or I'll spurn thine eyes
Like balls before me; I'll unhair thy head,
She hales him up and down.
Thou shalt be whipt with wire, and stew'd in brine,
Smarting in ling'ring pickle.
MESSENGER: Gracious madam,
I that do bring the news made not the match.
CLEOPATRA: Say 'tis not so, a province I will give thee,
And make thy fortunes proud; . . .

Unlike Constance's rant, the whole exchange is conceived in dynamic terms. Visually, the audience sees a queen so moved that she strikes a messenger twice, then hauls him about the stage before eventually drawing a knife on him. What it hears are short, eruptive speeches, in which polysyllabic words are avoided unless they can really be made to count. It also hears aggressive onomatopoeia, alliteration, and enjambment, together with interrupted lines ("Good madam, patience. / What say you? *Strikes him.* / Hence"). Cleopatra's iambic pentameter calling down pestilence has ferocity built into it, while phrases like "eyes / Like balls" and "I'll unhair thy head" pierce by their brevity. At the same time, however, Cleopatra's list of punishments soon exhausts itself and expires in the phrase "Smarting in lin'gring pickle."

Then a new, plaintive note is heard, beginning with "Say 'tis not so," and the deeper emotions of the exchange surface.

In a word, Cleopatra is hurt, and her hurt manifests itself in the sounds and silences of rage, frustration, humiliation, jealousy, and love. As the first shock passes, Cleopatra admits that she has demeaned herself by unjustly striking the Messenger, and she also acknowledges that Caesar has paid her back for praising Antony at his expense. But then come lines through which can be heard, from the mouth of a queen, female vulnerability *tout court:*

> Go to the fellow, good Alexas, bid him
> Report the feature of Octavia, her years,
> Her inclination; let him not leave out
> The color of her hair. Bring me word quickly.

Fear of a rival who is younger and perhaps prettier speaks through these lines: Cleopatra needs to know what the other woman is like in order to understand her apparent success in womanly terms. Finally, as Cleopatra leaves the stage, she says this:

> Let him for ever go—let him not, Charmian—
> Though he be painted one way like a Gorgon,
> The other way's a Mars. . . .
> . . . .
>   Pity me, Charmian,
> But do not speak to me. Lead me to my chamber.
>   *Exeunt.*

An essential part of Cleopatra's characterization is audible in the abrupt reversal of these lines: however Cleopatra judges Antony, she cannot stop loving him. She knows, even as she speaks, that Antony has long since ceased to be a Mars; but the wish continues to be father to the thought. Only the most profound love produces pathos of this order. Solitude is also audible in Cleopatra's lines and, possibly, tears that can only just be restrained ("But do not speak to me"). Since Cleopatra is in love, her fulfillment depends on her being part of a couple. But she exits alone except for Charmian, and it is aloneness that sounds through the "me" and "my" of "lead me to my chamber."

In the second chapter of *Elizabeth and Essex,* Lytton Strachey, the English essayist and popular historian, wonders out loud how he is to reach back over time to the Elizabethan period, for all that it is outwardly familiar. "The more clearly we perceive it," he says, "the more remote that singular universe becomes. With very few exceptions—possibly with the single exception of Shakespeare—the creatures in it meet us without intimacy; they are exterior visions, which we know, but do not truly understand."[9]

There is some truth in this. Anyone who has looked at pictures from Elizabethan times will acknowledge that, however well informed he or she is, the phrase "without intimacy" sticks. Even if the picture is of a well-documented figure like Queen Elizabeth herself, or Robert Devereux, second Earl of Essex, or of Henry Wriothesley, third Earl of Southampton, more of the beholder goes into the painted figures than comes back from behind the painted eyes. However, Strachey's wanting to exempt Shakespeare's characters seems right. Samuel Johnson's "just representations of general nature" provides one reason why, and just representation involves not least a knack of characterizing by means of small details. What Hamlet might eat has no dramatic importance, so it is left out of the play. But, in *Henry IV, Part One,* Falstaff's consumption is listed by Peto item by item (2.4), because Shakespeare wants to emphasize Falstaff's self-indulgence as Hal's mind is turning toward war. Peto's list includes "a capon . . . 2s. 2d," "sack, two gallons . . . 5s. 8d," and "anchoves and sack after supper . . . 2s. 6d." According to G. B. Harrison, a skilled City of London workman earned ten to fourteen pence a day,[10] so Falstaff's gluttony is self-evident. The play insists on Falstaff's great girth as well. Unless it matters, Shakespeare habitually omits his characters' physical appearance, but, since Falstaff's rotundity marks him out as a character unwilling to think beyond his own perimeter, in it goes. And in *All's Well That Ends Well,* Bertram's "arched brows, his hawking eye, his curls" (1.1) indicate very precisely the emotional shape of Helena's love. They also help account for her drastic comparison of the hind mated by the lion. That the Bertram of the play is not at all lionlike is a separate issue.

Shakespeare's characters also move and gesticulate revealingly. Many of the gestures are conventional. For example, in act 4, scene 6, of *King Lear,* when the blinded Gloucester addresses the gods before launching himself (as he thinks) over the edge of Dover Cliff to his death, it is apposite for him to kneel—hence the stage direction "*He kneels*"—and to raise his hands, too. But Shakespeare also knew that it is much easier for an actor to throw himself onto the stage from a kneeling position with his hands held out than it is for him to perform the same action from a standing position. (The "Dover Cliff" scene is discussed in chapter 8, section III.)

Then there are moments of pure Shakespearean inventiveness, such as when, in *Much Ado about Nothing,* Claudio makes as if to draw his sword on Leonato (5.1). Although Claudio denies doing any such thing, his rash action, his manifest untruthfulness, and his insolence to the elderly *signior* all highlight his callowness.

V

Plays on words and speech patterns as they contribute to characterization.

That Shakespeare could expect his audiences not just to listen but to listen closely is evidenced not least by his plays on words: they are everywhere, many of them are intricate, and these, especially, were probably delivered with deliberate care from the stage. Some might be thought to be indelicate.[11] The name "Jaques" in *As You Like It* was pronounced "jakes," and, then as now, a jakes was a privy. So the name connotes Jaques's unadorned view of life, but because it sounds funny, it also prevents the character from being taken as seriously as he takes himself. In *Much Ado about Nothing,* on the other hand, there is nothing indelicate about Dogberry's "Dost thou not suspect my years?" (4.2). "Ears" would have been heard through "Years," and, while Dogberry means "*re*spect," the audience has every right to find Dogberry's ears *su*spect, since he is an ass from his first entrance to his last exit.

Much Ado about Nothing is altogether a word-conscious play. Even its title is widely accepted as a pun, since, if "nothing" is understood as "no thing," the insinuation is that the play's much ado is vaginal in bias. (This is a variant of the joke in act 4, scene 2, of *A Midsummer Night's Dream,* when Flute says that a paramour is "a thing of naught"—"naught," which means "wickedness," being heard as "nought.") *Much Ado about Nothing* also contains two characterizing plays on words that are, perhaps, not always as fully appreciated as they should be, yet that indicate how much an audience could gain from listening closely.

The first of these plays on words falls into two parts and begins in act 2, scene 1. Claudio is persuaded that Don Pedro intends to marry Hero, and Beatrice describes him as "civil as an orange." The homophonic allusion is to a Seville orange, and Seville oranges were not only bitter, they were also yellow, the color of jealousy.[12] So although Claudio is a Florentine, not a Spaniard, the fruit characterizes him at this early juncture as given to bitterness and jealousy. When Claudio rejects Hero as his wife in act 4, scene 1, he exclaims to Leonato, "Give not this rotten orange to your friend." This time, Claudio is not civil, that is, well behaved, but the preestablished associations of the word "orange" with Claudio's character still apply. Consequently, Claudio effectively condemns himself out of his own mouth as he seeks to condemn Hero.

The second characterizing play on words occurs in act 3, scene 5, when Dogberry says, "'When the age is in, the wit is out.'" Like Escalus in *Measure for Measure,* Leonato needs to be visibly old, since he acquires the epithet "old." Furthermore, in act 2, scene 3, Benedick calls him "the white-bearded fellow," and in act 5, scene 1, Claudio rudely describes Leonato and his brother as "two old men without teeth." In fact, Leonato is likely to be holding his hat in his hands out of deference when he greets Don Pedro in act 1, scene 1, and that would allow his white hair to be seen. Even more than Escalus, Leonato is destined not to live up to his appearance: he is far from wise, and this discrepancy between what he looks like and how he is is consistent with a major theme of the play, namely, that appearances deceive. As for Dogberry, he, in his pride, is anxious to prevent Verges from receiving any credit for reporting the arrest of Borachio and Conrade to Leonato, so, since Verges is also old, he interrupts him with a characteristic corruption of the Elizabethan proverb "When ale is in, wit is out."[13] Nevertheless, Verges manages to speak of "as arrant knaves as any in Messina" before being cut out, so Leonato, despite being impatient to get to Hero's wedding, really ought to pursue the matter further. Instead, he leaves the examining of the prisoners to Dogberry, whom he knows to be a fool, and this makes him (Leonato) partly responsible for his daughter's shaming in the next scene. The play on "When ale is in, wit is out" is relevant in three ways. First, Dogberry's mangling of the proverb is one more verbal symbol of the general incompetence that should disqualify him from examining the "two aspicious persons" the Watch has "comprehended" ("aspicious" means "suspicious," and "comprehended" means "apprehended"). Second, while Dogberry intends his version of the proverb to apply to Verges, he is addressing "old" Leonato, and, in the eyes of the audience, he is thereby associating Leonato with foolishness at an important point in the play. Third, since, as has already been noted, Dogberry later asks, "Dost thou not suspect my years?" (4.2), his attempted aphorism about age and wit presumably applies to himself as well.

When Dogberry speaks, he always speaks in character, but, while his idiom is unique to him, speaking in character is not. All of Shakespeare's characters are differentiated by the way they speak, even very minor ones. In *Henry IV, Part One,* Prince Hal says that he is "so good a proficient in one quarter of an hour, that [he] can drink with any tinker in his own language" (2.4). Shakespeare's ear and quill are just as good: he can make any character speak "in his own language." Even nowadays, what is heard from the stage seems to emanate from within the nature of the character who is speaking, despite the fact that the pronunciations of Shakespeare's day, like many of his passing allusions, have become casualties of the passage of time. A reason for this is that, in art as in life, words that are spoken form patterns, and speech patterns are indicative of character. Here are some lines from *Twelfth Night* that show this clearly, though any play would serve as well. They are spoken by Sir Andrew Aguecheek during the letter scene:

> MALVOLIO: "Besides, you waste the treasure of your time with a fool-
> ish knight"—
> SIR ANDREW: That's me, I warrant you.
> MALVOLIO: "One Sir Andrew"—
> SIR ANDREW: I knew 'twas I, for many do call me fool. (2.5)

Sir Andrew's disposition fluctuates during the play, but, regardless of whether he speaks these lines triumphantly or regretfully, the audience can relate them to his earlier speech acts and recognize the speech pattern of a fool who, even when he is right, is incapable of rising above his foolishness. Relevant earlier speech acts by Sir Andrew include "I am a great eater of beef, and I believe that does harm to my wit" (1.3) and—in answer to Sir Toby's, "Does not our lives consist of the four elements?"—"Faith, so they say, but I think it rather consists of eating and drinking" (2.3).

Speech patterns are, by definition, larger than any single speech act, and, as Shakespeare moves his characters through his plays, he evidently intends their speech patterns to contribute substantially to their comprehensibility. This intention has a payoff that Shakespeare is unlikely to have foreseen but that retrospectively endorses his practice. Nowadays, thanks to the way English has changed over time, the details of individual speeches are sometimes hard to understand, however closely audiences listen. When that happens, a character's speech pattern often bridges the gaps. Not every word may be understood when he or she speaks, but the general idea still comes across.

Chapter 5

SCENES NOT SHOWN

I

Scenes not shown and dramatic priorities. How scenes not shown contribute to characterization. Different kinds of tellers.

To show or not to show, that is the question. Pacing, emphasis, and keeping the play's length within limits all compel omissions, and then there is the recurrent problem in Shakespeare of horses. So, for sometimes several reasons at once, Shakespeare's plays are full of scenes not shown. For example, in act 4, scene 1, of *A Midsummer Night's Dream,* (1) Shakespeare needs to move the plot beyond the point at which Titania is in love with Bottom; (2) Bottom cannot return to Athens to play Pyramus as long as he looks like an ass; (3) the cause of Titania's quarrel with Oberon—the changeling boy—is redundant following Titania's infatuation with Bottom; and (4) Shakespeare does not want the boy complicating matters after Titania's release from Oberon's magic. So, Oberon is given a brief speech detailing an offstage meeting with Titania. In it, Oberon's pity, Titania's change from pride to deference, the surrendering and disposal of the boy, and Oberon's consequential willingness to free Titania and Bottom from their spells follow one after the other. The speech lasts just twenty-five lines, and it enables the play to move forward by summarizing matters that don't need dramatizing.

Perhaps surprisingly, *A Midsummer Night's Dream* does *not* then move forward to the "nuptial" referred to in the play's opening line, since it, too, is not shown. Theseus says the marriage will be "by and by" (4.1); shortly after,

Snug enters with "Masters, the Duke is coming from the temple, and there is two or three lords and ladies more married" (4.2); and that is that. It looks as if Shakespeare wanted to keep the play's focus on *Pyramus and Thisby* and so ruled out a double climax. He must have sensed that *Pyramus and Thisby* would be a winner, and his interest in everything to do with playmaking would tilt him toward the play-within-the-play anyway.

The same sort of thing occurs in *Macbeth* and *The Winter's Tale,* and again the purpose seems to be to serve a dramatic priority. Macbeth murders for the crown, but his coronation goes unshown. Instead, like the weddings in *A Midsummer Night's Dream,* it is placed in an interstice between two scenes that *are* shown. After reports of violent unnatural events and of the hasty departures of Malcolm and Donalbain, Macduff tells Rosse that Macbeth is "already nam'd, and gone to Scone / To be invested" (2.4). The next scene then opens with Banquo musing, "Thou hast it now: King, Cawdor, Glamis, all" (3.1). Macbeth's coronation has taken place in between, but it is secondary to its accompaniments of disorder and suspicion, so disorder and suspicion are highlighted. In *The Winter's Tale,* the reunions and discoveries toward the end of the play would detract from Hermione's reanimation if they were staged in full. So three Gentlemen tell what they have witnessed elsewhere (5.2), and the play can move to its climax. It is worth noting that the Gentlemen's entrances are staggered. This is a favorite Shakespearean arrangement and more usually takes the form of messengers with bad news entering one at a time. Shakespeare knew the dramatic value of not having everything said at once.

A scene not shown can also contribute to characterization since, if a report is made, key words or actions can be emphasized. During the Sergeant's account of Macbeth's battlefield prowess (1.2), Macbeth is described as "brave" and "[l]ike Valor's minion," but he is also associated with the phrases "bloody execution" and "his head upon our battlements." This lays the basis for Macbeth's dual characterization as soldier and assassin, and anticipates his beheading in act 5. In a lighter vein, as Maria is preparing the stage for the letter scene in *Twelfth Night* (2.5), she says of Malvolio, "He has been yonder i' the sun practicing behavior to his own shadow this half hour." The key phrase is "this half hour." The extraordinary vanity it implies is just what Maria wants, since vanity is the vice in Malvolio that her vengeful scheme is intended to exploit (2.3). (Details of the letter scene are discussed in chapter 9, section I.)

When a scene is not shown but reported, the reactions of characters who *are* onstage can be highly revealing—a boon to any dramatist, since a play is a very compressed art form. First, their reactions can reveal a lot about themselves. But second, their reactions can reveal a lot about the nature of the play they are in. When in *Macbeth* the Sergeant brings Duncan the latest news of the revolt (1.2), he, like Rosse after him, makes Macbeth's valor the principal focus of what he says. As he speaks, the Sergeant is listened to by Duncan, Malcolm, Donalbain, and Lennox, and the most important of these is Duncan, since he is king, and a king's authority is supreme. Or so one might assume. Yet, crucially, Duncan does not enter the play first; he enters it second, after the Witches' first appearance. That is to say, Duncan's first entrance is in a preestablished context of which the audience is aware, though he is not. Understandably, Duncan conducts himself as if he had entered first: his demeanor is regal, and nothing is further from his thoughts than the supernatural. When he exclaims, "O valiant cousin, worthy gentleman!" what he reveals about himself is a spontaneous sense of gratitude. But what he reveals about the play he is in is that it has some kind of menacing incongruity to it. For how can Macbeth be "worthy" if, before Duncan speaks his name, the Witches have shown such a strong interest in him?

Macbeth is a play in which the unsuspected is everywhere. The reason is that, more than any other play by Shakespeare, including *Othello, Macbeth* is conditioned by the logic of evil. It is opened by the Witches, and their "Fair is foul, and foul is fair" means what it says: what appears fair is foul underneath, and, from the Witches' point of view, the more the foul dominates, the better. The evil they represent is insidious. Even when they are not on-stage, they represent a continuing threat, a fact that was probably symbolized during original performances of the play by the lingering smoke and smell of the firecrackers used to simulate stormy weather. (In *Cymbeline,* after Jupiter has thrown his thunderbolt and ascended again, Posthumus's father says, "He came in thunder, his celestial breath / Was sulphurous to smell" [5.4].) That smoke and smell would probably account for the Witches speaking of "the fog and filthy air" in act 1, scene 1, and they could well still be perceptible to the audience when Duncan first enters in act 1, scene 2, nominally in a different place in Scotland but still within the Witches' sphere of influence.

In such skewed circumstances, equivocation is a key concept: a crown successfully defended is a crown worth stealing, and gratitude can have fatal consequences. As has just been said, Duncan's first words about Macbeth express gratitude; so do his words to the Sergeant, as the latter is taken off to have his wounds dressed. It is gratitude, too, that moves Duncan to give Macbeth Cawdor's title; and it is in a spirit of gratitude that Duncan looks forward to going to Inverness with Macbeth. When he says to Macbeth, "I have begun to plant thee, and will labor / To make thee full of growing"

(1.4), he means exactly that. However, gratitude is a cousin to trust, and Duncan trusts too readily, despite the warning Cawdor provides. This gives evil its opportunity, and, by act 2, scene 2, when he is murdered, Duncan has had his victory, his gift, his gratitude, and his good intentions turned against him. Duncan's characterization is consistent to the end. Before going to bed for the last time, he sends presents to members of Macbeth's household and a diamond to Lady Macbeth as signs of gratitude for the hospitality he has received. He never learns that Macbeth is anything other than "worthy" or that, beneath her fair appearance, Lady Macbeth is foul.

Scenes that are reported, not shown, typically consist of three component parts: what is told, to whom it is told, and the teller. Tellers combine two things: their individual characteristics and the perspective that goes with their social situation. Society has changed so much since Shakespeare's day that the social situations of his characters are not always obvious to modern audiences. When the Falstaff of *The Merry Wives of Windsor* describes how he was thrown into the Thames (3.5), it is easy to hear his lines as the Elizabethan equivalent of a fat man slipping on a banana skin. But when, later in the play, he looks back on that event and on his beating as the witch of Brainford, what he fears is being ridiculed at court. "If it should come to the ear of the court," he says, "how I have been transform'd, and how my transformation hath been wash'd and cudgell'd, they would melt me out of my fat drop by drop, and liquor fishermen's boots with me" (4.5). Falstaff's fear reflects the vertical structuring of late sixteenth-century English society. His humiliations at the hands of the Windsor wives hurt socially as well as physically, and to understand that is to understand more completely lines like "Have I liv'd to be carried in a basket like a barrow of butcher's offal?" and "The rogues slighted me into the river" (3.5).

The Falstaff of *The Merry Wives of Windsor* leaves the play alive, well, and with Mistress Page's invitation to "laugh this sport o'er by a country fire" (5.5) in his ears. But the Falstaff of *Henry V* dies in disgrace and penury in Eastcheap, a location that has been a symbolic fixity in his life. The scene is not shown but reported by the Hostess, who is part of the Eastcheap milieu though not debauched by it:

> HOSTESS: Nay sure, he's not in hell; he's in Arthur's bosom, if ever man went to Arthur's bosom. 'A made a finer end, and went away and it had been any christom child. 'A parted ev'n just between twelve and one, ev'n at the turning o' th' tide; for after I saw him fumble with the sheets, and play with flowers, and smile upon his fingers' end, I knew there was but one way; for his nose was as sharp as a pen, and 'a babbl'd

of green fields. "How now, Sir John?" quoth I, "what, man? be a' good cheer." So 'a cried out, "God, God, God!" three or four times. Now I, to comfort him, bid him 'a should not think of God; I hop'd there was no need to trouble himself with any such thoughts yet. So 'a bade me lay more clothes on his feet. I put my hand into the bed and felt them, and they were as cold as any stone; then I felt to his knees, and so up'ard and up'ard, and all was as cold as any stone. (2.3)

Unforced compassion shines through every line. Even the discouragement of a deathbed conversion is an expression of care. The speech's key phrase is "to comfort him," and the tone throughout is sincere. But what gives this scene its special power is the Hostess's low status. Socially, she is far inferior to Falstaff. As young Jack Falstaff, he was page to Thomas Mowbray, Duke of Norfolk (*Henry IV, Part Two*, 3.2), and, as Sir John Falstaff, he is a knight, even if a decayed one, which is why, in *Henry IV, Part One*, the Hostess is obliged to say "setting thy knighthood aside" before calling Falstaff a knave (3.3). The Hostess would be inferior to many in the audience, too. And she is a woman in a social order dominated (with the exception of Elizabeth I) by men. And yet, if any character in Shakespeare flouts the convention that only the socially great can have great speeches, it is the Hostess. The speech to measure hers by is Gertrude's report of Ophelia's death by drowning in *Hamlet*. That speech begins, "There is a willow grows askaunt the brook" (4.7), and, in poised iambic pentameters and their modulations, it wends its polished way down to "muddy death." It is an object lesson in rhetoric. By contrast, the Hostess, as befits her standing, speaks in prose and artlessly mangles her words—"Arthur's bosom," not "Abraham's bosom," and "christom child" instead of "chrisom child," that is, a newly dead child in its white baptismal garment. Yet her prose has the sensitivity and beauty of great verse, even if it does not have its form. It is as if common humanity has found its voice, and, leaving aside the fact that *Hamlet* was written after *Henry V*, it says much for Shakespeare's sureness of touch that he can give the Eastcheap Hostess lines to equal or even surpass the Queen of Denmark's. (NB, one of the Hostess's most memorable phrases, " 'a babbl'd of green fields," is an emendation by Lewis Theobald of the 1623 First Folio's "a Table of greene fields." It is generally accepted as correct.[1])

If the Hostess's status precludes social involvement, that of Edmund of Langley, Duke of York, compels it. In *Richard II*, York is caught between the king and Henry Bullingbrook. He is a man of genuine feelings and of principles, but he lacks moral strength; so he gradually changes sides as the pendulum swings from Richard to his usurper, and it eventually falls to him to tell the audience, via his wife, of the entry of the victorious Henry and the defeated Richard into London (5.2). Bullingbrook is popular, and (a little ambiguously, though not to the minds of the Londoners) he is welcomed with the cry, "God save thee, Bullingbrook!" But Bullingbrook, ever aware of the need to create the right impression, conceals any triumphalism he might feel beneath a calculated show of humility:

> Whilst he, from the one side to the other turning,
> Bare-headed, lower than his proud steed's neck,
> Bespake them thus: "I thank you, countrymen."
> And thus still doing, thus he pass'd along.

The contrast with Richard is stark:

> As in a theatre the eyes of men,
> After a well-graced actor leaves the stage,
> Are idly bent on him that enters next,
> Thinking his prattle to be tedious,
> Even so, or with much more contempt, men's eyes
> Did scowl on gentle Richard. No man cried "God save him!"
> No joyful tongue gave him his welcome home,
> But dust was thrown upon his sacred head,
> . . . .
> But heaven hath a hand in these events,
> To whose high will we bound out calm contents.
> To Bullingbrook are we sworn subjects now,
> Whose state and honor I for aye allow.

York's lines are theater without the stage, and they eloquently contrast the pseudohumble victor and the humiliated king. Throughout the play, Richard is the more conspicuously theatrical of the two, yet Bullingbrook, too, is a player of parts: the wronged Duke of Lancaster, the loyal subject, the humble king. His lines never soar like Richard's, but their effect is precisely calculated. As a consequence, he may not steal the show, but he knows how to steal the crown.

Then there is York himself. Step by step, York moves from challenging Bullingbrook's return from banishment "[i]n gross rebellion and detested treason" (2.3) to proclaiming Bullingbrook "Henry, fourth of that name!" (4.1). And it is York who prompts Richard to resign his crown to Bullingbrook (4.1). By making York the teller, Shakespeare shows how far even a man of principle may travel if he floats with the political tide and persuades himself of the right pieties at the right times. It is true that weeping makes York break off his narrative of Bullingbrook and Richard entering London. But he weeps from within a new political arrangement that he has connived in. And his glib concluding couplets (quoted above) show that, to all intents and purposes, he is well adapted to it.

II

Dealing with horses. People in large numbers and large-scale settings. Scenes recalled from the more distant past.

Had Shakespeare wanted actually to stage Bullingbrook's entry into London, the biggest difficulty would have been the horse. Horses are everywhere in Shakespeare, but real ones are unsuited to use on stage, and that leads to a large number of ingenious responses. Richard III, unhorsed, famously offers his kingdom for one (*Richard III,* 5.4); Poins removes Falstaff's in *Henry IV, Part One* (2.2); and, at Forres (in *Macbeth*), the custom is to walk to the palace gate (3.3). These three horseless situations alone create the opportunity for a major sword fight—sword fights were spectacular and much-relished events on London's stages[2]—for high-grade clowning, and for the onstage ambush of Banquo and Fleance.

Of course, there are horses and horses, and not all of them are "proud steeds." This is Biondello describing Petruchio's in *The Taming of the Shrew* (Petruchio is arriving for his wedding):

> [H]is horse hipp'd, with an old mothy saddle and stirrups of no kindred; besides, possess'd with the glanders and like to mose in the chine, troubled with the lampass, infected with the fashions, full of windgalls, sped with spavins, ray'd with the yellows, past cure of the fives, stark spoil'd with the staggers, begnawn with the bots, . . . (3.2)

Not only does Shakespeare find it easier to describe the horse than to bring it onstage, he is free to make it as outrageous as he pleases, knowing that his audience is familiar with horses and their ailments and knowing also that, the more unprepossessing he makes the buildup to Petruchio's entrance, the more impressive, by contrast, Petruchio's forcefulness will be. (To pick out just three of the ailments Biondello cites, "hipp'd" is "lame at the hip"; "glanders" is a bacterial infection causing ulcers, abscesses, and discharge from the nostrils; and "the yellows" is jaundice.) Some of Petruchio's forcefulness shows itself in Grumio's account of the journey to his master's country house, and, once more, a verbally created horse has a central part to play: "[T]hou shouldst have heard how her horse fell, and she under her horse; thou shouldst have heard in how miry a place, how she was bemoil'd, how he left her with the horse upon her, . . . how he swore, how she pray'd that never pray'd before" (4.1).

People in large numbers and large-scale settings present essentially the same kind of challenge as horses in that, for entirely practical reasons, they cannot be put onstage either. In a battle scene in *Edward III* (conjecturally dated 1592/1593[3]), Edward, Prince of Wales, is reported as being surrounded and, seemingly, destined to be killed, for "[t]he snares of French, like emmets on a bank, / Muster about him" (3.5; "emmets" means "ants"). But, shortly afterward, there is a flourish, and the Prince of Wales comes onto the stage *"in triumph, bearing in his hand his shivered lance; his sword and battered armor carried before him, and the body of the* KING OF BOHEME, *wrapped in the colors."* During his reconstruction of what has happened, the prince speaks of "[t]he King of Boheme, father, whom I slew, / Whose thousands had intrench'd me round about, / And lay as thick upon my batter'd crest, / As on an anvil, with their ponderous glaives" (3.5; "glaives" means "swords"). None of this could possibly be staged detail for detail, yet the audience needs to know what has taken place, so the plasticity of the spoken word is used instead. Although the play appears to have been written or cowritten by Shakespeare early in his career, he had by that time already developed the full-bloomed language for which the choruses in *Henry V* are famous.

What works for a land battle also works for one at sea. In act 3, scene 1, of *Edward III,* Shakespeare has to decide how best to manage the naval Battle of Sluys. The scene onstage is set in the French camp in Flanders, and King John of France is boasting, "At sea we are as puissant as the force / of Agamemnon in the haven of Troy," when the Mariner enters to report, "The proud armado of King Edward's ships" is approaching. The Mariner is sent back to observe, cannon shot offstage signals a battle, then a retreat is sounded. This is the Mariner's cue to return to the stage, not just to report the French defeat but to provide the audience with a vivid blow-by-blow account of the battle that it has been unable to see for itself:

Purple the sea, whose channel fill'd as fast
With streaming gore that from the maimed fell,
As did her gushing moisture break into
The cranny cleftures of the through-shot planks.
Here flew a head dissever'd from the trunk;
There mangled arms and legs were toss'd aloft,

As when a whirlwind takes the summer dust
And scatters it in middle of the air.

This unshown scene surely exceeds the resources of any Elizabethan play-house.[4] However, image-rich language more than makes up for staging limitations, especially when patriotism lends a hand.

It is difficult to overestimate the implications of Shakespeare's mastery of scenes not shown for his theater, for what it gives him is virtually unlimited control over space, time, and mise-en-scène. Whatever his imagination requires, he has the means to communicate it, one way or another. Furthermore, scenes that are not shown but reported have the advantage of always being perfect, free from the compromises and snags that, as Shakespeare well knew, can beset live performances. For example, the flying head and mangled limbs mentioned by the Mariner in *Edward III* would be a lot less effective if props were used. A head as a prop needs an identifiable owner and its own dramatic moment if it is really to have any effect, as is the case when Macduff returns to the stage with Macbeth's severed head and exclaims, "Behold where stands / Th' usurper's cursed head: the time is free" (*Macbeth,* 5.9).

The land victory of the Prince of Wales in *Edward III* and the naval Battle of Sluys are still fresh in the memory of their tellers when they are reported, and this immediacy lends verve to what they say. But sometimes scenes from the more distant past have to be written in if a play is to be made to work. In *Hamlet,* little can happen until the prince learns of his father's murder by Claudius, so the scene is reprised in words that communicate location, time of day, the administering of the poison, its physical effects, questionable sexual conduct, and calculated deceit. The teller—the Ghost—is not neutral: it wants revenge, so it uses its privileged knowledge to bias the scene accordingly. By the time the Ghost is finished, Hamlet, like the audience, knows what has happened and what is expected of him. But because Hamlet is presented not just with information but with a depiction that he can imagine in the way his father wants him to, his reaction is intensified, and it generates enough energy to fuel his intentions for much of the rest of the play:

Yea, from the table of my memory
I'll wipe away all trivial fond records,
All saws of books, all forms, all pressures past
That youth and observation copied there,
And thy commandement all alone shall live

Within the book and volume of my brain,
Unmix'd with baser matter.

(1.5)

Othello, too, reaches back into a past antecedent to the action onstage since, with matrimonial murder due in act 5, Shakespeare needs to explain precisely how Othello and Desdemona came together in the first place. That Othello is the teller means that, as he recalls his frequent invitations to Brabantio's house, he reveals more about himself than he intends at a point in the play when the audience is still getting its bearings:

> These things to hear
> Would Desdemona seriously incline;
> But still the house affairs would draw her thence,
> Which ever as she could with haste dispatch,
> She'ld come again, and with a greedy ear
> Devour up my discourse. . . .
> . . . .
> My story being done,
> She gave me for my pains a world of sighs;
> She swore, in faith 'twas strange, 'twas passing strange;
> 'Twas pitiful, 'twas wondrous pitiful.
> She wish'd she had not heard it, yet she wish'd
> That heaven had made her such a man. . . .
> . . . .
> She lov'd me for the dangers I had pass'd,
> And I lov'd her that she did pity them.

(1.3)

What emerges from Othello's confident and uncomplicated recollections is that his experience of life, while unconventional, is limited: his adventures amount to dangers of one kind only, namely, external dangers. He is manifestly unaware of his enemy within—his susceptibility to jealousy—and no danger he has faced compares with Iago. Consequently, in the context of the play as a whole, Othello's initial confidence and innocence are ironic in character: he may be a military expert and the proposed defender of Cyprus, but, thanks to his inexperience and ingenuousness, he cannot defend himself. Othello also recalls awaking in Desdemona a combination of empathy and fascination; and her losing struggle between her domestic responsibilities and the attraction of Othello's stories sheds light on her readiness to deceive her father and take up with the exotic Moor. Complacently, Othello calls his reconstruction of the past "a round unvarnish'd tale" (1.3). Not the least of its effects is to evoke a love match that, while vulnerable, might well have prospered in kinder circumstances.

Of the tragedies that follow *Othello*—*Timon of Athens, King Lear, Macbeth, Coriolanus,* and *Antony and Cleopatra*—only the last two make an issue of the past. Coriolanus's "tender-bodied" time is recalled by way of his mother's reminiscences during conversation (1.3), and Antony and Cleopatra, two characters who have more past than future, are both given full scenic treatment. Throughout *Antony and Cleopatra,* what Antony has become is, to his detriment, compared to what he once was; that difference is spelled out early and clearly by Octavius Caesar in act 1, scene 4 ("to lank" means "to shrink"):

> Antony,
> Leave thy lascivious wassails. When thou once
> Was beaten from Modena, where thou slew'st
> Hirtius and Pansa, consuls, at thy heel
> Did famine follow, . . .
> . . . .
> Thou didst drink
> The stale of horses and the gilded puddle
> Which beasts would cough at; thy palate then did deign
> The roughest berry on the rudest hedge;
> Yea, like the stag, when snow the pasture sheets,
> The barks of trees thou brows'd. On the Alps
> It is reported thou didst eat strange flesh,
> Which some did die to look on; and all this
> (It wounds thine honor that I speak it now)
> Was borne so like a soldier, that thy cheek
> So much as lank'd not.

Although Octavius's words, like Othello's, conflate actions performed on different occasions, they have, again like Othello's, the "set piece" character of a single unshown scene; and Antony's former austerity and self-discipline are made all the more impressive by the extreme nature of the actions Octavius recalls from the past.

This, by contrast, is Enobarbus's account of the prelude to Antony's first meeting with Cleopatra:

> The barge she sat in, like a burnish'd throne,
> Burnt on the water. The poop was beaten gold,

> Purple the sails, and so perfumed that
> The winds were love-sick with them; the oars were silver,
> Which to the tune of flutes kept stroke, and made
> The water which they beat to follow faster,
> As amorous of their strokes. . . .
>
> (2.2)

Enobarbus's sumptuous tableau vivant is an accumulation of color, sensuousness, wealth, and seductiveness. It communicates the going soft Antony will resent but never escape from. In Enobarbus's words, "Other women cloy / The appetites they feed, but she makes hungry / Where most she satisfies" (2.2).

III

Controlling audience responses to scenes not shown. Film versions of Much Ado about Nothing, Macbeth, *and* Henry V.

It can easily happen that, when a play is being remembered, unshown scenes are recalled as if they were really present in the play and not imported into it by a trick of the mind. That can come about whether the play being remembered has been read or seen onstage. But if a film version is being recalled, what in the play was an unshown scene may be really remembered, since filmmakers, being visual people, have a fondness for plugging Shakespeare's gaps. Yet scenes not shown are not simply omissions; they are controlled parts of the play, and Shakespeare knew exactly how he wanted them registered, even though they are not acted out. This comes out very clearly in the deception scene in *Much Ado about Nothing,* Duncan's murder in *Macbeth,* and the Battle of Agincourt in *Henry V.*

Preparation of the deception scene in *Much Ado about Nothing* begins very early in the play. When Don Pedro undertakes to woo Hero on Claudio's behalf, he arbitrarily favors disguise over an orthodox approach:

> I know we shall have revelling to-night;
> I will assume thy part in some disguise,
> And tell fair Hero I am Claudio,
> And in her bosom I'll unclasp my heart,
> And take her hearing prisoner with the force
> And strong encounter of my amorous tale;
> Then after to her father will I break,
> And the conclusion is, she shall be thine.
>
> (1.1)

Almost immediately afterward, Antonio informs Leonato that one of his men has told him that Don Pedro is in love with Hero, that he intends to tell her so "this night in a dance," and that he will then ask Leonato for her hand (1.2). And in the next scene, Borachio informs Don John that he has heard it agreed "that the Prince should woo Hero for himself, and having obtain'd her, give her to Count Claudio" (1.3). Before act 1 is over, then, the unreliability of seeing and of hearing has been established. At the reveling Don Pedro refers to (2.1), Claudio is deliberately "mistaken" by Don John for Benedick. As if addressing an established confidant of Don Pedro, Don John claims that his brother is in love with Hero but should be dissuaded from the match. Claudio instantly believes Don John, despite what he knows about him. This demonstrates the power of suggestion.

All four elements—the unreliability of what is seen and heard, the power of suggestion, and misplaced trust in Don John's words—are included in the deception of Don Pedro and Claudio. It takes place at night, and the two victims are some distance off, making it easy for their eyes to be deceived. They hear Margaret, disguised as Hero, bidding Borachio "a thousand times good night" (3.3), by which means their ears are deceived. And they are predisposed to believe what they think they are witnessing because Don John has put it into their heads that Hero is "every man's Hero" (3.2). So competent is Shakespeare's delivery of this unshown scene—preparing the audience in a general way beforehand and having Borachio run through it beforehand in act 2, scene 2, and afterward in act 3, scene 3, and (more briefly) act 5, scene 1—that it is difficult to see what more its actual staging could achieve; though Kenneth Branagh's 1993 film adaptation, by showing simulated copulation, makes specific the sexual nature of Claudio's jealousy.[5]

As for the murder of Duncan in *Macbeth,* in the play itself it is relayed to the audience from within the complicated consciousness of its perpetrators (2.2). Presumably Shakespeare reasoned that staging the murder would lead to its physical details distracting from and adulterating its moral horror, as in fact happens in Roman Polanski's 1971 film version, in which Duncan is stabbed in a frenzy about the body, then in the carotid artery.[6] In the play, the scene in which the murder occurs is so written that the one thing *not* likely to preoccupy an audience is the mechanics of the murder. What normally embeds itself in an audience's consciousness is darkness, blood, the daggers, the drugged grooms, and selected lines like Macbeth's "But wherefore could not I pronounce 'Amen'?" or Lady Macbeth's "A little water clears us of this deed"—all expressors of the scene's tensions and heart of darkness. Not even when Macbeth later says of the dead Duncan, "His silver skin lac'd with his golden blood, / And his gash'd stabs look'd like a breach in nature" (2.3) is it likely that physical interest will dominate. More interesting by the time these superfine lines glide from Macbeth's tongue is what will happen to their dissimulating speaker.

Like Polanski's *Macbeth,* Laurence Olivier's film version of *Henry V* (1944) has become a classic.[7] Made during the Second World War in the months before D-Day, the film stresses the play's patriotic elements, and it is justly famous for its rendition of the Battle of Agincourt. But although there are "alarums" (calls to arms) in the play itself and although the chorus to act 4 speaks with exaggerated apology of "four or five most vile and ragged foils / (Right ill dispos'd, in brawl ridiculous)," onstage battle is conspicuous more by its absence than its presence. The stage direction to act 4, scene 4, includes "*[e]xcursions,*" that is, soldiers running onstage to skirmish. But these excursions are followed by the encounter between Pistol and the French Soldier (M. le Fer), a localized and squalid exchange concerned with ransom. When Pistol is onstage, chivalry disappears, mercy comes at a price, and posturing replaces valor. According to the Boy, Pistol is a coward even in matters of theft.[8]

Shakespeare's decision to keep the Battle of Agincourt almost entirely offstage allows him to deconstruct the phenomenon of war selectively in a rapid succession of scenes, since his great insight, from a playwright's point of view, is that war—even the illustrious Battle of Agincourt—is qualitatively divisible. That is to say, it can be heroic, base, glorious, murderous, patriotic, profitable, grievous, ascribable to God, or any mix of these. Such distinctions entail differentiated characterization throughout the cast: the good soldier Fluellen, the parasitic Pistol, the overweening Constable, the dignified Montjoy. And each character has his distinctive rhetoric.

Henry's own characterization partakes of the complex nature of war as Shakespeare sees it: as the battle approaches and unfolds, Henry shows humaneness, the common touch, awareness of the burdens of kingship, guilt with regard to his father, morale-raising bravura, generosity of spirit, ruthlessness, and piety. And the way he speaks changes accordingly, including some finely judged prose when he talks to Bates and Williams. Death, too, a constant of war, is represented in a variety of ways and invites a variety of responses. This is Exeter reporting the deaths of Suffolk and York ("haggled" means "mangled"):

> Suffolk first died, and York, all haggled over,
> Comes to him where in gore he lay insteeped,
> And takes him by the beard, kisses the gashes
> That bloodily did yawn upon his face.
> He cries aloud, "Tarry, my cousin Suffolk!

My soul shall thine keep company to heaven;
Tarry, sweet soul, for mine, then fly abreast,
As in this glorious and well-foughten field
We kept together in our chivalry!"

(4.6)

Exeter's report idealizes death in battle from an English point of view. Its ex-
alted style calls to mind the phrase that the eighteenth-century art historian
Johann Joachim Winckelmann used in describing Greek sculpture: "noble
simplicity and quiet grandeur."[9] But there is a realism to Exeter's lines as
well. It is communicated by "haggled," "gashes," and "bloodily." These are
the words of cut flesh, and the implication is that idealization of battle, while
inspiring, provides an incomplete account of what battle really is. To drive
this point home, Shakespeare has Henry conclude this scene with some unadorned realism of his own:

Alarum.
KING HENRY: But hark, what new alarum is this same?
The French have reinforc'd their scatter'd men.
Then every soldier kill his prisoners,
Give the word through.

(4.6)

This combination of lofty idealism and low realism is also present in the
speeches of the Chorus. They are discussed in chapter 10, section III.

The killing of the boys—another example of war's squalor—offends
Fluellen's principled conception of "the law of arms" (4.7), but pillaging the
king's tent justifies, in Gower's eyes, Henry's tit-for-tat throat-slitting order
and earns for Henry the partisan accolade "gallant":

GOWER: Besides, they have burn'd and carried away all that was in the
King's tent; wherefore the King, most worthily, hath caus'd every soldier to cut his prisoner's throat. O, 'tis a gallant king! (4.7)

After the battle, Montjoy is mindful of feudal order even among the dead:

For many of our princes (woe the while!)
Lie drown'd and soak'd in mercenary blood;
So do our vulgar drench their peasant limbs
In blood of princes . . .

(4.7)

And Henry, perhaps feigning piety, perhaps genuinely grateful that the Lord, after all, has not thought "upon the fault / My father made in compassing the crown" (4.1), attributes the disproportion of French and English losses to a divine wish that he should win: "O God, thy arm was here; / And not to us, but to thy arm alone, / Ascribe we all!" (4.8).

Whereas in his film version of *Henry V* Laurence Olivier uses the best cinema technology of his day, a large cast, and an aircraft-free Irish location to render the Battle of Agincourt and its buildup, Shakespeare uses dialogue, entrances, exits, and a wooden stage. The temptation, therefore, is to see in Shakespeare's achievement a triumph of genius over primitive resources. Shakespeare was always open to technical innovation, so what would he have achieved, one is tempted to ask, had he had today's film, television, and high-tech theaters at his disposal? Yet to ask such a question is rather like asking what Bach might have achieved had he had a Steinway—without adding that the great weakness of a Steinway is that it does not function like a harpsichord. In other words, there is no separating Shakespeare from his resources. His plays were and are successes, and the resources of his day were constituent to their success. The following extracts from the buildup to the Battle of Agincourt show this clearly. It makes no sense to think of them as low-tech, high-tech, or any-tech. They work because they report what is needed when it is needed and in an appropriately dynamic way:

ORLEANCE: The sun doth gild our armor, up, my lords! (4.2)

CONSTABLE: I stay but for my guidon; to the field! (4.2; "guidon" means "standard" or "standard-bearer")

BEDFORD: The King himself is rode to view their battle. (4.3)

SALISBURY: The French are bravely in their battles set, And will with all expedience charge on us. (4.3)

KING HENRY: Now, soldiers, march away, And how thou pleasest, God, dispose the day! (4.3)

The time before Agincourt also includes stillness, to invoke which Shakespeare uses words that replace sounds and actions with stationary images. This is Grandpré's report of "[y]ond island carrions, desperate of their bones" (4.2; he means Henry's army). His lines, complete with their reverse patriotism, transfer to any stage, Shakespearean or modern, without loss, because of their inherent quality. And because Grandpré's images are verbal rather than fixed on film or DVD, they never seem dated, even though a battle involving horses is a throwback to a long-gone age:

> GRANDPRÉ: The horsemen sit like fixed candlesticks,
> With torch-staves in their hand; and their poor jades
> Lob down their heads, dropping the hides and hips,
> The gum down-roping from their pale-dead eyes,
> And in their pale dull mouths the gimmal'd bit
> Lies foul with chaw'd-grass, still and motionless;

Unlike Shakespeare's Agincourt, Olivier's is informed by three interests only: patriotism, optimism, and the English hero/king (as played by himself). These interests are straightforward; a glorious victory satisfies them best, and that victory finds optimal expression in cinematic coups like an accelerating French charge and the sound of arrows shot by unarmored English bowmen. By contrast, Shakespeare's Agincourt is, like the play in which it occurs, complex, challenging, and, in the longer historical perspective, not optimistic at all. By leaving it unshown and reporting from it selectively, Shakespeare is able to present what he thinks matters in the manner and order he thinks best. There is no denying the play's patriotism. But patriotism is far from being its only important point.

Chapter 6

CONTROLLING THE
AUDIENCE'S RESPONSES (I)

Places; Times of Day and Night; The Bible

I

Mimesis and the uses of precise associations. Nighttime, darkness, and a clock in
Hamlet *that is not heard.*

> *Hoboys and torches. Enter* KING DUNCAN, MALCOLM, DONALBAIN,
> BANQUO, LENNOX, MACDUFF, ROSSE, ANGUS, *and* ATTENDANTS.
> DUNCAN: This castle hath a pleasant seat, the air
> Nimbly and sweetly recommends itself
> Unto our gentle senses.
> BANQUO: This guest of summer,
> The temple-haunting marlet, does approve,
> By his lov'd mansionry, that the heaven's breath
> Smells wooingly here; no jutty, frieze,
> Buttress, nor coign of vantage, but this bird
> Hath made his pendant bed and procreant cradle.
> Where they most breed and haunt, I have observ'd
> The air is delicate.
>   (*Macbeth,* 1.6)

Shakespeare's verse conveys the impression that Macbeth's castle is visible
to the naked eye, yet very little physical detail is actually provided. Anyone
asked to draw it on the basis of these lines would very quickly have to resort either to recollections of one or more castles they have seen for them-

selves or to improvisations derived from a general sense of what a castle looks like. These simple facts indicate the way Shakespeare handles mimesis.

"The concept of mimesis," Kenneth McLeish writes in *Aristotle,* "defies exact translation. It means setting up in someone's mind, by an act of artistic presentation, ideas that will lead that person to associate what is being presented with his or her previous experience."[1] In other words, descriptions like that of Macbeth's castle interact with what the audience brings to them, and this applies not just to physical features mentioned in those descriptions but to the affective vocabulary they include as well. Duncan begins with "This castle," thereby transforming a bare stage into a location; in response to his words, some people may imagine a full-fledged physical construction, particularly if they are reading the play, while others may have an entirely nonvisual experience. "Pleasant," "sweetly," "summer," "wooingly" and "delicate" generate positive associations, though "summer," it should be noted, suggests transience, too; "temple-haunting marlet" and "heaven's breath" connote harmony and God (a "marlet" is a "house martin"); and "pendant bed" and "procreant cradle" suggest security. If the castle's description had come at the beginning of the play, there might have been little more to say about it than that. But, like Duncan's first entrance in act 1, scene 2, it occurs in a prepared context. The castle's description, marlet and all, has been preceded by Lady Macbeth's raven and her thoughts of murder (1.5). That fact puts the audience in a position quite different from that of Duncan and Banquo, since it can compare outer appearance with inner reality and understand the castle to be a restatement by other means of the face that hides the mind's construction (1.4).

Because of the way Duncan and Banquo talk about the castle, they can easily be assumed to be looking at it by daylight, if their description is quoted out of context. But the play dictates otherwise. A messenger explicitly says, "The King comes here to-night" (1.5); and, shortly after, Macbeth likewise says, "Duncan comes here to-night" (1.5). So repeated, the word "to-night" is difficult to misinterpret, and it links directly to the stage direction to act 1, scene 6 (quoted above), which includes "*torches*" (meaning "torchbearers"). Torches and torchbearers are standard visual signifiers of darkness in Shakespeare's plays, even in daylight performances. So, either gathering or complete darkness is intended—both metaphors of evil.

Ceremony and sound are intended, too. As always during his brief time in the play, Duncan enters act 1, scene 6, as a king: he is preceded by attendants and heralded by "hoboys," that is, not modern oboes but loud outdoor instruments belonging to the shawm family.[2] Duncan's entrances express royal power even as their contexts assert that it is power within the reach of evil.

Since Shakespeare relies heavily on the generation of associations when he is creating his settings, it might be thought that he risks being imprecise. But the opposite is the case. Shakespeare chooses meticulously which details to provide, and their associations are, for his contemporaries if not always for posterity, mostly conventional and/or very obvious. That is, while Shakespeare depends on subjective responses, he takes pains to ensure that those responses are carefully managed. The darkness associated with Macbeth's castle is a case in point. In a general way, darkness and evil are an obvious pairing anyway. But just before Duncan's arrival, Lady Macbeth has said, "Come, thick night, / And pall thee in the dunnest smoke of hell, / That my keen knife sees not the wound it makes" (1.5). These lines make the significance of the darkness very precise indeed and lend a lethal second meaning to Duncan's "Fair and noble hostess, / We are your guest to-night" (1.6).

There is no need for the exact time of Duncan's arrival to be stated or tolled by the clock: "to-night" is definite enough. Its definiteness is important, since what it conveys is that, as certainly as night follows day, Duncan's murder will follow his arrival in Inverness. However, there are occasions when darkness gains in expressiveness because the time it is combined with is deliberately made *not* definite, imparting uncertainty. Near the beginning of *Hamlet,* Horatio says that Marcellus and Barnardo have seen a figure like Hamlet's father "on their watch, / In the dead waste and middle of the night" (1.2) and that he has since seen it himself. Consequently, act 1, scene 4, opens with Hamlet, Horatio, and Marcellus coming onto Elsinore's guard platform "'twixt aleven and twelf'" (1.2), as they believe, to wait for the apparition to return:

> HAMLET: The air bites shrowdly, it is very cold.
> HORATIO: It is a nipping and an eager air.
> HAMLET: What hour now?
> HORATIO: I think it lacks of twelf.
> MARCELLUS: No, it is strook.
> HORATIO: Indeed? I heard it not. It then draws near the season
> Wherein the spirit held his wont to walk.

Shakespeare's economy of means here is masterly. The cold, with just a hint of the grave and of wickedness about it, is established in two lines of the sort of talk people incline to when they have good reason to feel tense; nighttime is confirmed by reference to the clock striking; and, of course, midnight and the supernatural go together. Yet the precise time is not given, and that has a disturbing effect, because it signifies that something is not right.

Hamlet has to ask; Horatio has not heard the clock; Marcellus claims he has, but does not say how long ago; and Horatio, suddenly realizing the seriousness of things, concludes that the appearance of the Ghost could well be imminent. Hamlet's "hour" and the clock that strikes it belong to the reassuring normality of everybody's time. Therefore, that the hour is uncertain prepares the audience for a major intrusion of abnormality—the Ghost—and that preparation is enhanced if, as is likely, the audience itself has not heard a clock, in the form of a sound effect, despite what Marcellus claims. In the midnight lines of Hamlet, Horatio, and Marcellus, two Elizabethan experiences come together, the one unsettling the other. One is that of a clock striking, with its message that all is well (in *Henry IV, Part Two,* pleasure-loving Falstaff recalls having heard "the chimes at midnight" with Shallow [3.2]). But the other experience, possibly difficult to empathize with in an electrically lit age, is that of the night as a dangerous and haunted time.

Shakespeare seems to have found the combination of uncertain time and darkness a winner, since *Hamlet* is neither the first nor the last of his plays in which it occurs. As act 1 of *Julius Caesar* ends, the time, according to Cassius, is "after midnight" (1.3). Brutus begins act 2 by entering his orchard, and the sky is clouded over:

> What, Lucius, ho!
> I cannot by the progress of the stars
> Give guess how near to day. Lucius, I say!
> I would it were my fault to sleep so soundly.
> When, Lucius, when? Awake, I say! What, Lucius!

The familiar progress of the stars toward day stands for an orderly universe in harmony with an orderly society. Brutus is thinking through the rightness of killing Caesar when he enters, and the obscuring of the progress of the stars is a metaphor for his continuing uneasiness. As Brutus tries to reconcile his moral scruples with his sense of duty to Rome, the uncertainty within him is communicated, in transposed form, as uncertainty about the time and as sleeplessness:

> Since Cassius first did whet me against Caesar,
> I have not slept.
> Between the acting of a dreadful thing
> And the first motion, all the interim is
> Like a phantasma or a hideous dream.
> The Genius and the mortal instruments

Are then in council; and the state of a man,
Like to a little kingdom, suffers then
The nature of an insurrection.

(2.1)

This speech, incidentally, shows how Shakespeare thought of the individual and the state as analogous to each other.

When Shakespeare later came to write *Macbeth,* his masterpiece of equivocation, it was only fitting that he should return to darkness and uncertain time yet again. This is Banquo entering with Fleance at the beginning of act 2:

BANQUO: How goes the night, boy?
FLEANCE: The moon is down; I have not heard the clock.
BANQUO: And she goes down at twelve.
FLEANCE: I take't, 'tis later, sir.
BANQUO: Hold, take my sword. There's husbandry in heaven,
Their candles are all out. Take thee that, too.
                    (*Gives him his belt and dagger.*)
A heavy summons lies like lead upon me,
And yet I would not sleep. Merciful powers,
Restrain in me the cursed thoughts that nature
Gives way to in repose!
                    Enter MACBETH, *and a* SERVANT *with a torch.*
                              Give me my sword.
Who's there?
MACBETH: A friend.

Up to a point, Banquo's words are inscrutable: he doesn't specify which thoughts he is referring to, though "cursed" discloses their moral status. This kind of inscrutability, with its "wait and see" message to the audience, is ideally suited to characters still in the process of thinking things over and to situations that have started to form but that are still incomplete. Nevertheless, Banquo is not unknown to the audience when he enters at the dead of night. His ambition has been aroused by the Weïrd Sisters' promise that he would found a royal line, so his uncertainty about the time, like his reluctance to sleep, could well be an outward sign of an inner struggle with the hope—it is spelled out at the beginning of act 3[3]—that that promise, despite its sinister provenance, will come true. Banquo is also bothered by Macbeth's responses to the Weïrd Sisters: the crown has been mentioned, Banquo has seen Macbeth's "raptness" (1.3), and Macbeth has asked Banquo whether he hopes for his children to become kings (1.3). So, in a few brief lines, Banquo's dialogue with Fleance produces a realistic nocturnal setting; an awareness of moral conflict in Banquo; and a sense that Banquo and Fleance are at risk in an evolving situation. That sense is heightened by Banquo's disarming himself. It is heightened further when, in the dark, the "friend," still up and about at a suspect hour, meets them unexpectedly—Macbeth is on his way to murder Duncan—and Banquo has to ask for his sword back.

II

When the sun refuses to shine. The rising sun. Making sure that as many people as possible understand what is being said.

Just as Shakespeare uses the absence of moonlight and starlight to control the audience's understanding, so, too, does he use the absence of sunlight. Act 5, scene 3, of *Richard III* is dominated by time slipping away, the countdown beginning with Catesby's, "It's supper-time, my lord, / It's nine a'clock." After the ghosts of his victims have visited him in his dreams, Richard says, "The lights burn blue. It is now dead midnight. / Cold fearful drops stand on my trembling flesh." As Ratcliffe enters to inform Richard that his friends are already buckling on their armor, he also tells him, "The early village cock / Hath twice done salutation to the morn" (3 a.m.; cf. Capulet in *Romeo and Juliet,* 4.4: "the second cock hath crowed, / The curfew-bell hath rung, 'tis three a'clock"). And, after Richmond's oration to his soldiers, Richard hears a clock striking and orders:

> Tell the clock there. Give me a calendar.
> Who saw the sun to-day?
> RATCLIFFE: Not I, my lord.
> KING RICHARD: Then he disdains to shine, for by the book
> He should have brav'd the east an hour ago.
> A black day will it be to somebody.

Suppertime is shared time and part of everyday life, so Richard's refusal to sup signals that something is about to go wrong. Midnight means maximum darkness, and its epithet "dead," coupled with "cold fearful drops," is clearly anticipatory. And then there is "The lights burn blue." An uncanny phrase, it indicates the continuing presence of ghosts.[4] The village cock's early salutations to the morn signify naturalness untouched by human corruption. And the sun's refusal to shine is unmistakably a portent, since, if the royal symbol fails to shine, the king will not shine either. When Richard observes, "A black day will it be to somebody," he senses and fears what the audience knows and looks forward to, namely, that that "somebody" will be himself.

An obscured morning sun is a regretful symbol: it consists, from the point of view of the beholder, of something worse impeding or impairing something better. In *Romeo and Juliet*, that regret is shared between speaker and audience. As the play draws to a close, the Prince says, "The sun, for sorrow, will not show his head" (5.3), and the implication is that, while harmony has at last come about in Verona, the price has been too high. On the other hand, an unobscured sun generally points to things turning out well. This need not be straightforward. In expectation of the Battle of Shrewsbury, Henry IV speaks of the sun rising "bloodily" (*Henry IV, Part One*, 5.1). But there is little to impair Don Pedro's sunrise optimism as *Much Ado about Nothing* enters its final phase:

> Good morrow, masters, put your torches out.
> The wolves have preyed, and look, the gentle day,
> Before the wheels of Phoebus, round about
> Dapples the drowsy east with spots of grey.
>
> (5.3)

Don Pedro doesn't actually say what color his rising sun is: the mood Shakespeare wants to communicate is a benign one, so "gentle," "drowsy," and "spots of grey" are sufficient. Don Pedro is so at ease by this point in the play that he is speaking verse again, and he feels free to ornament his classical allusion to Phoebus with an elegant application of assonant synecdoche (part for the whole). However, given the social mix of Shakespeare's playhouse audiences, there would have been many listening to him who did not share his educated idiom and who, perhaps, had at best a sketchy idea of who Phoebus was. In *A Midsummer Night's Dream*, Bottom refers to "Phibbus' car" during his impromptu delivery of a rant (1.2), so he, a weaver who appears to have acting experience, might just know who "Phibbus" was, even if his mispronunciation of the name, like his mispronunciation of "Ninus" (5.1), indicates that any classical knowledge that he has would be fragmentary. But would the Snugs of London know—Snug, who needs the lion's part in good time, since he is "slow of study" (1.2)? They probably would not. Yet there is no reason why Don Pedro should not be intelligible well below his station. In addition to "the wheels of Phoebus," the torches are put out, the wolves are dispatched, "Good morrow" is said, and so is "day." In other words, Don Pedro's lines speak to different strata of the audience in different ways, and their sunrise gist should have been clear to anyone who could pay to get in and hear them.

III
Fading light in Timon of Athens, Macbeth, *and* Troilus and Cressida.

Like the rising sun, the setting sun is an archetypal image and, as such, it lends itself readily to key statements in Shakespeare's plays. These characteristically achieve their effectiveness by combining *analogy* and *association*. An image from *Timon of Athens* provides a simple example of this combination.

Timon depends on the respect and affection of others so much that he lavishes his fortune on gifts and entertainment. Apemantus, the cynic, knows that cupboard love lasts only as long as the largesse that inspires it, and he uses an image involving sunset to say so. It is the third line in the following quotation. It does not refer to an actual sunset in the play, but it enables the effectiveness of "real" sunsets in other plays to be understood better: "I should fear those that dance before me now / Would one day stamp upon me. 'T 'as been done; / Men shut their doors against a setting sun" (1.2). Apemantus's image uses an everyday idea—shutting doors at sunset—to make clear by *analogy* the more distant idea that fawners and flatterers refuse to help when good times change to bad. But if Apemantus is to be a dramatic counterweight to Timon, clarity alone is not enough: his image must carry an emotional charge as well. That emotional charge is provided by the monosyllabic word "shut," with its *association* of exclusion. In other words, Apemantus's image gains its clarity from *analogy* and its power from *association*. That is a potent combination, as it has to be, if it is to contrast with Timon's thinking and behavior. Apemantus's distant idea is not distant because it is startlingly original or difficult to grasp. It is distant because it is alien in the context in which it is expressed. Nevertheless, as the scene's conclusion shows, Apemantus can stand his ground against Timon. Apemantus's viewpoint may be extreme, but he has cool reason on his side.

"Cool reason," it will be recalled, is Theseus's phrase. It comes from act 5, scene 1, of *A Midsummer Night's Dream* and was discussed in chapter 4, section I. While no cynic, Theseus is, like Apemantus, naturally attracted to cool reason. When he reads that *Pyramus and Thisby* is "'[a] tedious brief scene'" and "'very tragical mirth,'" he makes two successive responses. His first response is analytical. "Merry and tragical?" he exclaims, fastening on the phrases' inner contradictoriness, "Tedious and brief? / That is hot ice and wondrous strange snow." His second response is to look for a way of reconciling the discrepancies his analysis has highlighted. "How shall we find the concord of this discord?" he asks, and, in seeking concord when faced with discord, Theseus brings out a characteristic that often goes with cool reason: it likes not just to explain things but to resolve them, to replace darkness with light. That sounds like a good thing, but it also implies a limitation that Shakespeare does not always want to accept.

That last sentence may raise eyebrows, given that Shakespeare brings light to every subject he treats and obviously sets out to do so. But Shakespeare's practice distinguishes sharply between wanting to replace darkness with light and wanting to apply light to darkness in order to show how dark it is. This is Macbeth contemplating the murder of Banquo and Fleance ("seeling" refers to the practice of stitching falcons' eyelids together as part of their preparation as hunting birds):

> Come, seeling night,
> Scarf up the tender eye of pitiful day,
> And with thy bloody and invisible hand
> Cancel and tear to pieces that great bond
> Which keeps me pale! Light thickens, and the crow
> Makes wing to th' rooky wood;
> Good things of day begin to droop and drowse,
> Whiles night's black agents to their preys do rouse.
>
> (3.2)

The replacement of pity by bloodshed, the deliberate violation of divine and social order by the taking of life—these are lucidly expressed analogously by "seeling," "scarf up" and "Cancel and tear to pieces that great bond." But the extraordinary three and a half lines beginning "Light thickens" are less easily reducible. As Macbeth speaks them, he willingly descends in thought from man to the level of a beast of prey, and, since his sense of right and wrong is intact, he implicitly declares a willing descent into wickedness as well. But such an analysis fails to exhaust these lines' effectiveness, and there is a powerful reason for this. It will be recalled that, in his explanation of mimesis, Kenneth McLeish writes that "it means setting up in someone's mind . . . ideas that will lead that person to associate what is being presented with his or her previous experience." But Macbeth is descending into murder, and that, even potentially, exceeds most people's previous experience. So, however much of Macbeth is illuminated as he speaks, something dark and disturbing is bound to remain. It is one of the great feats of these three and a half lines that they make that something real. Everything that Macbeth says in them is intelligible, but their intelligibility serves to clarify the dark point where he and the audience part company.

Nevertheless, McLeish is basically right, provided that "previous experience" is taken to include deeply buried emotions of a general kind. Just about everyone can respond to the idea of thickening light because of menacing associations that may well go back to childhood. And to this day, people avoid woods by failing light, not because of any known danger but because of the deep fears the idea of a wood at night provokes. It feels like an unsafe place, even if it isn't. That may explain why, while Macbeth understandably identifies himself with nocturnal predators, his hearers are more likely to identify with their victims. In his preceding speech, Macbeth has promised his wife "a deed of dreadful note." The depth-psychological effect of his lines after "light thickens" makes the word "dreadful"—that is, "full of dread"—mean what it says.

Yet, for all its darkness, *Macbeth* is a forward-looking play. Macbeth is never completely settled in authority, the play's undertow is toward things getting better, and, in act 5, brutality is defeated and order restored. It is a satisfying ending, because what is right has the last word. Is life really like that, however? Is there something in the balance between order and brutality that makes the eventual triumph of order inevitable? These questions are posed in act 5, scene 8, of *Troilus and Cressida* in the form of a contest between chivalry and its opposite; and the fact that it takes place in fading light indicates a pessimistic answer even more forcefully than the forebodings of Andromache and Cassandra that precede it in act 5, scene 3.

Chivalry is embodied by Hector. His ethical attitude to fighting is made clear in a preparatory exchange with Troilus:

> TROILUS: Brother, you have a vice of mercy in you,
> Which better fits a lion than a man.
> HECTOR: What vice is that? Good Troilus, chide me for it.
> TROILUS: When many times the captive Grecian falls,
> Even in the fan and wind of your fair sword,
> You bid them rise and live.
> HECTOR: O, 'tis fair play.
> TROILUS: Fool's play, by heaven, Hector.
>
> (5.3)

Troilus's contention is that warfare is organized brutality: if chivalry is persisted in, it simply invites destruction. Shortly afterward, Hector allows Achilles, who is out of condition, to escape with his life. It is a fatal mistake. As the day draws to a close, Hector, relaxing, removes his helmet and shield:

Enter ACHILLES *and* MYRMIDONS.

ACHILLES: Look, Hector, how the sun begins to set,
How ugly night comes breathing at his heels;
Even with the vail and dark'ning of the sun,
To close the day up, Hector's life is done.
HECTOR: I am unarm'd, forgo this vantage, Greek.
ACHILLES: Strike, fellows, strike, this is the man I seek.

HECTOR *falls.*

(5.8)

The scene has the starkness of a very unpleasant truth. As is recurrently the case in Shakespeare, the divided nature of man is on display. Above the line are civilization and generosity of spirit; beneath it are meanness and brutality. Hector's great error is to suppose that, in an inherently brutal situation, his own code of conduct places some kind of obligation on his adversary. But it does not, and Hector's death at sunset shows this in a direct and immediate way. Hector is unprotected, tired, and outnumbered; Achilles, avid to avenge Patroclus's death, would not have it any other way; brutality wins. It will be recalled that, in act 5, scene 7, Achilles had instructed his Myrmidons to proceed against Hector "[i]n fellest manner" ("fell" means "savage" and is intensified by the superlative form).

Achilles goes on to have Hector's body tied to his horse's tail and dragged across the battlefield. That is one individual's humiliation. But Shakespeare wants the death of Hector to be seen as more than that, so he has Achilles evoke nightfall a second time:

The dragon wing of night o'erspreads the earth,
And stickler-like the armies separates.
My half-supp'd sword that frankly would have fed,
Pleas'd with this dainty bait, thus goes to bed.

(5.8)

The imagery of these lines is polarized. On the one hand, there is the stickler, that is, the moderator or umpire in combat, who is there "to see fair play, and to part the combatants when they have fought enough."[5] The stickler stands for governance by rule and order, without which civilization is impossible. On the other hand, replete with negative associations, there is "the dragon wing of night" and its agent, Achilles, who stands for arbitrariness and force majeure. Hector's idealism, like the stickler's authority, belongs to the enlightened part of human nature, but, on its own, that part of human nature is always open to defeat by brutality just as, on his own, a Hector is always open to defeat by an Achilles and his Myrmidons. Evidently, then, there is nothing in the balance between order and brutality to make the triumph of order inevitable in all circumstances.

This point can be taken a little further. Achilles' victory is presented as repellent, whereas Hector's chivalry, like the office of stickler, is presented as desirable. This makes attractive the case for civilization as a bulwark against brutality. However, Shakespeare makes it clear that chivalry, because it is vulnerable, needs to be coupled with prudence, at least if it is to survive and be effective. To this end, he has Cassandra spell out to Hector that "vows to every purpose must not hold" (5.3), that is, vows have to take circumstances into consideration. She also spells out to Priam, in Hector's presence, that, if Hector falls, then Priam and Troy will fall, too. Nevertheless, Hector imprudently insists on fighting because he has given his word; and it remains for Troilus to confirm what his avoidable death means for Troy: "Sit, gods, upon your thrones, and smile at Troy! / I say, at once, let your brief plagues be mercy, / And linger not our sure destructions on!" (5.10).

IV
Times of the year and clock times. Death as an enigma. Biblical allusions.

Sunrise and sunset, daytime, nighttime, the chiming of the hours: Elizabethan and Jacobean audiences were nothing if not time conscious, and, in addition to the natural phases of the day and the orderly artificiality of clock time, Shakespeare's plays are filled with references to the seasonal, religious, and agricultural patterns of the year. These were, much more than nowadays, living systems for dividing up time.[6] In *Henry IV, Part One,* Falstaff is called "All-hallown summer" (1.2), a calendar-based description meaning young ways in an old body (All Hallows is November 1); and Francis, the drawer in the Boar's Head, dates his birthday as "about Michaelmas next" (2.4; Michaelmas is September 29), just as, in *Romeo and Juliet,* the Nurse dates Juliet's as Lammas-eve (1.3; Lammas-eve is July 31). Given the respective dates of All Hallows and Michaelmas, Shakespeare's audiences would know straight away when, in *The Merry Wives of Windsor,* Simple locates "All-hallowmas" before "Michaelmas," that his name is well chosen (1.1). And the double meaning in Poins's calling Falstaff "the martlemas" in *Henry IV, Part Two* (2.2), would be obvious to them, too: Martinmas (November 11) was when fattened livestock was killed for winter.[7] More than mere terminology is involved here. Shakespeare's words reciprocated the ways his audiences experienced their year and, consequently, helped them instinctively to orientate themselves in his plays.

Of all the forms of time that Shakespeare incorporates into his plays, clock time is probably the most assertive. "The invention and dissemination of mechanical time in the renaissance," writes John Kerrigan in his preface to *"The Sonnets" and "A Lover's Complaint,"*

> brought about a complete reordering of sensibility. . . . Those who explain the Elizabethan obsession with Time by invoking the iconography of Saturn and Chronos (the god of chronology) confuse symptoms with cause. Time the Devourer, Time the Revealer, Time in rags with his scythe and hourglass: such figures were elaborated because they gave writers and artists emblems in which they could encapsulate their hopes and fears. The roots of Time's symbolism lie . . . in the springs, coils, and pendula of renaissance machinery.
> . . . As clocks and watches became cheap and compact, however, during the sixteenth century, the new music of time—cold, mechanical, inexorable—encroached on the lives of ordinary men and women. Clocks appeared in homes and workshops. Labour began to be regulated by machinery; domestic affairs were organized around the dial's hand. . . . Clock time invaded men's lives, and was, indeed, for city-dwellers like Shakespeare, the matrix of living.[8]

Measured against the sundial, the mechanical timepieces of Shakespeare's day were not, in fact, completely accurate, but, in his plays, Shakespeare treats them as if they were and uses their chimed hourly preciseness to pinpoint important occasions and turning points. Macbeth arranges supper for "seven at night" (*Macbeth,* 3.1); the conspirators in *Julius Caesar* part at three—they "count the clock"—and Caesar is to be fetched "[b]y the eight hour" (2.1); in *Henry V,* the French ambassador is due to be heard at four o'clock (1.1); and Falstaff claims to have fought Hotspur "a long hour by Shrewsbury clock" (*Henry IV, Part One,* 5.4). The list could be extended much further. Only the Forest of Arden, it seems, has no clocks at all (*As You Like It,* 3.2).

Because of its regularity, clock time, if heard, can connote good order. In *Twelfth Night,* as Olivia half accepts the futility of trying to woo Viola, Shakespeare has a clock strike, and Olivia, mistress of an Elizabethan household despite its Illyrian setting, says, "The clock upbraids me with the waste of time" (3.1). But because of its one-way flow, time can also be linked to the way reputations routinely fade if they are not refreshed. In *Troilus and Cressida,* Achilles asks, "What, are my deeds forgot?" and Ulysses slyly explains,

> Time hath, my lord, a wallet at his back,
> Wherein he puts alms for oblivion,

A great-siz'd monster of ingratitudes.
Those scraps are good deeds past, which are devour'd
As fast as they are made, forgot as soon
As done. . . .

(3.3)

Finally, there is Time the Devourer. In *King John,* time is referred to as "Old Time the clock-setter, that bald sexton Time!" (3.1). In context, the idea is that, over time, men's expectations can turn out to be less secure than they initially seem. But "old," "bald," and "sexton" have recognizable associations with death.

If objective time is fixed, subjective time is flexible. As Rosalind puts it in *As You Like It,* "Time travels in divers paces with divers persons" (3.2). For Shakespeare, this truism was a liberation and an opportunity, for it enabled him to dramatize passages of time on the basis of how his audiences would experience them. Approximately twenty-two years are compressed into the four plays of the second Henriad; *The Winter's Tale* encompasses fifteen or sixteen years (the text has both numbers, though sixteen is the likelier, since it is repeated in act 5, scene 3); *Much Ado about Nothing* speaks of "a just seven-night" between Claudio and Hero's betrothal and their wedding (2.1); and in *Twelfth Night,* three days are said to pass between Viola's arrival at Orsino's palace and her first commission (1.4). When Shakespeare raises time's profile, it may well be to make its pressure felt. *The Comedy of Errors* is a race against the clock, and *Romeo and Juliet* is marked by time signals throughout.

Unusually, *The Tempest* comes close to real time. Act 1, scene 2, contains the following lines:

> PROSPERO: What is the time o' th' day?
> ARIEL: Past the mid season.
> PROSPERO: At least two glasses. The time 'twixt six and now
> Must by us both be spent most preciously.

Prospero's two o'clock ("two glasses") is the time an afternoon performance of *The Tempest* would normally start, and, augmented by music, it might well last four hours. Furthermore, as *The Tempest* nears its close, Alonso asks Ferdinand, presumably with a pun on "play," "What is this maid with whom thou wast at play? / Your eld'st acquaintance cannot be three hours"; and the Boatswain declares shortly afterward, "our ship— / Which, but three glasses since, we gave out split— / Is tight and yare" (both quotations from 5.1; "yare" means "ready to sail"). However, the least interesting form of time, from a dramatist's point of view, is a straight run of it as if from life. So, to spend the play's time "most preciously," Shakespeare includes the prehistory of the principal characters and a whirlwind courtship. In any case, Miranda and Prospero seem to have their own time. For Miranda, time is measured in terms of successive experiences; for Prospero, it is the stage-by-stage completion of his project that sets the pace. "Now does my project gather to a head," he says at the beginning of act 5, ". . . and Time / Goes upright with his carriage," meaning that Time now has less of a load to carry.

Specific clock times conventionally arouse specific associations. Midnight and three o'clock in the morning are dark hours suggesting evil: in *Macbeth,* "midnight" is used as an absolute epithet ("secret, black, and midnight hags" [4.1]), and in *Cymbeline,* Jachimo's exploration of Imogen's bedchamber and body takes place between midnight and three o'clock (2.2). Noon, on the other hand, is positive and so lends itself to powerful good/bad contrasts. In *King Lear,* Regan makes the stocking of Kent, Lear's servant, even more outrageous by postponing its termination from noon "[t]ill night, my lord, and all night too" (2.2); in *The Winter's Tale,* Leontes imputes to Hermione and Polixenes the wicked wish that noon were midnight (1.2); and, in *Antony and Cleopatra,* drunkenness appears much worse to Octavius Caesar for being "at noon" (1.4). By comparison, three o'clock in the afternoon seems anonymity itself, but there is one momentous exception: the birth of Falstaff. "My lord," he informs the Lord Chief Justice in *Henry IV, Part Two,* "I was born about three of the clock in the afternoon, with a white head and something a round belly" (1.2). Falstaff's afternoon launch into time anticipates his irregular habits in later life.

When time runs out, death results, and the importance of death to Shakespeare is testified to by the variety of his treatment of it. Among other things, it is the gateway to "[t]he undiscover'd country, from whose bourn / No traveller returns" (*Hamlet,* 3.1); a grievous intrusion (*Love's Labor's Lost,* 5.2); a source of grave digger's wit (*Hamlet,* 5.1); and a source of terror (*Measure for Measure,* 3.1). The reason for this variety is that, in his plays taken as a whole, Shakespeare treats death as something that is essentially enigmatic. That is to say, because it is not fully intelligible, it cannot be summed up in any single comprehensive statement, and so it is treated in a number of different ways instead, none of which says all that there is to say about it. Some of these treatments involve great verse. Hamlet's "For in that sleep of death what dreams may come, / When we have shuffled off this mortal coil, / Must give us pause" (3.1) or Macbeth's "And all our yesterdays have lighted fools / The way to dusty death" (5.5) are two cases in point. But death can be well served in prose as well, and one of Shakespeare's outstanding reminders of mortality is the reminiscing of Justice Shallow and Justice Silence in *Henry IV, Part Two:*

SHALLOW: Jesu, Jesu, the mad days that I have spent! And to see how many of my old acquaintance are dead!

SILENCE: We shall all follow, cousin.

SHALLOW: Certain, 'tis certain, very sure, very sure. Death, as the Psalmist saith, is certain to all, all shall die. How a good yoke of bullocks at Stamford fair?

SILENCE: By my troth, I was not there.

SHALLOW: Death is certain. Is old Double of your town living yet?

SILENCE: Dead, sir.

SHALLOW: Jesu, Jesu, dead! 'A drew a good bow, and dead! 'A shot a fine shoot. John a' Gaunt lov'd him well, and betted much money on his head. Dead! (3.2)

Like Hamlet's reflections on Yorick's skull (*Hamlet*, 5.1), these lines bring life and death together as absolute incongruities. Shallow's thoughts are as shallow as his name: they go round and round without profundity; and Silence can do no better. Their banalities are amusing, though their speakers don't intend them to be; but at the same time they amount to a disturbing challenge to the audience to do better.

They also instance Shakespeare's expectation that, in an age of biblical instruction and compulsory church attendance, his audiences would know their Bibles thoroughly and understand his allusions at first hearing. Shallow remembers Psalm 89 well enough: verse 48 runs, "What man liveth, & shal not se death? shal he deliver his soule from the hand of the grave?" But it takes an intimate knowledge of the Bible, including the Apocrypha, to spot that he reaches Lincolnshire's Stamford fair via Ecclesiasticus 38:25: "How can he get wisdome that holdeth the plough . . . and talketh but of the brede of bullockes?"[9] The joke, a clever one, is on Shallow and his flitting mind. (In the phrase "How a good yoke of bullocks at Stamford fair?" "How" means "What was the price of.")

On other occasions, Shakespeare's use of the Bible is, for modern audiences, rather more obvious. Two instances show this clearly. In *Romeo and Juliet,* Friar Lawrence says:

> The sweetest honey
> Is loathsome in his own deliciousness,
> And in the taste confounds the appetite.
> Therefore love moderately: long love doth so;
>
> (2.6)

This draws on Proverbs 25:16—"If thou have founde honie, eat that is sufficient for thee, lest thou be overful, and vomit it"—and the gloss in the margin of the Geneva Bible reads, "Use moderatly the pleasures of this worlde." The original injunction against immoderate pleasure is adapted as a timely warning to Romeo to temper his extremity of passion. And in *Measure for Measure,* Isabella says of Angelo:

> This outward-sainted deputy,
> . . . .
>   is yet a devil;
> His filth within being cast, he would appear
> A pond as deep as hell.

(3.1)

St. Matthew's Gospel 23:27 reads, "Wo be to you, Scribes and Pharises, hypocrites: for ye are like unto whited tombes, which appeare beautiful outwarde, but are within ful of dead mens bones, and of all filthines." St. Matthew's "outwarde"-"within" duality carries over onto Angelo, the hypocrite, and condemns his "filth" in moral terms. It is not known whether Shakespeare had any religious beliefs of his own, and it is generally held that his plays are not intended as the vehicles of doctrine. Nevertheless, allusions to the Bible are everywhere in them, and the very least that can be said is that, when Shakespeare makes such allusions, he can be generally confident not only *that* they will be understood but *how* they will be understood as well.

Chapter 7

CONTROLLING THE
AUDIENCE'S RESPONSES (II)

Long Plot Lines; Setting Up Situations Early; Risk Management; Two Storms

I

Long-range continuity in The Merry Wives of Windsor. *Getting Bottom and Titania together in* A Midsummer Night's Dream. *Establishing Hotspur's character early in* Henry IV, Part One. *Brutus's reasoning in* Julius Caesar.

In act 1, scene 2, of *The Merry Wives of Windsor,* Parson Evans sends Simple to Caius's house with a letter asking Mistress Quickly to act as intermediary between Slender and Anne Page. Caius returns unexpectedly, learns of Simple's errand, and the result is a challenge that the well-meaning Host of the Garter Inn frustrates by directing Caius and Evans to two different places. Caius and Evans feel that they have been made a laughingstock, so they plan revenge. In unparsonly fashion, Evans declares that he "will smite his noddles" (3.1), but, instead, they trick the Host into believing that his horses have been stolen.[1]

It is a good trick, for horses would represent a substantial capital investment on the Host's part, but matters don't end when the Host exclaims, "I am undone!" (4.5), even though they might appear to. For Fenton, needing the Host to help him marry Anne Page, offers him "[a] hundred pound in gold more than your loss" (4.6), and the Host, thanks to the trick played on him, is in no position to refuse. In other words, Shakespeare sustains a plot line from act 1, scene 2 to act 4, scene 6, the ultimate purpose of which is to dispose the Host to help Fenton—an action indispensable to the play's final phase. Furthermore, since the Host obviously needs some kind of explanation in exchange for his help, Fenton tells him what he and Anne Page intend on the one hand and what Master Page and his wife intend on the other—all in the hearing of the audience. (Fenton's words to the Host are discussed in chapter 8, section I.) Consequently, when the play's elaborate finale begins, its principal actions are already prepared, and the audience, in the know, can see what is just and what is ironical about them as they take place.

Advance preparation is something Shakespeare takes a lot of care over. Sometimes he uses an image that reaches forward into a given play. In *Coriolanus*, the central character is established well before the end of act 1 as a man of blood—that is, as a war hero who will be faced with an obligation to adapt to peace. In *Twelfth Night,* Viola asks, "Who governs here?" and the Captain replies, "A noble duke, in nature as in name" (1.2). That reply, to which "Orsino" and "bachelor" are soon attached, prepares the audience to see Orsino as a match for Viola before the play is out, by which time, in keeping with his romantic destiny, he will have changed from being a duke to being a count. A name can help, too. Borachio, whose name means "drunk" in Spanish ("*borracho*"), has no real reason to be drunk in *Much Ado about Nothing* except in act 3, scene 3, when, "like a true drunkard," he blurts out to Conrade and the overhearing Watch how Don Pedro and Claudio have been deceived about Hero. But—*in vino veritas*—if his is a drunkard's part from the start of the play, his loose tongue later is more believable.

One famous name can nowadays be misleading, however. Modern editions and productions of *A Midsummer Night's Dream* routinely include a character called "Puck." However, as Peter Levi writes, "Robin Goodfellow has become known as Puck through Shakespeare, but 'a puck' or 'the puck' is a general word, like 'an elf,' not a proper name, and that is how Shakespeare is using it, just as in the *Epithalamion* Spenser speaks of 'the Pouke,' a wicked imp."[2] These are Spenser's lines in full, and differences between the traditional puck and Shakespeare's reduced version are immediately obvious ("fray" means "frighten"):

> Ne let the Pouke, nor other evill sprights,
> Ne let mischivous witches with theyr charmes,
> Ne let hob Goblins, names whose sence we see not,
> Fray us with things that be not.
> Let not the shriech Oule, nor the Storke be heard:
> Nor the night Raven that still deadly yels
> Nor damned ghosts cald up with mighty spels
> Nor griesly vultures make us once affeard.[3]

Shakespeare's Puck—with a capital "P"—is not toned down arbitrarily from the diabolical figure of Elizabethan folklore; he is, like Theseus and Hippolyta, reduced very precisely to *A Midsummer Night's Dream*'s needs. During his introductory dialogue with the Fairy as act 2 begins, Puck emerges as a practical joker and as a misleader of night wanderers. Furthermore, whereas in *The White Goddess,* Robert Graves's study of folklore, Robin Goodfellow is associated with the ram,[4] Shakespeare keeps Puck categorically at a distance from the lovers by making him sexless, despite the fact that Puck conventionally attracts the pronoun "he" when the play is discussed (including here). Distant echoes of Puck's origins may be heard when he sets out after the hempen home-spuns in act 3, scene 1, and also in his speech in act 5 beginning, "Now the hungry lion roars, / And the wolf behowls the moon." But Puck spends most of *A Midsummer Night's Dream* under Oberon's direction. The result is more muddle than malignancy, and even the muddle stays within bounds.

Nevertheless, there is a crucial moment in the play when Puck intervenes on his own initiative, and it succeeds because Shakespeare has established well ahead of time exactly what *his* Puck is like. This intervention occurs in the section of the play that begins with Titania's defiant exit in act 2, scene 1, and that ends with Titania's "What angel wakes me from my flow'ry bed?" in act 3, scene 1. Thematically, its purpose is to ensure that Titania wakes up and falls in love with the transformed Bottom. Technically, its purpose is to get two independent plot lines to converge, and that is not as easy as Shakespeare makes it appear.

Titania has conveniently "forsworn [Oberon's] bed and company" when she exits, preferring to sleep apart on her bank where the wild thyme blows (2.1). That keeps Oberon out of the way once he has primed her to fall in love with the first creature she sees when she wakes up (he hopes that it will be something vile). Act 3, scene 1, has Peter Quince "coincidentally" leading his actors to the same vicinity for their moonlight rehearsal away from prying eyes, and Puck, equally "coincidentally," enters on his way back to Oberon just as the rehearsal is beginning. Puck's lines as he comes on spell out (1) that he doesn't know Bottom or the other actors; (2) that they are all near the sleeping Titania; and (3) that he is tempted not just to be an audience but to interfere, if the opportunity presents itself:

> What hempen home-spuns have we swagg'ring here,
> So near the cradle of the Fairy Queen?
> What, a play toward? I'll be an auditor,
> An actor too perhaps, if I see cause.

Bottom is excelling as an ass at the very moment of Puck's arrival—it is when he famously muddles "odious" and "odorous"—so Puck, associating a metaphorical ass with a literal one, sees his chance for some practical joking and (shortly after) nocturnal misleading; and, while all this is happening on-stage, someone with a mocked-up ass's head held ready to place over Bottom's is waiting behind the tiring-house facade. The head mustn't prevent Bottom from saying his lines clearly, so it might be a cap with long ears—in act 4, scene 1, Oberon tells Puck to "take this transformed scalp / From off the head of this Athenian swain." But the likelihood is that it is an elaborated imitation head, like the lion's head Bottom has envisaged for Snug earlier in act 3, scene 1. Such a head would allow half the face to be seen through the neck and would comply with the phrase Puck uses—"An ass's nole I fixed on his head"—when he relates to Oberon what he has been doing (3.2; a "nole" is a "noddle"). Bottom's "I must to the barber's, mounsieur; for methinks I am marvail's hairy about the face" (4.1) and Oberon's "Robin, take off this head" (4.1) point in the same direction. Either way, to get Bottom off the stage at exactly the right moment, with Puck invisibly following him, Shakespeare includes in Pyramus's script an exit line that might reasonably be there anyway, given the tenseness of the lovers' meeting. It has already been quoted at the beginning of chapter 3, and is "But hark; a voice! Stay thou but here a while, / And by and by I will to thee appear." Quince has already told Bottom to exit into the brake when he finishes his speech, and that is what Bottom does. When he returns—cued back on by Thisby's "'As true as truest horse, that yet would never tire'"—he is transformed, and his fellow actors flee the stage in fear, followed by Puck who, in his capacity as nocturnal misleader, intends to lead them hither and yon (Quince and the rest would be in the way if they stayed). To show that he is not afraid, Bottom starts to sing, walking up and down as he does so. This awakens Titania, who promptly falls in love with him. So the plot lines of Titania and Bottom are unobtrusively brought together; and although, when Titania initially leaves the stage in act 2, scene 1, the audience cannot foresee what will eventually happen, when it does happen, it appears as a logical outcome of the characterization and plot management that have preceded it.

Sustained plotting of this order presupposes plays based on coherent development from act 1 to act 5. For example, act 1 of *Henry IV, Part One,* prepares the audience not only for Prince Hal's and Falstaff's future behavior but for Hotspur's as well. In scenes 1 and 3, Shakespeare introduces Hotspur as a brave but self-centered and hot-tempered young man of poor judgment who is, quite unhistorically, of about the same age as Prince Hal (the real Hotspur was thirty-eight years old in 1402, twenty-three years older than the crown prince).[5] However, given what is in store for Hotspur later on, these first impressions of him require not just reinforcing but adding to as well. In act 2, scene 3, therefore, Hotspur reads a letter *"solus"* from an unnamed critic. In terms of the play's plot, the letter is superfluous. It is there solely to further define Hotspur and his situation in advance, which is why it is read out loud and commented on by him as well:

> Let me see some more. "The purpose you undertake is dangerous"— why, that's certain. 'Tis dangerous to take a cold, to sleep, to drink, but I tell you, my lord fool, out of this nettle, danger, we pluck this flower, safety. "The purpose you undertake is dangerous, the friends you have nam'd uncertain, the time itself unsorted, and your whole plot too light for the counterpoise of so great an opposition." Say you so, say you so? I say unto you again, you are a shallow, cowardly hind, and you lie. What a lack-brain is this! By the Lord, our plot is a good plot as ever was laid, our friends true and constant: a good plot, good friends, and full of expectation; an excellent plot, very good friends. What a frosty-spirited rogue is this!

Hotspur, temperamentally resistant to bad news, resorts to abuse and insistence to overwhelm the letter's central assertions that the opposition is too great and that he is likely to be let down. His insistence is an important characteristic; and "frosty"—another of Shakespeare's forward-looking words—will be used again by Worcester in act 4, scene 1, when news comes that Glendower, like Northumberland, will be absent from the Battle of Shrewsbury. But there is more to these lines than a reckless loser being pointed out early. Insistence can conceal inner doubts, and Lady Percy confirms as much when, in a conspicuously long and detailed speech, she links Hotspur to sleeplessness, pallor, "thick-ey'd musing," "curst melancholy," "beads of sweat," and "heavy business." Hers are the last major details to be added as far as Hotspur is concerned. Everything of importance to do with him has been disclosed to the audience by the time she finishes, including an important capacity for doubt. This means that he can be followed as a known quantity through the remainder of the play.

Around the time Shakespeare concluded his second Henriad, he returned to the theme of rebellion by dramatizing the conspiracy against Julius Caesar. One of the principal interests of the later play is how Brutus, the high-minded man of reason, unintentionally paves the way for Antony, the man of violence and civil war. Perhaps Brutus should distance himself from Cassius, who knows how to play on Brutus's anxiety about Caesar's ambition. But he does not do so, and, once Brutus is involved in the conspiracy,

Shakespeare needs to make clear to his audiences precisely why Brutus fails. A major part of the explanation is that Brutus's reasoning is poor when it needs to be good. To show that that is so, Shakespeare provides in act 2, scene 1, not one example but three.

1. Cassius proposes, "And let us swear our resolution." But Brutus argues that oaths are for the cowardly and the deceitful, not for honest Romans: they befit bad causes and would therefore contaminate "[t]he even virtue of our enterprise." So, there is no oath. Brutus's lofty arguments overlook the fact that even when men are convinced that they are in the right, they may still need some kind of solemn reinforcement beyond a giving of hands.

2. Crucially, Decius asks, "Shall no man else be touch'd but only Caesar?" and Cassius explicitly identifies Mark Antony as "a shrewd contriver" ("shrewd" means "evil" as well as "astute"). Brutus's reply is exquisite: the verse is balanced, the imagery is well chosen, and the reasoning is coherent. If form were everything, Brutus would carry the day:

> Our course will seem too bloody, Caius Cassius,
> To cut the head off and then hack the limbs—
> Like wrath in death and envy afterwards;
> For Antony is but a limb of Caesar.
> Let's be sacrificers, but not butchers, Caius.

3. When Cassius advances Mark Antony's love for Caesar as a reason to be wary of him, Brutus refuses to listen, dismissing Mark Antony as a man given to loose living.

What Shakespeare is demonstrating with this sequence is not just suspect individual judgments but a whole wrong approach: Brutus fails to build into his thinking the possibility that he might be wrong. He overrules when he should accommodate, he is decisive when he should be circumspect, he makes no contingency plans, and, above all, he shows no adequate awareness of unreason as a force antagonistic to and possibly more powerful than reason.[6] And so, when he is eventually challenged by Mark Antony, the "shrewd contriver" whose love for Caesar is "ingrafted" (2.1), he is seen not just to lose but to lose deservedly. (Brutus's defeat by Mark Antony is discussed in chapter 3, section IV.)

II

Parental and marital authority. Risk management in A Midsummer Night's Dream, Twelfth Night, *and* Othello.

Generally speaking, then, Shakespeare takes great care both to sustain long plot lines as the need arises and to use earlier parts of his plays to anticipate later parts. However, to deduce that Shakespeare was an invariably cautious dramatist would be incorrect. Some of his plotting entails taking considerable risks with his audiences' attention, then concealing those risks by good management.

Some risks are admittedly only nominal, since drama conventionally allows many an oddity for the sake of the play. Parents are a case in point. In real life, to have one or both parents living depends on nature and fortune, but having or not having parents in a play involves other imperatives. Hermia (*A Midsummer Night's Dream*), Juliet (*Romeo and Juliet*), and Desdemona (*Othello*) have living fathers, at least to start with, because the plot requires them to disobey paternal authority. But a deceased physician is Helena's allocation in *All's Well That Ends Well,* since that makes her a lowly placed dependent with healing skills who has no obvious right to aspire to a match with Count Bertram. And the Helena of *A Midsummer Night's Dream* is effectively fatherless, since Nedar, while named in act 1 and act 4, never comes into the play. There is, therefore, no one to prevent her nocturnal pursuit of Demetrius, which removes a major impediment from the play. In *Much Ado about Nothing,* Beatrice can happily make do with an uncle, as, less happily, Cressida can in *Troilus and Cressida.* But although Hero arguably needs a mother to counteract her dim-witted father, she is deliberately deprived of one by Shakespeare to maximize her vulnerability. (The 1623 First Folio edition's opening stage direction includes "*Leonato, Governour of Messina, Innogen his wife*"; she is also mentioned in the opening stage direction to act 2; but she plays no part in the play.)

No one in Shakespeare's audiences would object to such contrivances, even if they noticed them, but they would certainly register Shakespeare's female figures in terms of the law and practices of their day, and it is worth pursuing this point a little further, since it bears directly on the male/female economies of all the plays. This is how S. T. Bindoff describes the situation of women in Tudor England:

> In Tudor England, as in England down to very recent times, the inequality which affected the largest number of people was not a social, but a sexual, one. The woman of the time, whatever her rank in society, was treated as an inferior being, and her freedom of action was restricted at every turn. Prior to marriage she was an infant, to be watched over by parent or guardian. Her marriage, which was normally a business arrangement in which she had no say whatever, converted her into a *feme covert* and submerged her legal personality in that of her husband. Only as a widow could she hope to enjoy something approaching equality with man in the disposal of person and property. Such, at least, was the dictate of the common law.[7]

It is against this background that Hermia is expected to defer to Egeus (*A Midsummer Night's Dream*), Desdemona to Brabantio (*Othello*), Anne Page to Master Page (*The Merry Wives of Windsor*), Hero to Leonato, Beatrice (once betrothed) to Benedick (*Much Ado about Nothing*), and, post-Tudor, Hermione to Leontes (*The Winter's Tale*). In *The Taming of the Shrew,* Katherina notoriously asserts, "Thy husband is thy lord, thy life, thy keeper, / Thy head, thy sovereign" (5.2); in *A Midsummer Night's Dream,* Oberon has the magic, and Titania subordinates herself to him after her punishment for disobedience; and as late as *Henry VIII,* Queen Katherine of England, kneeling, points to deference, obedience, and duty as signs of having been "a true and humble wife" (2.4). (Katherine's deference moved Samuel Johnson to write, "The meek sorrows and virtuous distress of Katherine have furnished some scenes which may be justly numbered among the greatest efforts of tragedy."[8]) Nevertheless, Shakespeare consistently registers a tension between a daughter's duty and romantic love. *Romeo and Juliet* is the best-known example, but, in *A Midsummer Night's Dream,* Theseus overrules Egeus to prevent a mismatch, and, in *The Merry Wives of Windsor,* altogether one of Shakespeare's clearest statements on arranged marriages, Fenton speaks openly of Anne Page avoiding "[a] thousand irreligious cursed hours / Which forced marriage would have brought upon her" (5.5).

As indicated, however, Shakespeare also takes risks with his audiences' attention that go beyond the nominal. For example, in *A Midsummer Night's Dream,* Demetrius is destined to return to Helena at some point in the play, but, if he does so early, a major loss of dramatic interest seems inevitable. Yet, under the influence of Oberon's magic, Demetrius does exactly that:

> O Helen, goddess, nymph, perfect, divine!
> To what, my love, shall I compare thine eyne?
> Crystal is muddy. O, how ripe in show
> Thy lips, those kissing cherries, tempting grow!
>
> (3.2)

Helena now has everything she has been pursuing Demetrius for—much more, in fact, for there is no mistaking that these lines come from the heart. Nevertheless, if the play is not to run out of steam, such a mistaking is what Shakespeare has to make plausible in Helena, without being seen to do so. He achieves this in stages. In act 1, scene 1, he shows Helena to be lacking in self-esteem and envious of Hermia's attractiveness. In act 2, scene 2, Helena claims to be so ugly that Demetrius's running away from her is "no marvel." And when, in the same scene, Lysander declares his love for her,

her persuasion that she is rightly unattractive to Demetrius makes her dis-
believe out of hand that she is attractive to Lysander. Therefore, she concludes, Lysander must be making fun of her ("flout" means "mock"):

> Wherefore was I to this keen mockery born?
> When at your hands did I deserve this scorn?
> Is't not enough, is't not enough, young man,
> That I did never, no, nor never can,
> Deserve a sweet look from Demetrius' eye,
> But you must flout my insufficiency?

Given Helena's way of thinking, it seems only natural that, instead of rejoic-
ing that Demetrius loves her when he declares that he does, she should continue to believe in Hermia's superior attractiveness and conclude that Demetrius is part of a conspiracy to make fun of her. It seems only natural, too,
that, when Hermia joins Helena, Lysander, and Demetrius, she (Hermia)
should be likewise misunderstood, and the set-piece quarrel of act 3, scene
2, which is one of the play's great glories, is all set to reach its climax: "Lo!
she is one of this confederacy. / Now I perceive, they have conjoin'd all
three / To fashion this false sport, in spite of me." Shakespeare's thumb on
the scales is probably detectable only when the play is read. During performance, shrewd audience preparation and the plot's forward momentum
make it go unnoticed.

In *Twelfth Night*, Shakespeare is bolder still. In act 3, scene 4, Malvolio,
led on by Maria's forged letter, appears before Olivia, smiling and cross-
gartered. Olivia asks, "Why dost thou smile so, and kiss thy hand so oft?" and
all Malvolio has to do is produce the letter to explain why. But Shakespeare
wants to keep the letter back until act 5, so he diverts the audience's attention from the obvious response to Olivia's question with high-order stagecraft. He makes Malvolio quote from the letter as if, in his jubilation, he
knows it pretty much by heart. From Malvolio's point of view, remembered
quotations are all that are needed anyway. Filled with expectancy, he views
them positively as collusive reminders to Olivia of what he believes to be
her own willing words to him, so he feels no need at this time to back them
up with the letter itself; Olivia, having already been exposed to Maria's
"the man is tainted in 's wits" (3.4), is too amazed by Malvolio's bearing and
words to investigate what is happening, though, as mistress of the house, she
has the authority to do so; so no letter is produced. Malvolio is actually
made to say, "'[T]was well writ.'" But his words are preceded with "'Be not
afraid of greatness'" and followed straight away by "'Some are born great,'"

so Olivia's ill-focused "What means't thou by that, Malvolio?" goes unanswered. Before matters can be looked at more coolly, Shakespeare terminates the scene with the Servant entering to announce the return of Cesario; and the forged letter survives for later.

Skillful as the problem solving in *A Midsummer Night's Dream* and *Twelfth Night* is, the nonpareil of risk management occurs in act 4, scene 1, of *Othello*, in which Iago undertakes to show Othello Cassio laughing over past and future triumphs with Desdemona. In fact, the risk taking is double: Iago is at risk from Othello, should he fail to convince, and Shakespeare elects to run risks with his audience to advance his play at a critical moment. These risks include manipulating Othello's requirements, introducing a new character (Bianca), and giving Cassio a new characteristic (laughing when Bianca is mentioned)—all without forfeiting credibility and the play's momentum.

A key part of Shakespeare's preparation for Iago's mise-en-scène is Othello's demand for proof. Specifically, he says, "No, Iago, / I'll see before I doubt" (3.3), and, a little later, "Villain, be sure thou prove my love a whore; / Be sure of it. Give me the ocular proof" (3.3). The language matters. First, "see" and "ocular" indicate that Shakespeare, developing his source material, is working toward an essentially visual situation. Second, Othello uses "ocular" as anyone might, that is, as meaning visible and therefore objectively true; but Shakespeare has a significantly different meaning in mind, namely, the subjective one of "seeing is believing." Given Desdemona's purity, true ocular proof is in any case impossible for Iago to deliver. So, to make an illusion of ocular proof possible instead, Shakespeare has Othello adjust his demand a fraction: "Make me to see't; or (at the least) so prove it / That the probation bear no hinge nor loop / To hang a doubt on; or woe upon thy life!" (3.3). Two reasons consistent with Othello's psychology make this adjustment credible. First, by being less specific, it caters more easily to his perverse need for grounds to resist his love for Desdemona. Second, the "it" Othello wants to see is too close to "copulation" for his comfort. When Iago asks point blank, "Would you, the supervisor, grossly gape on? / Behold her topp'd?" (3.3), Othello balks and then effectively settles for Iago's "imputation and strong circumstances."

In the form that Shakespeare intends for it, Iago's ocular pseudoproof requires a new minor character in the play, namely, the off-white and indecorously clinging Bianca. She has to be off-white, since no respectable woman would cling as she does, and her clinging is part of the pseudoproof. Her debut appearance lasts just long enough for Cassio to give her Desdemona's handkerchief to copy, then Shakespeare, with Bianca's crucial second entrance in mind, has her exit with Cassio. To divert attention from the fact

that Bianca is really no more than an ad hoc expedient, Shakespeare elabo-
rates her first entrance with some care. Cassio, allegedly preoccupied by his
dismissal though apparently tiring of her as well, has been neglecting her.
This is enough to cover her absence from the play hitherto. Bianca, however, is given to haunting Cassio (he later emphasizes the point). Tired of
waiting for him, she has therefore set out for his lodging. This brings her onto
the stage, named and on cue, with every appearance of naturalness. That
Cassio is surprised by Bianca within the action of the play goes a long way
toward alleviating any surprise the audience may feel that she has been slot-
ted into the play at all:

> BIANCA: 'Save you, friend Cassio!
> CASSIO: What make you from home?
> How is't with you, my most fair Bianca?
> I'faith, sweet love, I was coming to your house.
> BIANCA: And I was going to your lodging, Cassio.
> What? keep a week away? seven days and nights?
>
> (3.4)

Cassio takes the opportunity to ask Bianca to copy Desdemona's handkerchief, and his request, which seems, at least in part, sincere, makes sense. The
handkerchief was patterned by a sibyl, so it looks interesting (3.4). And since
Cassio expects its owner to want the original back, the "honorable lieu-
tenant" (as he is called in the cast list) naturally wants a copy made as the
next best thing. Such work would be a woman's work; Bianca is available;
so Bianca gets the request. As to why Bianca, for all her suspicions, takes the
handkerchief with her, Cassio explains to her that he is waiting for Othello
and that he is anxious not to appear "woman'd" in Othello's eyes (3.4). In
short, Cassio presses her to leave (with the handkerchief) before she can
fully gather her thoughts. Knowing her temper, he prudently agrees to accompany her a little way as a sign of affection. That Bianca is not really mol-
lified when she exits lays the basis for an imminent return by her.

Cassio's prudent agreement to accompany Bianca a little way clears the
stage for Iago to enter with Othello (4.1) and to remind him, in a sexually
provocative way, of the missing handkerchief. This causes Othello to have a
fit, which coincides with Cassio's preannounced return to the stage to wait
for Othello. This fit is Iago's big chance, and Shakespeare makes it believable
by letting the audience see for itself what has brought it on. Iago gets Cassio temporarily to exit again, and, by the time Cassio returns, as Iago has
privately asked him to, Othello is in hiding, believing that Iago will make

Cassio talk about misbehaving with Desdemona. The emphasis is on what Othello will think he is seeing. (The parallels between this scene and the tricking of Claudio and Don Pedro in *Much Ado about Nothing* are strong ones.)

> IAGO: Do but encave yourself,
> And mark the fleers, the gibes, and notable scorns
> That dwell in every region of his face,
> For I will make him tell the tale anew:
> Where, how, how oft, how long ago, and when
> He hath, and is again to cope your wife.
> I say, but mark his gesture.
>
>   (4.1)

Of course, for this arrangement to work, it has to be made credible that Othello, who has just thrown a fit and whom Iago intends to craze, will nevertheless remain where Iago "encaves" him. Iago, therefore, preemptively makes an issue of Othello's manliness—"Marry, patience, / Or I shall say y' are all in all in spleen, / And nothing of a man"—and the tactic just about works. The striking word "encave" is deliberately chosen by Shakespeare. It recalls Othello's account of himself in act 1, scene 3, when he spoke of "antres vast" ("antres" means "caves"). Act 4, scene 1, reaches down into the violent and primitive part of Othello that "antres" and "encave" both suggest.

To round off his preparations, Shakespeare has to invest Cassio with a second new character trait. The first was his inability to hold his drink. The second is that "[h]e, when he hears of [Bianca], cannot restrain / From the excess of laughter" (4.1). It is natural enough that, if Cassio and Bianca are close, Iago will know her, too, but, even so, that Cassio has to laugh whenever he hears Bianca's name might well be regarded as an unacceptably blatant addition on Shakespeare's part. However, the audience is allowed no time to dwell on the matter. Its attention is moved forward by Cassio's return and by the future tense in Iago's "As he shall smile, Othello shall go mad" (4.1).

Bianca's subsequent return with the handkerchief is crucial because it seems to confirm the guilt of Desdemona and Cassio. It is a windfall moment for Iago, and he makes the most of it, but it, too, might be regarded as unacceptably blatant on Shakespeare's part. Shakespeare meets that difficulty with sovereign competence. Since the audience might well wonder at Bianca making her second entrance precisely when she does, he does no less than put that wondering into the play by having Cassio exclaim, "What do you mean by this haunting of me?" (4.1). This occasions a torrential release of in-character jealousy from Bianca, as if she has been brooding on the handkerchief since she last left the stage and can contain herself no longer. In other words, haunting and jealousy together provide such persuasive *reasons* for Bianca's return, complete with handkerchief, that any question of its *timing* is lost in the rumpus.

In sum, Iago's risk taking works because, opportunist that he is, he knows how to exploit, and how to remain one step ahead of, Othello's rising sentiments. And Shakespeare's risk taking works because all his artifices, including some distinctly blatant ones, are plotted with audience management and with movements on stage fully in mind. Even the need to have Iago alone with Othello after Othello's deception is fully thought through. Bianca exits with the same angry hurt that brought her on; and Cassio, prompted by Iago, decides that he must follow her to stop her railing in the streets. That removes Cassio to a safe distance, as far as Iago is concerned, and leaves Othello at his mercy.[9]

III

The storm in Julius Caesar. *Prospero's supernatural power compared with Shakespeare's powers as a dramatist.*

Much earlier in *Othello,* in act 2, scene 1, there is a storm. One of its purposes is to stagger the arrivals of Cassio, Iago, Desdemona, Emilia, and Othello in Cyprus so that the interactions of these characters can be spaced apart and given clear onstage display. It is also an agent of peace, since it disables the Turkish fleet. But the peace it brings about contains hidden mischief, for, as soon as Cassio affably engages with Desdemona, Iago says in an aside ("gyve" means "ensnare"): "He takes her by the palm; ay, well said, whisper. With as little a web as this will I ensnare as great a fly as Cassio. Ay, smile upon her, do; I will gyve thee in thine own courtship." As the characters land, they think they have left the storm behind them when, in fact, the real one is still to break.

Storms span virtually the whole of Shakespeare's career. His first known storm accompanies the spirit raising in *Henry VI, Part Two* (1.4); his most quoted storm is probably the one in *King Lear; Macbeth* contains enough evil for more than one; the one in *Pericles* transforms the stage into the deck of a ship in peril; and *The Tempest* is named after one. Some storms last longer than others. Shakespeare's first protracted storm—and, in all likelihood, his very first in the new Globe theater—dominates act 1, scene 3, of *Julius Caesar.*[10] It is a storm that places dramatic emphasis on Casca. Casca will eventually lead the stabbing of Caesar, so, in addition to symbolizing Rome's deteriorating political situation, the storm is an integral part of the presentation onstage of Casca's recruitment by Cassius as an assassin.

As thunder and lightning fill the stage, Casca's first words are to Cicero. Each character enters by a separate flanking door, and Casca's sword is drawn:

> Are you not mov'd, when all the sway of earth
> Shakes like a thing unfirm? O Cicero,
> I have seen tempests when the scolding winds
> Have riv'd the knotty oaks, and I have seen
> Th' ambitious ocean swell, and rage, and foam,
> To be exalted with the threat'ning clouds;
> But never till to-night, never till now,
> Did I go through a tempest dropping fire.
> Either there is a civil strife in heaven,
> Or else the world, too saucy with the gods,
> Incenses them to send destruction.

There is fear and trembling in these lines, and a sense of portentousness, too. But where that sense might lead initially remains open, since Cicero coolly distances himself from what Casca says. Not so Cassius, who enters as Cicero exits. Cassius has already singled Casca out as being, despite his blunt exterior, a man to carry out "any bold or noble enterprise" (1.2), and Cassius is not intimidated by the storm. He says so himself, rightly sensing that, in so doing, he will gain ascendancy over Casca. For Cassius is a manipulator, and the storm, combined with Casca's fear, is his opportunity.

The stage is supposed to be so dark when Cassius enters that he does not recognize Casca, who answers "A Roman" when challenged. That is better than a name: it identifies Casca as a patriot, a point Cassius can work on. Cassius puts it to Casca that the storm is tantamount to a divine warning that Rome is in danger from tyranny. Then he insinuates that Caesar is "prodigious grown, / And fearful," although he is "[a] man no mightier than thyself, or me" ("prodigious" means "ominous" and "fearful" means "fear-inducing"). Casca, finding that his own thoughts are following Cassius's allusions, names the name: "'Tis Caesar that you mean; is it not, Cassius?" With that, Cassius has Casca very near his hook, and it is an interesting question how Shakespeare meant the storm to mark this moment—with a sudden lull? Or with an intensification of noise and light? Cassius claims that the Romans have become effeminate in their endurance of Caesar and, after hinting talk of daggers, feigns indifference to the possibility that Casca is "a willing bondman" who might report him. As intended, this provokes Casca's "quick mettle" (1.2), and he commits himself to what is clearly a plan to assassinate:

> You speak to Casca, and to such a man
> That is no fleering tell-tale. Hold, my hand.
> Be factious for redress of all these griefs,
> And I will set this foot of mine as far
> As who goes farthest.

Casca is self-evidently no leader, but he is a useful follower under Cassius's influence. The nocturnal storm, like an unorthodox chorus, accompanies Casca step by step from the agitated staring and breathlessness Cicero comments on as Casca enters, through his ambiguous assertion to Cassius that "every bondman in his own hand bears / The power to cancel his captivity," to Cassius's "There's a bargain made." It makes clear that Casca, by committing himself to political assassination, however well motivated, is committing himself to a dark and fearsome act. As Cassius himself puts it: "And the complexion of the element / In favor's like the work we have in hand, / Most bloody, fiery, and most terrible." Casca is conceivably intended to hear these lines as a challenge; but an Elizabethan audience would hear in them a serious moral warning.

The storm, by its nature, also intimates to the audience that Casca, Cassius, and their co-conspirators may be set to release forces too great for them to control. In this regard, Cicero's parting words to Casca are as easy to overlook as they are difficult to dismiss. First, he says: "Indeed, it is a strange-disposed time; / But men may construe things after their own fashion, / Clean from the purpose of the things themselves." These lines emphasize that any gap between the way things are and the way they might be interpreted would create a dangerous opportunity for willfulness and error. Then Cicero adds: "Good night then, Casca; this disturbed sky / Is not to walk in." Casca should listen carefully, since one meaning of Cicero's leave-taking is that rash commitment is to be avoided.

Finally, while most of Shakespeare's storms imply things going to the bad, not all of them do: the storm in act 3 of *The Winter's Tale* presages improvement, as does the one that opens *The Tempest*. Since *The Tempest* is a highly theatrical play, it comes as no surprise that the storm the play's title refers to is highly theatrical, too, though that can only be known ex post facto, since an audience unfamiliar with the opening of *The Tempest* has no way of knowing, until Prospero explains, "There's no harm done" (1.2), that the storm it

has been watching is not all it seems to be. However, after Prospero's explanation, some kind of before-and-after comparison is inevitable. One result
of such a comparison is an associating of Prospero with power: he can make
and unmake storms, and issues of power accompany him through the play.
Another result is an enhanced alertness to not just the storm but the entire
play as an artifact. In that case, the question of power is transferred from
Prospero, the mostly visible character, to Shakespeare, the invisible dramatist. Prospero's power, being magic, is supernatural. That distinguishes it from
Shakespeare's, which derives from two sources. First, Shakespeare, the play
maker, can view his play in terms of where he wants to get to as well as
where he is coming from, whereas the audience can only follow what is
presented to it in the order and in the manner of Shakespeare's choosing.
Second, Shakespeare knows from long experience the ways audiences react
to stage reality, so he can control those reactions with confidence. Both kinds
of knowledge place Shakespeare in such a position of advantage that the
word "power" is no exaggeration. It might be argued that Shakespeare's
power is relatively greater during the opening of *The Tempest* than subsequently in the play, since the presentation of the storm amounts to outright
deception. But deception is a large topic in Shakespeare's plays and deserves,
therefore, a chapter to itself.

Chapter 8

UNTRUTHFUL BEHAVIOR

Telling and Acting Lies in The Merry Wives of Windsor, Romeo and Juliet, Much Ado about Nothing, All's Well That Ends Well, Measure for Measure, King Lear, Cymbeline, *and* The Winter's Tale

I

Anne Page, the successful liar. Deception and its exculpation in The Merry Wives of Windsor.

FENTON: Hark, good mine host:
To-night at Herne's oak, just 'twixt twelve and one,
Must my sweet Nan present the Fairy Queen;
The purpose why, is here; in which disguise,
While other jests are something rank on foot,
Her father hath commanded her to slip
Away with Slender, and with him at Eton
Immediately to marry. She hath consented.
Now, sir,
Her mother (even strong against that match
And firm for Doctor Caius) hath appointed
That he shall likewise shuffle her away,
While other sports are tasking of their minds,
And at the dean'ry, where a priest attends,
Straight marry her. To this her mother's plot
She (seemingly obedient) likewise hath
Made promise to the doctor. . . .

. . . .

HOST: Which means she to deceive, father or mother?
FENTON: Both, my good host, to go along with me.
(*The Merry Wives of Windsor,* 4.6)

The Merry Wives of Windsor is not the first play in which Shakespeare is prepared to countenance untruthful behavior as an expedient. In act 4, scene 1,
of *Romeo and Juliet,* Friar Lawrence tells Juliet, "Go home, be merry, give
consent / To marry Paris," and she effectively does that, onstage, in the next
scene. She claims to repent of the sin of disobedient opposition and, kneeling, says that she will in the future be ruled by her father. Juliet's untruthful
behavior is inherently ambiguous. On the one hand, she is behaving untruthfully in the name of love. That speaks for her. On the other hand, she
is deceitfully compounding divergence from her father's authority. That
speaks against her. Because Juliet's untruthful behavior will turn out to be
unsuccessful, it leaves unaddressed a number of questions, two of which are
whether deception in the name of disobedience could ever succeed in practice and whether it could ever be justified in principle. "Be merry," by the
way, is not just a casual piece of dialogue. It links with the Nurse's "See
where she comes from shrift with merry look" (4.2) to form an embedded
stage direction, and it is there to ensure in performance the forced cheer
Juliet's scene with her parents requires.

Anne Page's untruthful behavior in *The Merry Wives of Windsor* is treated
differently. That it is not shown onstage stops it from seeming like shame-
lessness, which could make an audience think ill of it. Rather, Fenton's buoy-
ant reporting of it puts it across as something integral to a play moving in
the right direction and as something right in itself as well. For, by the time
The Merry Wives of Windsor is finished, it will have shown that deception can
succeed and that it can invite approval, too. In fact, without Shakespeare's
preparedness to incorporate deception that invites approval into his plays,
not only *The Merry Wives of Windsor,* but also *Much Ado about Nothing, All's
Well That Ends Well, Measure for Measure, Cymbeline,* and *The Winter's Tale,*
would simply not exist. Nor would the "Dover Cliff" scene in *King Lear,*
which is discussed in section III of this chapter.

As in *Romeo and Juliet,* what lies behind the deceit in *The Merry Wives of
Windsor* is a forced marriage. G. B. Harrison writes, "The father was the
head of the family and its ruler. His absolute right to dispose of his daughters in marriage was indeed questioned but the picture of the Capulet family is not far from the fact."[1] Master Page is lower down the social scale than
Capulet, but, that said, Harrison's words apply to him, too. Peter Levi notes
that *The Merry Wives of Windsor* is set "far in the past, when Eton was a small,

isolated chapel in the fields."[2] But there is no sense of historicizing in the play, and Shakespeare's contemporaries would not have regarded the issue of Anne Page's marriage as obsolete. It is not, however, an issue that Shakespeare treats evenhandedly. He presents arguments for, as well as against, a forced marriage, but the structural bias of *The Merry Wives of Windsor* is unmistakably against it.

Page wants his daughter to marry for material gain, and his position is credible by Elizabethan standards. Slender may live like "a poor gentleman born" (1.1), but he is a good prospect. "He will make you a hundred and fifty pounds jointure" (3.4), Shallow tells Anne Page. A jointure, according to T. W. Craik, "was the part of the husband's estate which he settled on his wife in the marriage-contract. It provided for her income if she were widowed. If Slender has £300 a year he probably has capital assets worth about £6,000. The common-law entitlement of a widow was one-third of her late husband's total estate. Slender's widow would be entitled to an income of £100 a year, so a jointure bringing in £150 a year is generous."[3] Understandably, Page thinks that Slender is an attractive investment. He is therefore happy to use a ruse to enforce his paternal authority and head off any possible interference by his wife or by Fenton.

Where Slender's wealth is hereditary and in land (4.4), Dr Caius's is professionally earned and in money. He has powerful friends at court as well (4.4). These reasons make Mistress Page's preference for the French physician understandable. Given her husband's authority as head of the family, Mistress Page has to look to a ruse of her own if she is to have her way.

Like Portia in *The Merchant of Venice,* Anne Page has a trio of suitors, but the third, Fenton, is actively out of favor with Master Page. Fenton himself explains why:

> He doth object I am too great of birth,
> And that my state being gall'd with my expense,
> I seek to heal it only by his wealth.
> Besides these, other bars he lays before me,
> My riots past, my wild societies,
> And tells me 'tis a thing impossible
> I should love thee but as a property.
>
> (3.4)

Social disparity, fortune hunting, and wild living—the last creating a faint link with the Prince Hal of *Richard II* and *Henry IV, Part One*—are not the things a Windsor citizen would want for his daughter. What counts in

Fenton's favor, however, is that, like Petruchio in *The Taming of the Shrew*, he is attracted by money but then falls in love (3.4), whereas what counts against Slender and Caius is that they are personally intolerable. When Slender and Caius are seen and heard onstage, the implicit question is: Who could possibly want his or her daughter to marry either one of them? That question reveals the bias of the play: of the three candidates for Anne Page's hand, Fenton is the only one who is agreeable. And Fenton stands for marriage for love. A secret contract is mentioned late in the play, but what really matters if the play's bias is to be fulfilled is, first, getting Anne Page and Fenton married and, second, getting their marriage vindicated. Since Fenton cannot gain acceptance by asking for it, and since he and Anne Page know that time is pressing, they resort to a swiftly applied ruse of their own, and it works because Anne Page has been prepared to lie without misgivings. So, by the end of the play, they are married.

Their marriage then has to be vindicated, and that is itself a two-part undertaking. The moral rightness of behaving untruthfully has to be argued, and the elder Pages have to express their acceptance of a marriage for love that neither wanted. Unless both conditions are met, the marriage will seem blemished and the play will not work. With regard to the moral rightness of behaving untruthfully, Shakespeare has Fenton assert, without being contradicted, "Th' offense is holy that she hath committed, / And this deceit loses the name of craft" (5.5). The key word is "holy," and the implication is that, by bringing about a good worthy of divine approval, the deception in question is freed from the moral censure that it would normally attract. With regard to the issue of parental acceptance, Shakespeare has Fenton and, more importantly, Ford speak *before* Master Page and his wife adopt a final position. Fenton goes first. Apparently addressing both the elder Pages, he claims that they "would have married [their daughter] most shamefully, / Where there was no proportion held in love" (5.5). It then falls to Ford, the respectable Windsor citizen who knows the value of money and who has relearned the value of love, to close off further debate by underwriting Fenton's position: "Stand not amaz'd; here is no remedy. / In love, the heavens themselves do guide the state; / Money buys lands, and wives are sold by fate" (5.5). Only then is Page allowed a response, and, as soon as he (followed by his wife) accepts Fenton as his son-in-law, the need to pursue further the issue of paternal authority is removed from the play.

But are matters really as settled as they seem when the play ends? Clearly, the question of Page's authority is fudged, since Page could theoretically have reacted very differently. That he gives in, albeit reluctantly, allows Shakespeare to have his cake and eat it, too, in the sense that he can make disobedience successful without seriously challenging the standard social order. Such things are possible in comedies, and all the signs are that Shakespeare expected his audiences to accept his way of handling things. It will be recalled that, in *A Midsummer Night's Dream,* Theseus's overbearing of Egeus's will (4.1) achieves the same effect.

However, the question of the moral justifiability of deception is not so easily dispatched. In the Geneva Bible, Proverbs asserts that "[t]he bread of deceit is swete to a man: but afterwarde his mouth shalbe filled with gravel" (20:17), and Revelations states flatly, "[A]ll liars shal have their parte in the lake, which burneth with fyre and brimstone" (21:8). Neither deception nor lying is to be taken lightly.

The fact is that, in plays besides *The Merry Wives of Windsor,* Shakespeare holds lying and its exculpation very close together, and a need to anticipate disquiet and even resistance on the part of his audiences may well explain why he does so. In *Much Ado about Nothing,* Friar Francis advocates lying— "And publish it that she is dead indeed" (4.1)—then spends thirty-four lines detailing why it will be a good thing. In *Cymbeline,* Pisanio tells Imogen, "I'll give but notice you are dead" (3.4), then justifies his lie immediately by detailing his plan to get Imogen close to her husband. And in *The Winter's Tale,* Camillo persuades Florizel to pass himself off as Perdita's husband on the grounds that harmony will follow (4.4). Nor are these the only examples. In *All's Well That Ends Well,* the Widow speaks of "this deceit so lawful" (3.7), and, in *Measure for Measure,* the Duke, having told Isabella to lie to Angelo "with a plausible obedience," is quick to assert that "the doubleness of the benefit defends the deceit from reproof" (3.1). So much explicitly justified lying suggests two linked conclusions. The first is that Shakespeare saw life as being so shaped that lying cannot be excluded categorically if good is to be achieved. The second is that, because of lying's moral dubiousness, he felt that a positive case for it needed to be made when it was turned to. Whether Shakespeare succeeds in defending his deceits from reproof is an open question. But, as a dramatist alert to the utility of untruthful behavior, he evidently felt the need to try.

II

Connections between lying and drama. The bed tricks in All's Well That Ends Well *and* Measure for Measure.

As lying and drama are both forms of make-believe, it comes as no surprise when lying assumes some of drama's appurtenances. This, for example, is how Friar Francis organizes things in *Much Ado about Nothing:*

Your daughter here the princes left for dead,
Let her awhile be secretly kept in,
And publish it that she is dead indeed.
Maintain a mourning ostentation,
And on your family's old monument
Hang mournful epitaphs, and do all rites
That appertain unto a burial.

(4.1)

Like a sequence in a play, this proposal is a fiction; its intended effect is calculated; it entails acting under direction; and it uses props. As Friar Francis
speaks, lines from *A Midsummer Night's Dream* might distantly stir in the memory of those who know the play, with Peter Quince saying, "But, masters,
here are your parts" and Bottom adding, "Take pains, be perfit" (1.2). Pisanio
(*Cymbeline*) and Camillo (*The Winter's Tale*) go further: both are attentive to
costuming; Pisanio gives instruction in deportment and in voice delivery;
and Camillo, who takes on the role of script writer, explicitly uses the tell-
tale phrase "[t]he scene you play" as he briefs Florizel (4.4). In *All's Well That
Ends Well,* Helena's explanation and justification to the Widow of the bed
trick she has in mind are of a piece with play making (3.7), as are the Duke's
explanation and justification to Isabella of his bed trick in *Measure for Measure* ("frame" simply means "prepare"):

> Go you to Angelo, answer his requiring with a plausible obedience,
> agree with his demands to the point; only refer yourself to this advan-
> tage: first, that your stay with him may not be long; that the time may
> have all shadow and silence in it; and the place answer to convenience.
> This being granted in course—and now follows all—we shall advise
> this wrong'd maid to stead up your appointment, go in your place. If
> the encounter acknowledge itself hereafter, it may compel him to her
> recompense; and here, by this is your brother sav'd, your honor un-
> tainted, the poor Mariana advantag'd, and the corrupt deputy scal'd.
> The maid will I frame, and make fit for his attempt. (3.1)

Effectively, the Duke articulates a mise-en-scène in miniature; as he speaks,
Isabella visualizes it as a Shakespearean boy actor or a modern actress might
and responds, "The image of it gives me content already"; and the Duke is
himself playing the part of a friar, having earlier been coached in the role by
Friar Thomas (1.3). It is not difficult to see the link between an untruthful
scenario like the Duke's and an untruthful scenario like Iago's when he has

Othello watch Cassio laugh about Bianca (*Othello,* 4.1): both are fictions of calculated intent, the important difference between them residing in the motive. And it is not difficult to see that an untruthful scenario within a play, whether it be intended for good or for ill, and the play in which it occurs share a common fictionality. This last point is implied early in *Measure for Measure* when Vincentio declares, "I love the people, / But do not like to stage me to their eyes" (1.1). On the one hand, Vincentio is a "real" duke about to become a make-believe friar; on the other hand, he is, and is known by the audience to be, not a real duke at all but part of the fictional cast of *Measure for Measure.*

The mendacious "Dover Cliff" scene in *King Lear* is one of Shakespeare's very great fictions-within-a-fiction, but, before moving on to it, it is worth dwelling for a moment on the bed tricks in *All's Well That Ends Well* and *Measure for Measure.* By the standards of ordinary life, the bed tricks are artifices that exceed all credibility, yet, to their onstage perpetrators, that is, Helena and the Duke respectively, they are totally reliable. Further, they appear to take place in secret, and they are associated with the dark. Artifices that exceed offstage credibility but that are credible onstage serve as reminders that a stage play is an idiosyncratic medium with a lexis and semiotics of its own; it need not be like life in order to be true to life. That the bed tricks appear to take place in secret shows how important social checks are on immoral intent. And that they are associated with the dark shows, in addition to the fact that wrongdoing is occurring, how gullible people can be when they think that they are most in control. In *Twelfth Night,* Feste, disguised as Sir Topas the curate, takes his text from Exodus 10:21–23 (the ninth plague of Egypt), to declare that "there is no darkness but ignorance" (4.2). It is in the darkness of ignorance that Bertram and Angelo are ensnared.

III

The "Dover Cliff" scene in King Lear.

The good hoped for from well-intentioned untruthfulness varies from play to play. Friar Lawrence wants to resolve the calamity he has helped bring about, Friar Francis and Anne Page foresee happy marriages, and Helena wants Bertram back with her. In *Measure for Measure,* the Duke sees problems solved for Mariana, Isabella, and Claudio, and, equally justifiably, he sees problems created for Angelo. None of these plays is unserious—far from it— but, equally, none has anything like the dramatic intensity and austere hopefulness of the scene in act 4, scene 6, of *King Lear* when Edgar leads Gloucester to believe that he has plunged off Dover Cliff. The scene, a dramatic tour de force, can be considered under four headings: (1) Gloucester and Edgar; (2) suicide; (3) setting the scene; and (4) staging death.

1. *Gloucester and Edgar.* Although he is not normally so described, Gloucester is a hero, not in the antique sense of a demigod but in the modern sense of someone whose unexceptional progress in life is crossed by a challenge that is as dangerous to rise to as it is wrong to shirk. Many heroes (and heroines) of this sort arose in Nazi-occupied Europe, and, if truth be told, most people would rather read about them than have been them. Gloucester's principled defiance of Cornwall and Regan costs him his sight, and mocking words from Regan make him realize that, metaphorically, he has been blind to Edgar's probity (3.7). Ailing and remorseful, he wishes for death, and Edgar, out of love, intends for him the psychological trauma, though not the fact, of suicide in order to cure him. The result is lying on a grand scale from Edgar, belief in a real location on the part of Gloucester, and, from the audience's point of view, a lucid demonstration of how to construct a fiction on an open Shakespearean stage. Edgar justifies his untruthful behavior by saying, "Why I do trifle thus with his despair / Is done to cure it."

2. *Suicide.* Shakespeare takes suicide very seriously, both as an extreme remedy and as a sin. Like Romeo, Juliet, and, possibly, Lady Macbeth, Ophelia represents it as the ultima ratio of the distressed (*Hamlet,* 4.7), and both Hamlet (1.2) and Imogen (*Cymbeline,* 3.4) speak of a divine prohibition. In fact, there is no explicit biblical prohibition, but Shakespeare and his contemporaries assumed that suicide was a breach of the sixth commandment, "Thou shalt not kil" (Exodus 20:13).[4] Shakespeare's word for suicide is "self-slaughter." Jay L. Halio notes that *King Lear* is "neither wholly pagan nor wholly Christian."[5] It is noticeable that, as the despairing Gloucester prepares to throw himself forward, Shakespeare puts "mighty gods" in the plural into his mouth.

3. *Setting the scene.* Edgar, in the role of Poor Tom, is dressed as a peasant, his clothes being, like an actor's, put on for the part. Shakespeare emphasizes the point. "And bring some covering for this naked soul," Gloucester commands the Old Man in act 4, scene 1, and the Old Man says, "I'll bring him the best 'parel that I have." Edgar also resembles a playwright transforming an open stage as he strives to transform the terrain he is leading his father across into a specific dramatic location. In order to induct Gloucester out of everyday reality and into the special reality of fiction, Edgar resorts to selective suggestion and to Gloucester's declared memory of Dover Cliff as "a cliff, whose high and bending head / Looks fearfully in the confined deep" (4.1). With a spot reached that is safely away from the real cliff's edge, Edgar—actor and playwright in one—mimetically sets the scene (to "leap upright" is to straighten up suddenly and risk losing one's balance):[6]

EDGAR: Come on, sir, here's the place; stand still. How fearful
And dizzy 'tis, to cast one's eyes so low!
The crows and choughs that wing the midway air
Show scarce so gross as beetles. Half way down
Hangs one that gathers sampire, dreadful trade!
Methinks he seems no bigger than his head.
The fishermen that walk upon the beach
Appear like mice; and yond tall anchoring bark,
Diminish'd to her cock; her cock, a buoy
Almost too small for sight. The murmuring surge,
That on th' unnumb'red idle pebble chafes,
Cannot be heard so high. I'll look no more,
Lest my brain turn, and the deficient sight
Topple down headlong.
GLOUCESTER: Set me where you stand.
EDGAR: Give me your hand. You are now within a foot
Of th' extreme verge. For all beneath the moon
Would I not leap upright.

(4.6)

The location exists by virtue of being asserted, and Gloucester is warned to
go no further, as if the cliff edge were really near. Vertigo—a common experience—is invoked, with its suggestion of vertical distance. Birds are
placed along a vertical line of sight, too. They are reduced in size, as if by
perspective, and their being visible at all implies that the light is good. "Sampire" ("samphire" in today's English) is a plant associated with cliffs and is
similarly placed by Edgar "half way down," its gatherer visualized in proportion and from the top. Fishermen and boats go with coastal areas, so they
are supplied, too, and distanced appropriately. Finally, the sound of waves
might be expected, so they are mentioned as well, Edgar blocking any further difficulty from his father by saying that they are too far down to be
heard. Edgar's speech exhibits a significant division between content and
form. Its content provides realistic detail in a plausible downward sequence,
as if a "real" Edgar were talking to a "real" blind father; but, since Edgar is
also a character in a play, its form is the blank verse of the playhouse. If
Gloucester had his sight, he would know Edgar's fiction for what it is, as the
audience does; but he is without it, so he remains imprisoned in Edgar's
make-believe. That, as it turns out, is to his advantage. After his "fall," the deception is continued, and he abandons thoughts of suicide. This vindicates
Edgar's untruthfulness, though, realistically, he cannot permanently subdue
his father's desire to die. Initially, Gloucester says:

I do remember now. Henceforth I'll bear
Affliction till it do cry out itself
"Enough, enough," and die.

But his resolution wavers in act 5, scene 2, when he says, "No further, sir, a man may rot even here."

4. *Staging death.* At its simplest, Gloucester's fall is an actor falling onto a rush-covered stage from a kneeling position, but, in the fiction Edgar constructs in Gloucester's mind, it is a one-way plunge to death. Since staged experiences are in principle there to be shared with the audience, the audience is implicitly invited to share this experience, too, even though, as Shakespeare knows in advance, an invitation involving death cannot be fully met. Why this is so can be explained by means of an ad hoc distinction between two terms that nowadays commonly overlap: "simulation" and "imitation."

Simulation, which in modern times is associated with things like flight simulators, and imitation, which is associated with activities like mimicking birdcalls, both aspire to reproduce reality exactly. But—for our present purposes—the big difference between simulation and imitation is that, whereas the makers of flight simulators know what real flying is, encode that knowledge in programs, and mediate that knowledge to their users by artificial means, imitators of birdcalls may well have no knowledge of what those birdcalls mean: the surface characteristics of the sounds are enough in themselves. Now, while the surface characteristics of death can be known, imitated, and mediated to others, death itself is, in Shakespeare's plays, "the undiscover'd country, from whose bourn / No traveller returns" (*Hamlet,* 3.1). That is to say (as explained in chapter 6, section IV), Shakespeare treats death in his plays as being beyond human knowledge, and what is beyond human knowledge is impossible to simulate in the sense of the word that is being used here. How an audience understands Gloucester's hitting the stage and lying there—a solemn and challenging moment in performance— depends principally on what it projects from itself onto the prone figure in front of it. For, however good the acting, the experience of death will not be transmitted to the audience by Gloucester's make-believe, and one insinuation of this complex moment in the play is that the experience of death cannot be transmitted by *any* play's make-believe, since it is an experience which, for the living, is absolutely unknowable. Edgar makes the essential point neatly when he says, as Gloucester "falls," "Had he been where he thought, / By this had thought been past."

Edgar's eventual success in the "Dover Cliff" scene is due to the two capabilities identified in *A Midsummer Night's Dream* by Theseus when he is reflecting on lovers, madmen, and poets: cool reason and strong imagination. Edgar knows what he wants to achieve, he imaginatively conjures up the appropriate location (once he gets into his stride), and he delivers his lines purposefully. That he *needs* to be successful is a symbol of how topsy-turvy things have become since Lear's abdication, since the son's having to assume governance over the father is an inversion of what should be the case, given Gloucester's robustness when the play opens. Nevertheless, the fact that Edgar is eventually as successful as he can be in the circumstances is not intended by Shakespeare to conceal the fact that he (Edgar) is, so to speak, drafted into the twin roles of actor and playwright for the occasion. On the contrary, Shakespeare deliberately emphasizes Edgar's amateur status in the lead-up to his big speech. In doing so, he adds a touch of what Bertolt Brecht, the twentieth-century German dramatist and innovator, called *Verfremdung* (alienation), so that the audience's appreciation of the scene is sharpened by its consciousness of what is being done technically.

When Edgar sets off with Gloucester for Dover, Edgar's exit line is "Poor Tom shall lead thee" (4.1). This underscores the fact that Edgar is continuing a part *that he cannot yet relinquish.* Shakespeare was familiar from his own experience with bad professional actors—apart from *Hamlet,* he alludes to them in *Richard II* (5.2), *Julius Caesar* (1.2), and *Troilus and Cressida* (1.3)— but Edgar is an amateur, and he commits the amateur's fault of letting his role slip and his real social status show. Gloucester, noticing him starting to slip out of his part, says, "[A]nd thou speak'st / In better phrase and matter than thou didst" (4.6). Edgar is not the only amateur in Shakespeare to show through in this way. In *As You Like It,* Orlando notices that Rosalind's accent is "something finer than you could purchase in so remov'd a dwelling" (3.2); and in *Twelfth Night,* Viola so conducts herself that Olivia has no trouble accepting her gentle birth (without perceiving that she is a woman, however). Olivia explains, "Thy tongue, thy face, thy limbs, actions and spirit / Do give thee fivefold blazon" (1.5; a "blazon" is a coat of arms). Without knowing it, she is endorsing Viola as a replacement for herself as Orsino's eventual bride.

As a playwright, too, Edgar has his shortcomings. He has the right idea: he wants to generate a sense of place in his father's mind. Unfortunately— and there is a direct link here to the problem with moonlight in *A Midsummer Night's Dream*—he doesn't initially know how to manage it:

> GLOUCESTER: When shall I come to th' top of that same hill?
> EDGAR: You do climb it now. Look how we labor.
> GLOUCESTER: Methinks the ground is even.

EDGAR: Horrible steep.
Hark, do you hear the sea?
GLOUCESTER: No, truly.
EDGAR: Why then your other senses grow imperfect
By your eyes' anguish.

                                                        (4.6)

It takes know-how to place ideas in the mind. In *A Midsummer Night's Dream,* the hempen home-spuns, working with an indoor setting in prospect, underestimate the creative power of words, so Bottom proposes importing real moonlight through a casement of the great chamber window (3.1). An actor dressed as Moonshine is actually an improvement on this, since it is a step toward art, even if only a small one. Edgar, working away from a theatrical setting, overestimates the creative power of words, so they founder on reality. Shakespeare, whose judgment of what words can and cannot do is precise, would not have made Edgar's mistake, any more than he would have made Bottom's. But, having shown what not to do, Shakespeare then shows how things should be done by lending Edgar true poetic power—and Gloucester is taken in.

IV

Parting thoughts on Friar Lawrence, Friar Francis, Pisanio, Camillo, and Paulina.

Edgar's need to assist his father because things have gone to the bad instances a fundamental pattern to be found in other plays by Shakespeare that would not normally be compared with *King Lear.* It is a pattern that consists of a relatively inferior character, motivated by goodwill, fostering goodness by whatever means seem best, including untruthful behavior. Most consistent with this pattern are Friar Francis in *Much Ado about Nothing,* Pisanio in *Cymbeline,* and Camillo in *The Winter's Tale.* They have been mentioned before in this chapter as justifiers of lying and as characters with links to playwriting. They are minor characters, so they always come some way down the cast list. But they matter because their function, and the structure of the plays they appear in, are both in line with a general idea expressed by Friar Lawrence in *Romeo and Juliet,* namely, that "vice [is] sometime by action dignified" (2.3). That was an immensely important idea for Shakespeare, even though Friar Lawrence is too imprudent to be its best agent.

So important are the interventions of these minor characters that, when they happen, they are heralded by their own distinctive form of words and, it must be assumed, by appropriate gestures as well. Friar Lawrence establishes the pattern in *Romeo and Juliet* by commanding Romeo, "Thou fond mad man, hear me a little speak" (3.3). In *Much Ado about Nothing,* this becomes Friar Francis's "Hear me a little" and "Pause awhile" (4.1). In *Measure for Measure,* the Duke, disguised as a friar, instructs Isabella, "Therefore fasten your ear on my advisings" (3.1). In *Cymbeline,* Pisanio gets as close to an order as his position allows with "Good madam, hear me" and "Good lady, / Hear me with patience" (3.4). And in *The Winter's Tale,* Camillo intrudes "Be advis'd" and "Then list to me" (4.4) into Florizel's agitated talk. After these imperatives, an intention involving untruthful behavior is set out in detail. Part of Duke Vincentio's is quoted above in section II, and part of Friar Lawrence's will be quoted now. It comes from an earlier moment in the play than Friar Lawrence's recommendation that Juliet drug herself. Romeo has been banished for killing Tybalt, and the intention is that Romeo and Juliet should conceal their marriage for the time being.

> FRIAR LAWRENCE: Go get thee to thy love as was decreed,
> Ascend her chamber, hence and comfort her.
> But look thou stay not till the watch be set,
> For then thou canst not pass to Mantua,
> Where thou shalt live till we can find a time
> To blaze your marriage, reconcile your friends,
> Beg pardon of the Prince, and call thee back
> With twenty hundred thousand times more joy
> Than thou went'st forth in lamentation.
>
> (3.3)

The rhetoric of Friar Lawrence anticipates that of Friar Francis, Duke Vincentio, Pisanio, and Camillo in that it sets out optimistically what is to be done and what results are expected. This provides Shakespeare with a fixity he can move the rest of the play toward, or away from, depending on the kind of play he is writing. In the case of Friar Lawrence, the play is a tragedy, so it moves away from his words in clearly discernible stages: the need for the drugged sleep will not be long in coming, and that will be followed by bad news from Friar John, Romeo's suicide, Friar Lawrence's abandonment of Juliet, and Juliet's suicide. On the other hand, *Much Ado about Nothing* is a comedy, so it largely moves toward what Friar Francis sets out. And the same is, with appropriate qualification, true of the two tragicomedies and the helpers in them: Pisanio in *Cymbeline* and Camillo in *The Winter's Tale.* In fact, Camillo's guiding words to Florizel have a strong family resemblance to those spoken by Friar Lawrence to Romeo, even though some fifteen years separate *The Winter's Tale* from the earlier play and even though the two speeches occur in plays moving in opposite directions:

> CAMILLO: Methinks I see
> Leontes opening his free arms, and weeping
> His welcomes forth; asks thee there, son, forgiveness,
> As 'twere i' th' father's person; kisses the hands
> Of your fresh princess; o'er and o'er divides him
> 'Twixt his unkindness and his kindness: th' one
> He chides to hell, and bids the other grow
> Faster than thought or time.
>
>   (4.4)

Friar Lawrence is part of a tragedy, so he has less control over people and events than his optimism requires, whereas Camillo is part of a tragicomedy. That means that, even if he errs in points of detail, his optimism will turn out to be justified. The play's structure is on his side.

While Friar Lawrence, Friar Francis, Pisanio, and Camillo are not all equally successful, there is a manifest need, since they are would-be agents of good, for the sincerity that they bring to their roles as deceivers to be beyond question. Pisanio, perhaps the least known of them, speaks for the others when he says, "Wherein I am false, I am honest; not true, to be true" (*Cymbeline,* 4.3). Pisanio is selflessness itself, which makes him a rather touching figure when he is wrongly blamed, but there is no reason in principle why helpfulness should not be blended with self-interest, since self-interest can be a good motivator. Camillo shows that that is so. He is principally benevolent, but he has personal hopes as well, so Shakespeare makes Camillo's personal hopes conterminous with his hopes for Florizel and gets the best of both worlds:

> CAMILLO: Now were I happy if
> His going I could frame to serve my turn,
> Save him from danger, do him love and honor,
> Purchase the sight again of dear Sicilia
> And that unhappy king, my master, whom
> I so much thirst to see.
>
>   (4.4)

Camillo's characterization as an altruistic deceiver is made all the clearer by the contrasting presence of Autolycus in the play. Even when he is helping others, Autolycus has no other end in view than helping himself: "If I had a mind to be honest, I see Fortune would not suffer me: she drops booties in my mouth. I am courted now with a double occasion: gold and a means to do the Prince my master good; which who knows how that may turn back to my advancement?" (4.4).

Since Friar Lawrence, Friar Francis, Pisanio, and Camillo are all male characters, the question naturally arises whether Shakespeare ever envisaged a female helper of the same sort, and the answer comes in the form of Paulina, Antigonus's wife and widow in *The Winter's Tale*. Paulina, who remains in Sicilia while Camillo operates in Bohemia, is given the important dual function of keeping Leontes' thoughts away from remarrying for the sake of an heir and of returning Hermione to him when he is ready. Paulina's helpfulness toward Leontes combines maternal authority with misleading reminders of Hermione. And while untruthful behavior is far from being a female monopoly, Paulina brings to hers a wily coquetry that a male character would find difficult, if not impossible, to carry off:

PAULINA: Will you swear
Never to marry but by my free leave?
LEONTES: Never, Paulina, so be bless'd my spirit!
PAULINA: Then, good my lords, bear witness to his oath.
CLEOMINES: You tempt him overmuch.
PAULINA: Unless another,
As like Hermione as is her picture,
Affront his eye.
CLEOMINES: Good madam—
PAULINA: I have done.
Yet if my lord will marry—if you will, sir,
No remedy but you will—give me the office
To choose you a queen. She shall not be so young
As was your former, but she shall be such
As (walk'd your first queen's ghost) it should take joy
To see her in your arms.
LEONTES: My true Paulina,
We shall not marry till thou bid'st us.
PAULINA: That
Shall be when your first queen's again in breath;
Never till then.

(5.1)

This is truly the art of benevolent deception. Paulina means what she says, but she does not say what she means. By the time she finishes with Leontes, she, a lady at court with no formal authority, has the emotional ascendancy over her king that the plot requires. By contrast, the machinations of Friar Lawrence, Friar Francis, Pisanio, Camillo, and Duke Vincentio are far less insinuating and far more propositional in character.

By means of Camillo on the one hand and Paulina on the other, Shakespeare achieves the balance between organization and influence that the design of *The Winter's Tale* requires; and so it makes sense for Leontes to order Camillo to marry Paulina in the aftermath of his reunion with Hermione, Polixenes, and Perdita. On the page, this might seem to be little more than tidying up. On stage, however, the logic of their marriage is far more apparent. Paulina and Camillo have both contributed to making that reunion possible, and both are party to the joy when it takes place. It also makes sense for Paulina to be ordered to lead the whole assembly off the stage. Having benevolently misled Leontes and kept faith with Hermione, she has the right to lead the rest into a wiser future in which, it is hoped, untruthful behavior will no longer be necessary.

Chapter 9

STAGING DECISIVE MOMENTS

The Letter Scene in Twelfth Night, *the Observation Scene in* Troilus and Cressida, *and Leontes' Denunciation of Hermione to Camillo in* The Winter's Tale

I

The letter scene in Twelfth Night *(2.5): zoning the stage and making Malvolio's manner of thinking clear.*

"First, good Peter Quince, say what the play treats on; then read the names of the actors; and so grow to a point" (*A Midsummer Night's Dream*, 1.2). The form of Bottom's line and its content go together. The content is an argument for orderly progression toward a conclusion; an orderly progression toward a conclusion is what the line's form actually is; and anyone hearing or reading the line is made aware by its form just how good a thing orderly progression is.

In advocating orderly progression, Bottom is of one mind with Shakespeare, for whom *growing* to a point is axiomatic. The big difference between the two is that Shakespeare's mind is more complicated than Bottom's, so his progressions are more complicated, too. As the three examples discussed in this chapter show, Shakespeare's progressions can include a divided stage and more than one perspective. How such devices are deployed varies from play to play. The first example comes from *Twelfth Night*.

By the time the letter scene in *Twelfth Night* takes place, the audience knows a number of important things about it. First, its motive is revenge. In act 2, scene 3, Malvolio has upbraided Sir Toby and Sir Andrew for being noisy late at night, and they want him paid back for his high-handedness. Second, Malvolio has threatened to report Maria to Olivia for abetting the merry-making, though she was actually trying to quiet things down. This makes her want revenge, too. Third, the point of vulnerability in Malvolio to be attacked is his vain belief that "all that look on him love him" (2.3). Fourth, Maria's weapon is to be a letter, forged by her to make it look as if Olivia is among those who love him. Fifth, the expected outcome is that Malvolio will look like an ass. To stress this last point, Sir Andrew is given the feed line "And your horse now would make him an ass," to which Maria replies, repeating the key word, "Ass, I doubt not" (2.3). By preparing the scene in this way, Shakespeare puts process on a par with product. If the audience knows in advance *what* is to be achieved and *why*, it will be more sensitive to the *how* of that achievement as it is played out on the stage.

Crucial to that *how* is the way Malvolio thinks, so it, too, is pointed out in advance. Following Viola's first visit to her in act 1, scene 5, Olivia summons Malvolio and gives him a ring, saying, "Run after that same peevish messenger, / The County's man. He left this ring behind him, / Would I or not. Tell him I'll none of it" (1.5). Malvolio, having been offstage, does not know this is not true. When he catches up to Viola, Viola, possibly to protect Olivia, says, "She took the ring of me, I'll none of it" (2.2), to which Malvolio replies, "Come, sir, you peevishly threw it to her; and her will is, it should be so return'd." But that is not what Malvolio has been told: Malvolio has caught the word "peevish" and induced the rest. The primary purpose of this scene is to open Viola's eyes to the fact that Olivia has fallen in love with her. But it also shows Malvolio to have the kind of mind that moves easily beyond available data to versions of reality he finds congenial.

Sir Toby and Sir Andrew actually want to see retribution visited on Malvolio, not just hear about it. This determines their presence onstage during the letter scene, along with that of Malvolio himself. Feste (who was originally intended by Maria to make the third but who may already have exited when she details her plan[1]) is somewhere between Orsino's palace and Olivia's house. This creates a space for Fabian, one of Olivia's servants, and his inclusion is a shrewd move on Shakespeare's part. Fabian's passport into the play is a grudge against Malvolio for making trouble between himself and Olivia over some bear baiting, but he is more detached than the others, so he can plead for peace as Sir Toby and Sir Andrew threaten to let their emotions run away with them. He can also be more of an observer, and the result is embedded stage directions that state exactly how Malvolio is to conduct himself following his entrance in act 2, scene 5. They are: "Contemplation makes a rare turkey-cock of him. How he jets under his advanc'd plumes!" ("contemplation" means "fantasizing," and "jets" means "struts"); "Look how imagination blows him"; and "Now is the woodcock near the gin." Fabian is a credible knower of hunting dogs as well. The importance of that will emerge shortly.

Because Malvolio is to be watched, the playing area has to be zoned. Overall, it represents Olivia's garden—one sign among others that the play is set in warm weather—but, within it, a location needs to be identified as the vengeance seekers' hiding place, though they must, of course, remain audible and in full view of the audience. Andrew Gurr connects *Twelfth Night* with the Globe, and one obvious hiding place there would be behind a stage post, with or without a prop to represent the box tree Maria indicates (the densely leaved *buxus sempervirens*).[2] Having Maria maneuver them smartly toward a stage post would be one way of handling the fact that Sir Toby, Sir Andrew, and Fabian are already onstage when Malvolio is said to be approaching. By the time he enters, if the scene is to work, they need to be out of his notional line of sight, and Maria needs to be already exiting through the other flanking door.

However, the play is known to have been performed in London's Middle Temple Hall on February 2, 1602 (that is, not Twelfth Night—January 6—which is nowhere mentioned in the play, but Candlemas). Located on the north side of the Thames, the Middle Temple was an Inn of Court, that is, a place of residence and instruction for students of law, and the hall itself was completed circa 1573. "It is," writes Anthony Arlidge, the Middle Temple's first twenty-first-century master of the entertainments, "a magnificent late Gothic hall, measuring about thirty-five metres in length and thirteen metres in width, . . . The Hall is topped with a superb double hammer-beam roof, supported by external buttresses. . . . At the east end there is a finely-carved screen. It has two wide entrances with a gallery above."[3] It is tempting to imagine the play being performed in front of the screen, which, with its two doorways, strongly resembles a tiring-house facade, and C. Walter Hodges does precisely that. In a line drawing of the letter scene as it might have been played in Middle Temple Hall by candlelight, he places the vengeance seekers behind a row of smallish shrubs—not a tree—between the two doorways, while Malvolio finds the letter in the middle of the rush-covered playing area.[4] Unfortunately, as Arlidge points out, there are "technical objections" to a performance in front of the screen. One is that dignitaries present at the feast when *Twelfth Night* was put on would have found their entrance procession impeded by a stage set up in front of the doors (unlike Hodges, Arlidge includes the possibility that a stage was built for the occasion). Another is that the high table was at the opposite end of the hall from the screen and, therefore, quite a distance from it. A third is that the open fire in the middle of the hall would have been lit in February. It had no chimney, the smoke escaping through the lantern above it, and that smoke would have further impaired the view from the high table. If, as Hodges envisages, seating was arranged in a U shape, with the screen across the open end of the U, the fire would not have been seriously in the way. Arlidge notes, however, that it was not consonant with the importance of dignitaries for them to move their seats.[5]

All things considered, then, Arlidge concludes, "Although the fact of the performance of *Twelfth Night* is certain, precisely how it was performed is far from clear."[6] Nevertheless, the text itself provides important information about performance that is relevant to the Globe as well as to Middle Temple Hall. Maria's appropriately horticultural "I will plant you two" (2.3) to Sir Toby and Sir Andrew suggests a single static hiding place from which to observe Malvolio without his seeing them. Her "Get ye all three *into* the box-tree" (2.5; italics added) indicates that actually getting them behind either a stage post or a prop is intended. The fact that the comments of Sir Toby, Sir Andrew, and Fabian have to be fully audible to the audience suggests that the actors are situated near one edge of the playing area rather than at the back. And while Fabian's "Ay, and you had any eye behind you, you might see more detraction at your heels than fortunes before you" (2.5) locates their hiding place behind Malvolio, "behind" need not mean on a straight line between Malvolio and the back of the playing area, given the in-the-round nature of an Elizabethan performance; "behind" is a power arrangement as well as a physical location, so the important thing is that the vengeance seekers be behind Malvolio's back in relation to where Malvolio is looking when he delivers his lines. Finally, although the audience needs to see the vengeance seekers as being separate from Malvolio, it also needs to see them and their victim as a unit. This seems to rule out using the gallery as a hiding place, although both the Globe and the Middle Temple Hall had one.[7] Arlidge adds that uncertainty about original performance practice allows a modern director flexibility. That is true, but it should not be taken to mean that a modern director has a completely free hand. Shakespeare's instinct for staging is such that the letter scene's *relative* positionings are clear, and to ignore them is to ignore the scene's tight internal organization.

When Malvolio finally picks up the forged letter—it has been lying in the open since Maria threw it down—he is confronted with what he takes to be reliable clues and with the letters "M.O.A.I.":

> MALVOLIO: By my life, this is my lady's hand. These be her very c's, her u's, and her t's, and thus makes she her great P's. . . .
>
> . . .

MALVOLIO: (*Reads.*) "To the unknown belov'd, this, and my good wishes":—her very phrases! . . . And the impressure her Lucrece, with which she uses to seal. 'Tis my lady. . . .

MALVOLIO: "M.O.A.I. doth sway my life." Nay, but first let me see, let me see, let me see.

FABIAN: What dish a' poison has she dress'd him!

SIR TOBY: And with what wing the staniel checks at it!

MALVOLIO: "I may command where I adore." Why, she may command me: I serve her, she is my lady. Why, this is evident to any formal capacity, there is no obstruction in this. And the end—what should that alphabetical position portend? If I could make that resemble something in me! Softly! M.O.A.I.—

. . .

M—but then there is no consonancy in the sequel that suffers under probation: A should follow, but O does.

. . .

And then I comes behind.

FABIAN: Ay, and you had any eye behind you, you might see more detraction at your heels than fortunes before you.

MALVOLIO: M.O.A.I. This simulation is not as the former; and yet, to crush this a little, it would bow to me, for every one of these letters are in my name.

Having Malvolio think out loud and in stages foregrounds the *manner* of his thinking and, to make sure that there is absolutely no missing its defectiveness, Shakespeare does three things. He has Malvolio ignore a *warning;* he introduces an *analogy;* and he effects a *comparison.*

The *warning* inheres principally in the letters "c," "u," and "t," though it is reinforced by "great P's." Malvolio is so struck by the letters' resemblance to Olivia's handwriting that he fails to read them as "cut" (a sexually allusive word which also means "stupid") and as "great pees" respectively.[8] Sir Andrew helps make it clear that a foolish cast of mind is implied by this failure when he asks, "Her c's, her u's, and her t's: why that?" and the audience, following the spelling as Malvolio should, easily hears the full word, answers his question on its own, and extends the answer beyond Sir Andrew to Malvolio.

The *analogy* comes from Fabian, the servant versed in the ways of animals. After "M.O.A.I." has been reached, he says, "The cur is excellent at faults." A fault in its first meaning here is a gap in the scent of a hunted animal, so a dog that is excellent at faults is one that can follow an interrupted scent.[9] By analogy, then, Malvolio should have a talent for following a trail with faults in it. But the second meaning of "faults," as "mistakes," turns praise of his excellence at faults into criticism of his faulty reasoning. In abstract terms, Malvolio's faulty reasoning can be described as mistaking induction for deduction. An audience of lawyers schooled in argument would have no difficulty in deconstructing Malvolio's reasoning abstractly, while less educated members of a playhouse audience would easily grasp Fabian's hunting allusion.

The *comparison* Shakespeare effects is made possible by the zoning of the playing area. In one zone are the vengeance seekers. They know what is really the case. In the other zone is Malvolio, applying his own brand of reasoning to the forged letter under their scrutiny. The audience, seeing both zones simultaneously, is able to compare Malvolio's thinking point by point with what is really the case and register the differences. These differences show Malvolio to be an ass in perhaps the most powerful way possible: they show him thinking like one. Before Maria's deception is completely played out, he will be acting like one as well.

II

Cressida opts for Diomedes and Troilus opts for revenge in the observation scene in Troilus and Cressida *(5.2). A divided playing area, the observation scene's subdivisions, and divided rhetoric from Cressida and Troilus.*

On the basis of the evidence currently available, *Troilus and Cressida* may originally have been performed privately at one of London's Inns of Court or publicly at the Globe.[10] Either way, the playing area would have been divided for the observation scene (5.2), with Diomedes and Cressida in the center, Troilus and Ulysses to one side where they can see Diomedes and Cressida, and Thersites either at the back toward the doorways or, more likely, on the other side from Troilus and Ulysses, from which position he can see and comment on Ulysses, Troilus, Cressida, and Diomedes. The audience, of course, would see and hear them all. The end effect is to transform the open playing area into an enclosed place of trial for Cressida and into a place of judgments, too—judgments *from* Ulysses, Troilus, and Thersites, and judgments *on* all the characters, including Cressida, from the audience. In *Twelfth Night,* the stage is zoned to reflect the fact that the vengeance seekers have Malvolio where they want him, in both senses of the phrase. But "zoned" is too static a word to apply to the observation scene in *Troilus and Cressida.* Its organization requires three interlinked loci of action, and the audience's attention is moved among them as the scene unfolds, while always being returned to Cressida until she exits. The observation scene has a strong sense of time and place created for it, too. As it becomes imminent, Ulysses tells Troilus to follow Diomedes' torchbearer to Calchas's tent (5.1). This signifies, using the standard symbolism of nighttime, that things are about to go bad in an alien place associated with betrayal. And, as the scene takes place, Ulysses tells Troilus, "This place is dangerous, / The time right deadly." His words apply metaphorically as well as physically to Troilus, and metaphorically to Cressida.

Each of the characters has been prepared in advance. The cynical Thersites is already convinced that Cressida is "a Troyan drab" (5.1); and Ulysses has brought his persuasion that Cressida is wanton either from the kissing scene itself or from Cressida's apparently compromised exit from it with Diomedes (4.5; Cressida's exit with Diomedes is discussed in chapter 4, section III). Troilus's love for Cressida, while exuberant, is consistently self-referenced. He is in love, but he doesn't give love selflessly in the form of transpersonal concern for Cressida, not even when she is to be handed over to the Greeks. This means that, as he watches Cressida move conclusively toward Diomedes, he will keep himself firmly at the emotional center of what is happening. To this trait must be added his sexual rivalry with Diomedes, which begins in act 4, scene 4, when Cressida is about to be handed over. What Troilus really expresses at that point in the play is not care that Cressida should be well looked after but unwillingness to be bested by the Greek.

Cressida's precarious situation in the early part of the play as the daughter of a traitor in the doubtful care of Pandarus is duplicated and intensified when Diomedes becomes her guardian.[11] Before her relationship with Troilus had been consummated, she had been able to generate a limited amount of power by "holding off" (1.2). That is less of an option with Diomedes, who is more insistent than Troilus and who, if faced with a refusal, can simply abandon her. From every point of view, then, Diomedes is an intimidating and coercive figure. Nevertheless, Cressida's exit soliloquy at the end of the observation scene expresses genuine attraction to him. As explained in chapter 4, section III, this attraction appears to have set in as early as the preliminaries to her handing over in act 4, scene 4.

The observation scene up to and including Cressida's exit soliloquy effectively falls into seven parts, during which pressure on Cressida is progressively increased. The first and last parts are a prelude and postlude, respectively, and the fifth part, in which Cressida hands over Troilus's sleeve, is the longest. All the parts show stagecraft of a very high order and are discussed individually below. As they succeed each other, Troilus's development is straightforward, but Cressida's poses difficulties since, in the observation scene as elsewhere, it is not always easy to tell when her reluctance is feigned and when it is authentic. A helpful approach is to note what Cressida says and does and the reactions she provokes, before attempting to decide what her words and deeds really signify about her, rather than trying to read a pre-formed understanding of her into the scene. Given that a tactical sense is part of Cressida's characterization, an overpreoccupation with her is always possible, and that can distort the balance Shakespeare obviously intended between her and the watching Troilus.

The prelude (from the beginning of act 5, scene 2, to Troilus's "Cressid comes forth to him," line 5) has Diomedes imperiously enter the empty stage after his torchbearer to demand Cressida. Since Calchas is *"within,"* Diomedes shouts. This demonstrates his power and Cressida's weak position, too, since her father, who is powerless, has no option but to defer to Diomedes. Meanwhile, Troilus, Ulysses, and Thersites take up position in the shadows away from the torchbearer. Only then does Cressida enter—"to him," as Troilus puts it, already starting to bristle with rivalry.

Part 2 (to Troilus's "Thy better must," line 33) begins with Cressida ingratiating herself with Diomedes as they whisper—this brings them suspiciously close together and allows Troilus, Ulysses, and Thersites to voice their individual thoughts. In particular, the whispering prompts Ulysses' "She will sing any man at first sight," which reinforces Troilus's growing dismay and chimes with Thersites' prejudice that "any man may sing her." But it is possible that Cressida is trying to ingratiate herself *out* of a sexual commitment without, however, losing Diomedes. Her uncooperativeness provokes Diomedes' first outburst of impatience and proposed departure. Cressida's key line at this point is "Sweet honey Greek, tempt me no more to folly." "Tempt" suggests wanting to comply as well as wanting to resist, while "folly" suggests a recognition that no good would follow, were temptation succumbed to. Implicitly, Cressida's vocabulary signals that a radical choice still awaits her rather than that one has already been made. Troilus, meanwhile, feeling that he is being made a fool of, has an outburst of impatience that parallels Diomedes' but that is differently motivated. Diomedes cannot get what he wants, but Troilus is afraid that he (Diomedes) can.

Part 3 (to Diomedes' "Fo, fo, adieu, you palter," line 48) has Cressida calling Diomedes back near her, and an embedded stage direction shows that she whispers in his ear again. This further enrages Troilus, but Diomedes' renewed determination to leave continues the possibility that, once more, Cressida is trying to escape a sexual commitment, not collude in one. If that is so, she is trapped between Diomedes' exasperation and Troilus's impatience, and the staging will show this.

Part 4 (to Troilus's "I am all patience," line 64) has Cressida calling Diomedes back to her yet again. Cressida strokes Diomedes' cheek, and this is once more interpreted by Troilus as meaning the worst. Cressida, under discernible pressure, agrees to Diomedes' demand, and it now definitely looks as if she is crossing, or has crossed, a line of resistance within herself, since, when Diomedes asks for a token of surety, it is Troilus's sleeve that she will fetch. Thersites' "Fry, lechery, fry!" is simplistic, but it points to a willingness in Cressida that cannot now easily be disputed.

Part 5 (to Diomedes' "Thou never shalt mock Diomed again," line 99) has Cressida reentering with Troilus's sleeve. She could have fetched anything, but the sleeve it is. It reminds her of what remains of her love for Troilus, and it brings out the nature and quality of that love as well. As to its nature, she says, "He lov'd me," not the other way around. It is a salient characteristic of Cressida that she needs to *feel* loved. During her discussion with Troilus about their imminent separation, she had had a flash of fear that she was not loved (4.4); and the rose-tinted image of Troilus the sleeve inspires in her is of his lying on his bed with her glove thinking of her. As to the quality of her love for Troilus, when the sleeve is snatched from her by Diomedes, she declares, "He that takes that doth take my heart withal." This is a line of notable shallowness and, for that reason, is arguably the single most important line in the play as far as Cressida's characterization is concerned. It is not surprising that it is followed by a show of indecision on Cressida's part, since shallowness and indecision go together. First comes resignation ("Well, well, 'tis done, 'tis past"); then comes a flickering back to Troilus ("And yet it is not"). Diomedes, feeling that he is being made a fool of, bids her what looks very much like a final farewell. If it is that, Cressida has no option but to commit herself one way or the other.

Part 6 (to Cressida's "I prithee come," line 106) sees Diomedes prevented from leaving for the last time to put the overwhelming question, and Cressida, with misgivings of no great magnitude, surrenders. "Surrenders" suits both the play's military context and Cressida's immediate situation. She has been coerced, but not absolutely; she has said no, but not resolutely; she has recalled her love for Troilus, but that has not been enough; she has admitted that Diomedes will never love her as well as Troilus has; she has shown a resigned sense that things have moved on; and she accepts that she will be "plagued." Her decision to surrender is therefore a mixed and shallow one, but a decision to surrender it is.

The postlude, which consists of Cressida's exit soliloquy, underlines her shallowness. First, her transition from Troilus to Diomedes defies the name of love. Love and the doggerel couplet "Troilus, farewell! one eye yet looks on thee, / But with my heart the other eye doth see" are poles apart. A comparison with *Twelfth Night* shows this clearly. For obvious reasons, Olivia's sentiments are wasted on Viola-as-Cesario, but when she tells "him," "Cesario, by the roses of the spring, / By maidhood, honor, truth, and every thing, / I love thee so" (3.1), she speaks a language that is different in kind from Cressida's. Second, in a way designed rather to evade than accept responsibility, Cressida owns up to being fickle in her affections. Thersites goes too far when he uses the word "whore," since that implies no scruples whatsoever, but, all in all, Cressida's exit looks like the start of a slippery slope.

Certainly, Shakespeare, like his audience, thought of Cressida as someone destined to come to a bad end. Her faithlessness is hinted at by Lorenzo in *The Merchant of Venice* (5.1); in *Twelfth Night,* Feste recalls that Cressida was a beggar (3.1); and in *Henry V,* Pistol speaks of "the lazar kite of Cressid's kind" (2.1; "lazar kite" means "diseased prostitute"). Nevertheless, the observation scene in *Troilus and Cressida* is intended to emphasize the dynamic of Cressida's present situation, not the fixity of her future reputation. Shallow Cressida may be, but that makes her mutable, and that, in turn, makes her dramatically interesting in a way that Thersites' uncomplicated "drab" and "whore" do not. Each component of Cressida's characterization has a claim on the audience's attention, and each, if it is allowed to expand in the mind, brings it own kind of instructiveness with it. As an anonymous prefatory epistle in the 1609 quarto edition (second state) of *Troilus and Cressida* puts it, "And all such dull and heavy-witted worldlings as were never capable of the wit of a comedy, coming by report of them to [Shakespeare's] representations, have found that wit there that they never found in themselves, and have parted better witted than they came, feeling an edge of wit set upon them more than ever they dreamed they had brain to grind it on."[12] The writer, presumably male, phrases himself generally. But if one of Shakespeare's contemporaries praises his plays as being there to be learned from, later generations could do worse than see them in the same way.

Considered purely in terms of plot, the observation scene could end soon after Cressida's exit: a brief vow from Troilus to pursue the triumphant Diomedes would be enough. Shakespeare implies as much. Ulysses states, "All's done, my lord," and Troilus answers, "It is." But such brevity would prevent the psychological process that results in Troilus's opting for revenge from being made fully intelligible to the audience, so Ulysses is made to ask, "Why stay we then?" and Troilus, by answering, "To make a recordation to my soul / Of every syllable that here was spoke," gives himself the opportunity to think out loud and in detail. Although Troilus should technically stay where he is as he does so, it would be good theater for him to move with Ulysses toward the position just vacated by Cressida, so that his divided soliloquy could succeed hers from the same onstage location (despite Ulysses' presence, Troilus's speech is tantamount to a soliloquy). This would symbolize that Troilus's decision to seek revenge is consequent on Cressida's decision to go with Diomedes. It would also symbolize a break between past and future and a break within the insubstantial Troilus-and-Cressida unity of the play's title as well:

> TROILUS: To make a recordation to my soul
> Of every syllable that here was spoke.
> But if I tell how these two did co-act,
> Shall I not lie in publishing a truth?
> Sith yet there is a credence in my heart,
> An esperance so obstinately strong,
> That doth invert th' attest of eyes and ears,
> As if those organs had deceptious functions,
> Created only to calumniate.
> Was Cressid here?
> ULYSSES: I cannot conjure, Troyan.
> TROILUS: She was not, sure.
> ULYSSES: Most sure she was.
> TROILUS: Why, my negation hath no taste of madness.

Troilus is clear-sighted. He might speak of "a credence in my heart" and "[a]n esperance so obstinately strong," but he knows full well that his eyes and ears are not "deceptious." What he is expressing in the self-referencing way he has is his reluctance emotionally to separate himself from Cressida, despite knowing factually that that separation has already taken place. This initial division between heart and head is then developed by Troilus in lines that take division as their theme and that are themselves part of a division. That is, he formulates his thoughts about division with his head, but just beneath the surface, there is the pressure of his feelings.

To take his thoughts first:

> If there be rule in unity itself,
> This was not she. O madness of discourse,
> That cause sets up with and against itself!
> Bi-fold authority, where reason can revolt
> Without perdition, and loss assume all reason
> Without revolt. This is, and is not, Cressid!
> Within my soul there doth conduce a fight

Of this strange nature, that a thing inseparate
Divides more wider than the sky and earth,
And yet the spacious breadth of this division
Admits no orifex for a point as subtle
As Ariachne's broken woof to enter.

Troilus's thoughts on division are, for all their formal intricacy, clear in their essentials.[13] Logically, unity is, by definition, one and the same in all circumstances, so, whatever is not one and the same in all circumstances is not unity. If Cressida were consistent with her past, "This was not she" would be a true statement. But Troilus has to accept that Cressida has become inconsistent with her past and that therefore, in a manner of speaking, she now is and is not the same person. However, if her situation is formulated like that, a logical impossibility seems to arise, namely a discontinuity in unity. Logic, being logical, automatically revolts against illogicality, but "without perdition," that is, without forfeiting its logicality—on the contrary, logic actually affirms its logicality by so doing. Troilus knows full well that he is using "is" in two different ways when he exclaims, "This is, and is not, Cressid!" but that does not matter, since the apparent paradox helps him externalize the fight in his soul. Unlike logic, Troilus has to accept discontinuity in Cressida, and, unlike logic again, he has to respond to the feelings that go with that acceptance.

The longer Troilus speaks, the greater the pressure his feelings generate. Effectively, they divide into pain and hatred. The pain is associated with Cressida and degenerates into disgust, while the hatred, which predominates, is directed at Diomedes, the sexual winner. Cued by Ulysses, Troilus makes his consequential opting for revenge known to the audience in clear analytical terms ("fancy" means "love"):

Ay, Greek, and that shall be divulged well
In characters as red as Mars his heart
Inflam'd with Venus. Never did young man fancy
With so eternal and so fix'd a soul.
Hark, Greek: as much as I do Cressid love,
So much by weight hate I her Diomed.
That sleeve is mine that he'll bear on his helm.
Were it a casque compos'd by Vulcan's skill,
My sword should bite it. . . .

These self-dramatizing words recall a remark made by Hector earlier in the play, namely, that revenge, like pleasure, has "ears more deaf than adders to the voice / Of any true decision" (2.2). "True" here means "not to be faulted objectively," as when a bell rings true or a wall is true to a plumb line. But Troilus's opting for revenge is shown by Shakespeare to be not true in that sense, since it is pure self-indulgence. If "[t]he venom'd vengeance" (5.3) makes Troilus successful in battle, it also makes him reckless. And in the last scene of the play as it is normally published nowadays,[14] Troilus, sensing that the death of Hector is the beginning of the end, nevertheless evokes the Greek tents and then bursts out (the "great-siz'd coward" is Achilles and "inward woe" superadds Achilles' killing Hector to Cressida's desertion):

> I'll through and through you! and, thou great-siz'd coward,
> No space of earth shall sunder our two hates.
> I'll haunt thee like a wicked conscience still,
> That mouldeth goblins swift as frenzy's thoughts.
> Strike a free march. To Troy with comfort go;
> Hope of revenge shall hide our inward woe.
>
> (5.10)

This is the language of obsession. It is energetic, but it is also disproportionately subjective, and so it diminishes the speaker. To witness Troilus declaiming these lines is to witness an ignoble figure puffed up by noise and gesture. Fittingly, Troilus's last action as he leaves the play is to lash out at the ailing Pandarus.

III

The growth of Leontes' jealousy in The Winter's Tale. *Movement around the Globe's platform stage. Leontes' denunciation of Hermione to Camillo (1.2) and Camillo's rebuttal. The importance of good acting to a right understanding of the play's opening.*

The Winter's Tale is known to have been performed at the Globe, since it was seen there by a Dr. Simon Forman (1552–1611) on Wednesday, May 15, 1611. Forman's notes on what he saw "at the glob [sic]" have been preserved and begin, "Observe ther howe Lyontes the kinge of Cicillia was overcom wth Ielosy of his wife with the kinge of Bohemia his frind that came to see him. and howe he Contrived his death and wold have had his cup berer to have poisoned. who gave the king of bohemia warning therof & fled with him to bohemia."[15] Forman obviously found it easy to recognize kings for what they were, to retain a sense of place as the play moves between Sicilia and Bohemia, and to hear Leontes' asides as they were spoken from the stage to the audience. He proves, if proof be needed, that the Globe really worked as it is nowadays assumed to have done. He also seems to have had no trouble with Leontes' becoming jealous. The credibility of that process must therefore have been part of his experience of act 1, scenes 1 and 2, that Wednesday afternoon in 1611. Although it is no longer possible to recover every nuance of an original King's Men's performance, much of Forman's experience remains available through the text of the play.

The Winter's Tale opens with Camillo and Archidamus making their way forward from one of the flanking doors in the tiring-house facade. They could well be costumed to indicate their respective nationalities. As they speak, the audience hears the phrase "great difference betwixt our Bohemia and your Sicilia" in the play's first sentence and subsequently learns that, while the two kings were close as boys, they have diverged as adults. Division is thereby established early, though its significance is not. The hint is also there that Leontes' generous hospitality is a form of would-be dominance, since it subjects Polixenes to pressure.

The decisive second scene is long and moves in phases. Despite Hermione's pregnancy and despite the fact that it is an indoor scene (Hermione will speak of going into the garden), it looks as if it was written to be played standing, since it is physically and psychologically mobile. Leontes, Polixenes, and Hermione would have their attendants, who would, from a respectful distance, be ready to respond to instructions, and who would move as the principal characters move. Mamillius would possibly be in the care of ladies, as he is in act 2, scene 1—the "they" of his "I am like you, they say" at 1.2.208 could well refer to nonspeaking attendants on stage with the boy. Counting in Camillo as well—his reentrance is discussed below—this makes for a fairly populous platform stage, and that allows for an emphasis on the changing relative positions of Leontes, Hermione, and Polixenes. As Leontes marginalizes himself psychologically, he will spend time at the edge of the stage in order to deliver his asides. He may additionally use the stage posts to accentuate his separateness.

Hermione's pregnancy is unmistakable. This is disclosed in act 2, scene 1, by the Second Lady, who says, "She is spread of late / Into a goodly bulk." The boy actor playing Hermione may well have been short, since an embedded stage direction in act 1, scene 2, requires Hermione to look up to Polixenes at line 183 ("How she holds up the neb! the bill to him!") and in act 5, scene 3, Camillo says that Hermione "hangs about [Leontes'] neck." If so, the pregnancy could really have been made to stand out, in both senses of the phrase. A consequence of its "goodly bulk" is that, when Polixenes opens act 1, scene 2, with "Nine changes of the wat'ry star hath been / The shepherd's note since we have left our throne / Without a burthen," the coincidence between Polixenes' nine months' stay at Leontes' court and Hermione's advanced condition is visibly there for Leontes to misinterpret (the "wat'ry star" Polixenes speaks of is the moon, and "burthen" means "occupant").

Hermione, as befits her subordinate status, speaks late. She is cued in with Leontes' "Tongue-tied our queen?" and, as will shortly become clear, the abruptness of his question combines with his "our" (a royal plural) to imply uneasiness about who really possesses her. As Hermione, at Leontes' bidding, seeks to change Polixenes' mind about leaving, she moves from addressing Leontes to addressing Polixenes directly. She does this when she reaches "Yet of your royal presence I'll adventure / The borrow of a week" in the following quotation, and she would presumably exert some female charm as well, since she accuses Leontes of proceeding "too coldly." (Double slashes indicate where Hermione turns from Leontes to Polixenes, then back to Leontes, then back to Polixenes again. A "distaff" is a stick used in spinning.)

> To tell he longs to see his son were strong;
> But let him say so then, and let him go;
> But let him swear so, and he shall not stay,
> We'll thwack him hence with distaffs.
> //Yet of your royal presence I'll adventure
> The borrow of a week. When at Bohemia
> You take my lord, I'll give him my commission
> To let him there a month behind the gest
> Prefix'd for 's parting; //yet, good deed, Leontes,
> I love thee not a jar o' th' clock behind
> What lady she her lord. //You'll stay?

In exchange for getting Polixenes to stay another week, Hermione volunteers to let Leontes stay in Bohemia as Polixenes' summer guest a month longer than the official date set for his return to Sicilia. But then, realizing that Leontes might misinterpret this as a wish to have him away from her, she addresses him directly again from "yet, good deed, Leontes." "Good deed" means "in truth," and Hermione's "I love thee not a jar o' th' clock behind / What lady she her lord" means that her love for Leontes will stand any comparison, a "jar" being a tick of a clock. That she has to say such things at all suggests that Leontes habitually needs reassurance about her feelings toward him. When, after the period in the last line of the above quotation, she goes on to ask, "You'll stay?" she returns her full attention to

Polixenes. At that point, Leontes can be assumed to move away from them, since, shortly afterward, Polixenes agrees to stay as Hermione's guest, but, some thirty lines later, Leontes still has to ask, "Is he won yet?" It may be that Leontes feels displaced when Hermione returns her attention to Polixenes. He may also want to observe from a distance the behavior of what he regards as a suspect pair. The one possibility does not cancel the other.

After Polixenes agrees to stay, Leontes' physical remoteness pretty much obliges Hermione to continue conversing with her guest, though the text suggests that she may well look for Leontes before continuing. Polixenes says that he will stay as Hermione's guest, not her prisoner, to which Hermione replies: "Not your jailer then, / But your kind hostess. Come, I'll question you / of my lord's tricks and yours when you were boys." The period between "hostess" and "Come" marks a clear halt followed by a new beginning, and it provides ample opportunity for Hermione to look around in vain for some kind of approving sign from Leontes, since she has accomplished what he says he wants. In default of such a sign, Hermione, good hostess that she is, moves onto a new subject, and the conversation she then conducts with Polixenes is indispensable to the play, which is why Shakespeare creates the opportunity for it. It is one of the many conversations in Shakespeare's plays that are there principally to be overheard by the audience, and its theme is that, as children grow up, they naturally pass from innocence to sexuality, and that that passage can entail promiscuity. The joke that Hermione and Polixenes share, as between one sophisticated adult and another, is that, in marrying, Polixenes and Leontes succumbed to sexual temptation by their wives; Hermione teasingly extends the joke by implying, without believing it to be true, that they could since have succumbed extramaritally as well.

Sexuality, being natural, is everywhere, and that includes in other parts of *The Winter's Tale.* Act 2, scene 1, has Mamillius already taking note of women's faces. Florizel, like Ferdinand in *The Tempest,* has to insist that his sexuality is under control ("[M]y desires / Run not before mine honor, nor my lusts / Burn hotter than my faith" [4.4]). And the Shepherd deplores sexuality, saying, "I would there were no age between ten and three-and-twenty, or that youth would sleep out the rest; for there is nothing in the between but getting wenches with child, wronging the ancientry, stealing, fighting" (3.3). It is also in the audience: sexuality is one of respectability's great shared secrets. And, as a consequence of his passing from boyhood into manhood, it is in Leontes, too. In short, what Hermione and Polixenes say about sexuality and promiscuity as they converse on stage is meant to be acknowledged by the audience based on its own worldly wisdom, and that acknowledgement primes the audience to understand, once Leontes has made clear why he is out of temper, that he has combined his general sexual awareness with his awareness of the friendliness between Hermione and Polixenes to conclude that his pregnant wife has been unfaithful to him.

However, while Leontes' conclusion must be understandable, it must not be believable, if the play is to work. In the last analysis, Hermione must be above suspicion, even though she displays an open and sexually confident personality in her dealings with Polixenes. This makes Shakespeare heavily reliant on his actors in the early part of the play. Even when Hermione gives her hand to Polixenes, or when she takes his arm, they must so conduct themselves that, although Leontes speaks of "paddling palms and pinching fingers" and of "[holding] up the neb! the bill to him!," there is a divergence between what the audience sees and the way Leontes interprets it. Furthermore, no one onstage must give any indication of anything untoward being known. That is, there must be nothing to support Leontes retrospectively when he asserts, "They're here with me already, whisp'ring, rounding: / 'Sicilia is a so-forth.'" ("A so-forth" is Leontes' pained euphemism for "a cuckold.")

Leontes eventually denounces Hermione to Camillo, because, in his jealousy, he wants Camillo to poison Polixenes. That denunciation must obviously be tête-à-tête, so some stage clearing is called for ahead of time, beginning with Hermione, Polixenes, and their attendants. Their removal is cleverly done. Leontes says that he wants to walk with young Mamillius away from Polixenes and his "graver steps"; Hermione, as hostess, is charged with looking after Polixenes, since he is their guest; deferring to Leontes' wish for separateness with his son, Hermione proposes going into the garden; and Leontes, in an aside, claims Shakespeare's cleverness for himself by revealing that he is "angling," that is, in modern parlance, that he is giving Hermione and Polixenes enough rope to hang themselves with.

Mamillius and any attendants are distanced by the command "Go play, boy, play," though the boy obviously wants to come back. This balances the stage between Leontes, his son (poised between innocence and sexuality), and Camillo. Leontes' first words to Camillo are "What? Camillo there?" and they might be taken to mean that he is calling Camillo back onto the stage. However, the stage direction at the head of act 1, scene 2, has Camillo reenter at the beginning of the scene with Leontes, Hermione, Mamillius, Polixenes, and attendants, despite the fact that he has only just exited with Archidamus. And when Camillo eventually speaks, it is clear that he has been onstage during Leontes' and Hermione's attempts to get Polixenes to stay. Leontes' "What? Camillo there?" therefore suggests, rather, that he has just

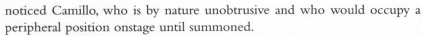

noticed Camillo, who is by nature unobtrusive and who would occupy a peripheral position onstage until summoned.

Before Camillo is brought into the action, however, Leontes behaves as if he is alone and reveals his innermost thoughts in what amounts to a soliloquy:

> There have been
> (Or I am much deceiv'd) cuckolds ere now,
> And many a man there is (even at this present,
> Now, while I speak this) holds his wife by th' arm,
> That little thinks she has been sluic'd in 's absence,
> And his pond fish'd by his next neighbor—by
> Sir Smile, his neighbor. . . .
>
> . . . .
>
> Be it concluded,
> No barricado for a belly. Know't,
> It will let in and out the enemy,
> With bag and baggage.

This soliloquy does four things. First, it parallels the earlier dialogue about sexuality between Hermione and Polixenes, but in a solipsistic and diseased manner, since it is the product of one man's secret jealousy and fear. Second, it claims—undeniably—that promiscuity is widespread, although not everyone is aware of being deceived. Third, it addresses the audience directly, thereby inviting its endorsement of what is being claimed and quite possibly causing embarrassment, too. Fourth, it confirms to the audience Leontes' persuasion that he is himself to be numbered among the cuckolds. When Leontes has finished, Mamillius comes back to him. This possibly distracts Leontes from his brooding and causes him to catch sight of Camillo. Leontes is plainly filled to the brim with jealous thoughts at this time, and he is used to sharing confidences with Camillo; so he sends his son off the stage and begins to pressure Camillo, who is now alone with him, into seeing things his way (remaining attendants would have to look studiously uninvolved).

By divulging his suspicions to another character, Leontes subjects their credibility to two external tests. First, Leontes asks Camillo,

> Ha' not you seen, Camillo
> (But that's past doubt; you have, or your eye-glass
> Is thicker than a cuckold's horn), or heard
> (For to a vision so apparent rumor
> Cannot be mute), or thought (for cogitation

Resides not in that man that does not think)
My wife is slippery? . . .

Camillo's answer is a flat denial. He is a character of integrity, he has first-hand knowledge of Hermione and Polixenes, he has been onstage since the beginning of act 1, scene 2, and he answers with a straightforward "Good my lord, be cur'd / Of this diseas'd opinion, and betimes, / For 'tis most dangerous." Second, Leontes' question goes over Camillo's head to the audience. Has *it* seen or heard anything that might lead it to believe that Hermione is not as she should be? In practice, audiences consistently incline to Camillo's point of view, even at this early stage of the play, showing that Shakespeare gets the balance of dialogue, movement, and tones of voice just right. In other words, the opening of *The Winter's Tale* is so written that, if it is properly performed, it *must* be understood in the clear-cut way Shakespeare wanted it to be. That is no small triumph, given that clandestine promiscuity is one of its major ingredients.

Chapter 10

PROLOGUES AND CHORUSES

I

Some general remarks about prologues and choruses. The Presenter (Prologue) to Henry IV, Part Two.

Prologues and choruses are to be found in *Romeo and Juliet; Henry IV, Part Two; Henry V; Troilus and Cressida; Pericles; The Winter's Tale; The Two Noble Kinsmen;* and *Henry VIII.* They span, therefore, most of Shakespeare's career, but, at the same time, they are too few to count as routine inclusions in the plays he either wrote or coauthored. The word "prologue" can refer both to a speech introducing a play and to the character delivering that speech. The word "chorus" can also refer either to a speech or to a character. The Chorus normally recurs within the play he is in—Shakespeare's Prologues and Choruses are all male—to set a scene, pass comment, or carry the plot forward. (In this chapter, if the character is referred to, a capital "P" or "C" is used, and if a speech is referred to, lowercase letters are used.) In *Romeo and Juliet,* the prologue is delivered by the Chorus, as it is in *Henry V,* in which the Chorus describes himself as "Prologue-like." The prologues and choruses in *Romeo and Juliet; Henry IV, Part Two; Henry V;* and *Troilus and Cressida,* together with the chorus that begins act 4 of *The Winter's Tale,* are all confidently attributed to Shakespeare; the choruses in *Pericles* are probably by Shakespeare, though the issue is not yet closed; the prologue to *The Two Noble Kinsmen* is usually attributed to John Fletcher;[1] and the prologue to *Henry VIII* is arguably by Shakespeare, though it, too, has been attributed to

Fletcher.[2] Technically, Shakespeare's most interesting prologues and choruses are those in *Romeo and Juliet, Henry V,* and *Pericles.* They are discussed in detail in sections II, III, and IV of this chapter.

As soon as he comes onstage, a Prologue is meant to be recognizable for what he is. He conventionally wears a black velvet cloak, and he enters on his own after a trumpet has sounded three times. In Thomas Heywood's *The Foure Prentises of London* (c.1594[?]), the 1st Prologue asks, "Do you not see this long blacke velvet cloake upon my backe? Have you not sounded thrice? . . . Nay, have I not all the signes of a Prologue about me?"[3] As indicated, the Prologue's basic function is to introduce the play to the audience. In *Hamlet,* when Ophelia wonders whether the dumb show she has just seen explains what the play is about (3.2), the Prologue enters, and Hamlet says, adding his own meaning, "We shall know by this fellow. The players cannot keep counsel, they'll tell all." In the event, the Prologue in *Hamlet* is distinctly brief. On the other hand, Peter Quince, who is preceded by a fanfare, gets twenty-five lines to detail the plot of *Pyramus and Thisby,* in addition to a preliminary ten lines for courtesies (*A Midsummer Night's Dream,* 5.1). The ten lines for courtesies are garbled, presumably out of nervousness. That is part of the scene setting: Philostrate has reported that Quince and his company are "[e]xtremely stretch'd," that is, not very able; Theseus speaks of great scholars, let alone artisans, becoming tongue-tied in his presence; and the performance of *Pyramus and Thisby* will shortly earn mocking comment from the newlyweds. But Prologues are generally no strangers to nervousness. The 1st Prologue in *The Foure Prentises of London* asks, "Do I not looke pale, as fearing to be out in my speech?"[4] And in Thomas Dekker's *The Guls Horn-Booke* (1609), the gallant, being advised on how to behave in a playhouse, is told to sit on the stage where he can be seen, but, "Present not your selfe on the Stage . . . untill the quaking prologue hath (by rubbing) got culor into his cheekes, and is ready to give the trumpets their Cue, that hees upon point to enter" (chap. 6).[5]

Prologues are a rarity in modern theater, but Shakespeare could routinely write the word "prologue" into his dialogue and know that he would be understood. Thus, in *The Merry Wives of Windsor,* Falstaff's account of his intended seduction of Mistress Ford includes the words, "after we had embrac'd, kiss'd, protested, and, as it were, spoke the prologue of our comedy" (3.5); Iago, speaking of Cassio's drunkenness to Montano, says, "'Tis evermore the prologue to his sleep" (*Othello,* 2.3); and in *Macbeth,* the new Thane of Cawdor reflects in an aside, "Two truths are told, / As happy prologues to the swelling act / of the imperial theme" (1.3). It was a word no audience in Shakespeare's day would have thought twice about.

Although the Prologue was a standardized character, Shakespeare varied his own Prologues according to his needs. The Prologue to *Henry IV, Part Two,* is a case in point (following the 1623 First Folio, modern editions usually call him the "Presenter" and his opening of the play the "Induction"). Shakespeare needed some way of linking the beginning of *Henry IV, Part Two,* to the ending of *Henry IV, Part One.* He could have used dialogue, but he opted to use a Prologue instead: the allegorical figure Rumor. Rumor follows logically on a big event like the Battle of Shrewsbury, which ended *Henry IV, Part One,* and he is just the right kind of striking figure to begin a play with anyway. His costume would be crimson, and his introductory stage direction reads *"Enter* RUMOR, *painted full of tongues."*[6] *"Enter"* is, in fact, an understatement, since Rumor's first contact with the audience is stentorian. It must have rung round the Curtain, where *Henry IV, Part Two,* arguably was premiered sometime after March 1598, but before the end of the year. The Lord Chamberlain's Men were dependent on the Curtain at this time, since the lease on the Theatre had expired, the indoor Blackfriars theater was unavailable to them, and the Globe had yet to be built.[7]

> Open your ears; for which of you will stop
> The vent of hearing when loud Rumor speaks?
> I, from the orient to the drooping west
> (Making the wind my post-horse), still unfold
> The acts commenced on this ball of earth.

One of Rumor's functions is to move the audience from one place to another. Geographically, the transition is from "the royal field of Shrewsbury" to Northumberland's "worm-eaten" castle at Warkworth via—a neat touch of realism—"the peasant towns" that lie between the two. Symbolically, the transition is from the death of Hotspur to the beginning of the end of rebellion as a national threat. As Rumor delivered his lines, he would have moved about the stage in order to address his in-the-round audience. Precisely how he moved is not possible to say, but it is likely that he gestured from east to west as he delivered "from the orient to the drooping west," and that he indicated by his body language the speed and lightness of the wind.

Rumor is not necessarily a liar, so he can be used to report accurately the ending of *Henry IV, Part One,* thereby putting the audience of *Henry IV, Part Two,* in the picture ("run before" means that Rumor precedes the truth by outpacing it):

> I run before King Harry's victory,
> Who in a bloody field by Shrewsbury

Hath beaten down young Hotspur and his troops,
Quenching the flame of bold rebellion
Even with the rebels' blood. . . .

So, the audience of *Henry IV, Part Two*, now knows what is really the case, and it will shortly be told that Rumor has been "noising abroad" that Prince Hal and Henry IV have been vanquished by Hotspur and Douglas respectively. Rumor's advance comparison of what is true and what is being noised abroad heightens the dramatic quality of the opening of the play proper. Northumberland, whom Rumor describes as "crafty-sick," enters "*in a night-cap and supporting himself with a staff*" (1.1). Initially, he is cheered by a false report from a lord (Lord Bardolph), who was not present at the Battle of Shrewsbury but who claims to have spoken with a gentleman who has allegedly come from there. This report is then corrected, and, in full view of the audience, Northumberland has to adjust to the news of his son's death and to the realization that the rebels' situation has deteriorated badly. Rumor's exit couplet is, "From Rumor's tongues / They bring smooth comforts false, worse than true wrongs." With it, his introductory functions are fully accomplished. (The "[t]hey" Rumor speaks of are messengers bringing heartening but untrue information.)

II

The Chorus's prologue to Romeo and Juliet *and his return to the play at the beginning of act 2.*

Although it is believed to have been written for the Theatre, *Romeo and Juliet* was probably, like *Henry IV, Part Two*, performed on the open platform stage of the Curtain. The lines used by the Chorus, acting as Prologue, to introduce the play follow. The stage would probably be hung with black to indicate a tragedy. (The lines containing the phrase "but their children's end" mean that it takes the children's deaths to end the parents' feuding.)[8]

Two households, both alike in dignity,
In fair Verona, where we lay our scene,
From ancient grudge break to new mutiny,
Where civil blood makes civil hands unclean.
From forth the fatal loins of these two foes
A pair of star-cross'd lovers take their life;
Whose misadventur'd piteous overthrows
Doth with their death bury their parents' strife.

The fearful passage of their death-mark'd love,
And the continuance of their parents' rage,
Which, but their children's end, nought could remove,
Is now the two hours' traffic of our stage;
The which if you with patient ears attend,
What here shall miss, our toil shall strive to mend.

The Chorus's first word after his stylized entrance is "Two." It draws attention to the fact that division is fundamental to the play. "Verona" transforms the stage nominally into an Italian city and conceptually into an area in which "fair" and "civil" will be pitted against "blood" and "unclean." A modern audience might well instinctively concentrate on the eponymous lovers, but the Chorus places a different emphasis. His approach is situational before it is individual, so he refers to the lovers not by name but functionally, using the word "lovers" itself and "star-cross'd." The phrases "parents' strife" and "parents' rage" on the one hand and "but their childrens' end, nought could remove" on the other provide the broad terms of reference of the tragedy to come. They include Romeo and Juliet, but they are not restricted to them.

The play's emphasis on situation has three consequences. First, Romeo and Juliet must indeed be characterized strongly and accurately as individuals, if their "piteous overthrows" are to have their intended effect; but, second, they must also be at all times inseparable from the plot, since they are essential to its overall development. Third, consistency of form requires that, if the play begins by prioritizing situation, it must end in the same way. And that is what happens. As the "two hours' traffic" nears its end, Prince Escalus is given lines that reiterate the prologue's situational emphases:

Where be these enemies? Capulet! Montague!
See what a scourge is laid upon your hate,
That heaven finds means to kill your joys with love.
And I for winking at your discords too
Have lost a brace of kinsmen. All are punish'd.

(5.3)

The form of the prologue is a sonnet, that is, it is orderly as well as concise. In part, the prologue's formal orderliness contrasts with the tragic disorder to come, and in part it signals a value to be aspired to as the play closes. In siding with order and deploring disorder, prologue and play express a common morality. As the audience listens to the prologue and then experiences the play, it is effectively invited to assent to that morality as it forms its judgments.

Although the Chorus describes a dramatic situation, he does not do so in a dramatic way. This is because he relies on statement. This raises the question of how Shakespeare generates so much forward momentum in the body of the play as he develops the material set out in the prologue. The answer is that he treats it propositionally. This becomes clear if the prologue is rethought on an "if-then" basis: *if* there is parental strife and *if* Romeo and Juliet actively persist in their love, *then,* one way or another, misfortune will follow, which will *then* bring their parents together. As soon as what the prologue says is construed in that way, the play's forward movement becomes much more understandable. Not just movement, but *forward* movement, since that is the kind of movement writing on an "if-then" basis naturally brings about. No audience can mistake the point of transition from statement to drama in *Romeo and Juliet,* since it is violent. As the Chorus leaves the stage at the end of his prologue, Sampson and Gregory burst on carrying swords and bucklers. Everything about them makes them different from the Chorus, including their lively dialogue in prose and respective demeanors. It is not that they are different characters, it is that they belong to a different idiom. They are dramatic, and the way the audience perceives the stage and everything on it changes radically with their entrance.

The Chorus makes a single return to the stage, and it is a return that has not always been well received. Even its location is disputed, though that would not normally have affected performance, which was continuous. It usually opens act 2, but G. Blakemore Evans argues for its concluding act 1.[9] As to its value, this is Samuel Johnson: "The use of this Chorus is not easily discovered; it conduces nothing to the progress of the play, but relates what is already known, or what the next scenes will show; and relates it without adding the improvement of any moral sentiment."[10] But is Johnson right, especially if the play is thought of as being performed, not read?

By the time the Chorus makes his second entrance, the play has established a triple context for him to return to. First, Romeo has moved on from his earlier love for Rosaline, whom, in his immaturity, he had believed to be matchless "since first the world begun" (1.2). Second, his new love—Juliet—is actually in the play, and he is loved by her as well. Third, their love is marked by danger. The sonnet form is preferred in the Chorus's second appearance, as in his first, but the tone is more drastic this time. His opening lines, "Now old desire doth in his death-bed lie, / And young affection gapes to be his heir," are harsh and meant to be so, since an important part of their purpose is to allude to the irruptive nature of Romeo's love for Juliet. In act

1, scene 2, Old Capulet explains to Paris (and the audience) that he thinks that Juliet is too young to marry just yet but that he sees her eventual marriage as a part of his plans for his inheritance. From Capulet's point of view, it is a humane line of thought and one he is perfectly entitled to. But Romeo, though acting out of love, not greed, is poised to intrude on it.

Juliet is treated more gently by the Chorus. Her key word is "tender," that is, she is loving, but she is also very young and a novice in love at this stage of the play. The rift between the Capulets and the Montagues makes any meeting with Romeo as dangerous as it is difficult. Ironically, it is the very power of their love that puts the lovers at risk, by making them want to be together. That is why the Chorus speaks of "[stealing] love's sweet bait from fearful hooks." His metaphor enhances the line Juliet had spoken just before he came onstage: "My grave is like to be my wedding-bed" (1.5), a line already echoed by the Chorus's "death-bed."

In sum, the second appearance of the Chorus draws together the threads of the play at a critical point, foreshadows the tragedy to come, and creates a distance between the audience and the doomed pair that makes understanding and judging them easier. Therefore, Johnson's evaluation is open to challenge. As with the Chorus's first exit, his second exit needs to be taken in conjunction with what follows it. As the Chorus leaves the stage this time, Romeo enters alone and speaks just two lines before Benvolio and Mercutio come on, namely, "Can I go forward when my heart is here? / Turn back, dull earth, and find thy centre out" (2.1). These lines express one of the play's most important decisions, since without it—and Romeo's acting on it—the tragedy could not happen. The Chorus's second exit is his last, since the tragedy is now set up to proceed without further interruption. Jill L. Levenson draws attention to the theory that Shakespeare originally planned more choric interventions but changed his mind.[11] Unlike Romeo, he made the right decision.

III

The power of the Chorus in Henry V. *His layered meanings. Nym and Bardolph as characters beneath the range of the Chorus's rhetoric.*

Henry V is believed to have been written in the earlier part of 1599. By then, the timber frame of the out-of-lease Theatre had been disassembled and transported south of the Thames, to be reconstructed as the Globe. Consequently, *Henry V* could have been premiered at the Curtain. In that case, the prologue's "unworthy scaffold" and "wooden O" would apply to that theater's aging timbers—it was first erected in 1577—as does, perhaps, Rumor's "worm-eaten" in *Henry IV, Part Two*. On the other hand, the prologue's now-famous phrases may have been destined for their first public hearing in the new Globe after its opening in the summer of 1599.[12] Either way, the choruses in *Henry V* were written with the physical construction and limitations of the Elizabethan playhouse very much in mind. By contrast, *Romeo and Juliet*'s two choruses see no need to make a technical issue of "our stage" and what surrounds it.

Whether the Chorus of *Henry V* is assumed to be in the Curtain or the Globe, he is the single point of focus of everybody watching, including the groundlings looking up at him from around the edge of the stage. As he speaks, so the audience listens, and, as he moves, so its eyes follow him. This arrangement generates choices. If, as the Chorus looks out at those watching him, he sees paying customers on whom he is dependent, then his attitude to the audience will be deferential. This is the case in *Romeo and Juliet*. If, on the other hand, he sees the audience as a body of people dependent on him, and if he wishes to emphasize his ability to transform by means of words the real or alleged shortcomings of the playhouse that audience is in—as does the Chorus in *Henry V*—he will express power over the circumstances of the playhouse and an aspiration to control the audience. That the Chorus in *Henry V* favors the imperative mood is no coincidence: it is of a piece with his characterization. It is true that the Chorus concludes his prologue by entreating the audience's patience. But he prefaces that entreaty by describing himself as "Prologue-like," that is, he is temporarily assuming a role that is out of character.[13] Presumably Shakespeare expected a change of demeanor and tone of voice as the Chorus becomes deferential.

The generalizations made in the preceding paragraph can be followed through in detail. In the prologue to the play, the audience is required to "[s]uppose," "[p]iece out," and "[t]hink," just as, in the chorus to act 3, it is required to "[f]ollow, follow!," "[g]rapple [its] minds to sternage of this navy," and "[w]ork, work [its] thoughts." Provided that the audience complies, space and time can be compressed; the unities of place, time, and action can be disregarded; a small cast can represent large numbers; selected versions of reality can be created; and socially lowly actors can be transformed into kings for an afternoon—even though, outside of the theater, they would not be allowed to dress above their station. As he introduces act 2, the Chorus assumes jurisdiction over transport and weather as well (in the days before steam and diesel, power over the weather at sea was no small matter):

> There is the playhouse now, there you must sit,
> And thence to France shall we convey you safe,

> And bring you back, charming the Narrow Seas
> To give you gentle pass; . . .

Authority over light and dark is added to the Chorus's capability as he opens act 4: "Now entertain conjecture of a time / When creeping murmur and the poring dark / Fills the wide vessel of the universe." Obviously, the Chorus expects no resistance to his commands. His authority is that of a live performer with a tale to tell, and, just by entering the playhouse, the audience signifies a willingness in principle to subordinate itself to that authority. However, even the Chorus has his limits. When he introduces act 5, he finds himself confronted with data in such abundance that they defy presentation "in their huge and proper life." His response is a variation on his theme that a play is a "mockery" of true things—"mockery" meaning a reduced and acted-out version, but also a version containing criticism. He openly admits that he has had to leave things out, and, above all, he draws attention, in a way that mocks himself and Henry alike, to his role as manipulator of king and history ("Callice" is "Calais"):

> Vouchsafe to those that have not read the story,
> That I may prompt them; and of such as have,
> I humbly pray them to admit th' excuse
> Of time, of numbers, and due course of things,
> Which cannot in their huge and proper life
> Be here presented. Now we bear the King
> Toward Callice; grant him there; there seen,
> Heave him away upon your winged thoughts
> Athwart the sea. . . .

The insinuation contained in the word "story" is that the play is a *version* of *The Life of Henry the Fifth* (to give the play its usual fuller title). This insinuation is expanded in the Chorus's epilogue:

> Thus far, with rough and all-unable pen,
> Our bending author hath pursu'd the story,
> In little room confining mighty men,
> Mangling by starts the full course of their glory.

The sequence is clear. First comes Henry V himself; then Henry V as recorded historically and remembered in the popular mind; then Shakespeare working up his own selective account; and, finally, the enactment of that account

in the enclosed here and now of the Curtain or the Globe. The emphasis
on a version would be even stronger if Shakespeare, the "bending author,"
were taking a bow, though "bending" might just refer to studying and writing (and manipulating).

The version of Henry V the Chorus implants in the minds of his audience is a layered one, in keeping with the body of the play.[14] On top is the
epilogue's "star of England," the victor of Agincourt, who achieved "the
world's best garden," that is, France, and who is contrasted with Henry VI,
during whose weak reign France was lost again (the epilogue's "Which oft
our stage hath shown" refers to Shakespeare's *Henry VI* plays). This Henry V
is honorifically associated with "the mirror of all Christian kings" (act 2),
"young Phoebus" (act 3; it means "rising sun," the sun being a royal symbol), "fleet majestical" (act 3) and "conqu'ring Caesar" (act 5). However, the
epilogue also explains that Henry achieved this garden by means of his
sword, and the sword stands for a more critical layer of meaning, since it includes the idea of taking by force.

The Chorus's introduction to act 3 shows even more clearly than his epilogue how he modulates from one layer to the other as he speaks. First, he
asks the audience to imagine an idealized version of Henry and the English
fleet setting sail from Hampton (Southampton) for Harflew (Harfleur):

> Suppose that you have seen
> The well-appointed king at Hampton pier
> Embark his royalty; and his brave fleet
> With silken streamers the young Phoebus fanning.
> Play with your fancies: and in them behold
> Upon the hempen tackle ship-boys climbing;
> Hear the shrill whistle which doth order give
> To sounds confus'd; . . .

This is followed by an account—once more to be imagined—of the siege
of Harfleur:

> Work, work your thoughts, and therein see a siege;
> Behold the ordinance on their carriages,
> With fatal mouths gaping on girded Harflew.
> Suppose th' embassador from the French comes back,
> Tells Harry that the King doth offer him
> Katherine his daughter, and with her, to dowry,
> Some petty and unprofitable dukedoms.

> The offer likes not; and the nimble gunner
> With linstock now the devilish cannon touches,
> *Alarum, and chambers go off.*
> And down goes all before them. Still be kind,
> And eche out our performance with your mind.

Lines like these remove the innocence from the imagining the Chorus demands from the audience. They retain the requirement to supplement the shortcomings of the playhouse but, as they pass from "silken streamers" and "young Phoebus" to "The offer likes not" and "the nimble gunner," they add an invitation to judge morally. "Devilish" is no casual adjective; it is strongly reinforced by the reality of cannon being fired; and there is carnage in the Chorus's lines, too. All of this adds up to brute military force. That force is pervasive. It is present in the sword hidden by "crowns imperial" referred to in the chorus to act 2;[15] it is present in Henry's peace talks with Burgundy (5.2) and in his telling Katherine, "I love France so well that I will not part with a village of it; I will have it all mine" (5.2); and it is present at the beginning of the play in the prologue:

> Then should the warlike Harry, like himself,
> Assume the port of Mars, and at his heels
> (Leash'd in, like hounds) should famine, sword, and fire
> Crouch for employment. . . .

The association with Mars lends Henry heroic grandeur; but his glamour is relativized, if not removed altogether, by the association with dogs and destruction. It is reasonable to suppose that these highly theatrical words, which additionally mark Henry as a player of parts, were written with hand gestures in mind that would take the audience down the moral decline from Mars to the crouching dogs.

It has become a commonplace that the choruses in *Henry V* and the play itself are not entirely conterminous. An indication of this can be found in the transition from the end of the chorus introducing act 2 to act 2, scene 1. That chorus states that the playhouse—audience and all—is about to be transported to Southampton, and, in its buildup, which includes the phrase "the mirror of all Christian kings," it tells of "honor's thought / [Reigning] solely in the breast of every man." There are dark notes, too, of course. The armorer is thriving, people are shortsightedly selling pastures to buy horses, and Expectation is putting an attractive gloss on the true nature of war. However, when the second Chorus exits, the scene is not Southampton but

London, and the stage direction reads, "*Enter* CORPORAL NYM *and* LIEU-TENANT BARDOLPH."

Some productions therefore relocate the second appearance of the Chorus so that it precedes act 2, scene 2, which *is* set in Southampton. But a conjectural emendation of the Chorus's exit couplet from "But *till* the King come forth, and not till then, / Unto Southampton do we shift our scene" to "But *when* the King come forth" etc. (italics added) abrogates the difficulty by suspending the advertised transfer to Southampton until Henry is due to reappear onstage in act 2, scene 2.[16] This is a true "performance" solution and aligns itself exactly with Shakespeare's layered conception of his play. It allows Nym and Bardolph to come onstage at a telling moment and, by being what they are, counterpoint the Chorus's assertion that "honor's thought / Reigns solely in the breast of every man." With their low-life entrance, the play's rhetoric plummets, too, from the Chorus's well-formed verse spoken solo to uncouth dialogue in prose. Up to a point, it can be said that the Eastcheap characters of the play do what the Chorus does: subvert gung-ho ideas with negative ones. But not even the crouching dogs of the prologue match Nym, Bardolph, and, shortly afterward, Pistol. Their squalor is lower than the Chorus's rhetoric can reach. This increases that squalor's impact. When Bardolph declares, "By this sword, he that makes the first thrust, I'll kill him; by this sword, I will" (2.1), the focus on violence becomes acute. When Pistol exclaims, "Let us to France, like horse-leeches, my boys, / To suck, to suck, the very blood to suck!" (2.3), he drags right down Henry's "Cheerly to sea! The signs of war advance! / No king of England, if not king of France!" (2.2). And when Nym asks, "Shall we shog? The King will be gone from Southampton" (2.3; "shog" means "get moving"), he makes it crystal clear to the audience that, by being part of the royal enterprise, he, Pistol, and Bardolph are also part of the way it is to be understood.

IV

The contested authorship of Pericles. *A brief plot summary and a discussion of John Gower, the Chorus. Shakespeare's use of Gower to distinguish between narrative and drama.*

Ben Jonson thought of *Pericles* as a moldy tale, but he was wrong: it is beautiful, accessible, and technically accomplished. It could have been written in 1606, but it is more likely to have been written in 1607 and premiered in 1608.[17] It is known to have been performed at the Globe,[18] and it made full use of that theater's large stage, flanking doors, central opening, and capacity for sound effects, including music. In act 5, scene 1, Diana, the "goddess argentine," makes an entrance. It is possible that she was lowered from the "heavens" and raised again on a trapeze.[19] If not, the central opening would be appropriate to her grandeur. Considered as part of Shakespeare's development as a dramatist, *Pericles* looks back to *Much Ado about Nothing* in that it shows how love can be intensified by separation and reunion: Pericles, unlike Claudio, is not jealous, but he comes to believe that his wife and daughter are dead, and he is then movingly reunited with them. Both plays also feature an empty monument. But if *Pericles* looks back, it looks forward as well, since it forms, together with *Cymbeline* and *The Winter's Tale,* a distinctive threesome of tragicomedies. All three present love as a mature and binding emotion.

Pericles was popular in its day, but, nowadays, despite a willingness to revive it, it counts among Shakespeare's lesser-known plays. This may be because of a widespread but not universally held belief that acts 1 and 2 are not by Shakespeare. This controversy, which has arisen because there is a clear heightening of the drama from the beginning of act 3, has yet to be resolved. (In this chapter, John Gower, the Chorus, is treated as Shakespeare's creation throughout.) Those who believe that Shakespeare wrote the whole play claim, with fair justification, that it offers a unified experience. Peter Levi, while accepting some outside influence, undoubtedly speaks for many when he says, "At every rereading it [*Pericles*] has grown in my estimation, and I still find it among the most moving of all Shakespeare's plays. The simplicity of its means rivals that of *Timon,* and its pure, direct reliance on poetry never ceases to astonish."[20] Nevertheless, *Pericles'* relative obscurity confronts any account of Shakespeare's plays with a dilemma: to ignore it is to ignore a significant achievement, but to talk about it in any detail is to risk talking in a vacuum. The solution adopted here is to provide a brief summary of the play, introduce the Chorus (John Gower), then discuss the most important things he says.

Prince Pericles of Tyre discovers the incestuous relationship between Antiochus, king of Antioch, and his daughter. To escape death, he sets sail for Tharsus (Tarsus) and is subsequently shipwrecked off Pentapolis (southeast Greece),[21] where he marries Thaisa, daughter of King Simonides. Learning that Antiochus is dead and that Tyre is impatient of his absence, Pericles sets sail for Tyre. During a storm, Thaisa appears to die in childbirth. Her "body," sealed into a chest, is buried at sea and washes ashore at Ephesus, where, unknown to Pericles, it is revived by an Ephesian lord named Cerimon. Before reaching Tyre, Pericles entrusts his baby daughter, the aptly named Marina, to the care of Cleon, the governor of Tharsus, and his wife, Dionyza.

After fourteen years, Dionyza, acting out of jealousy, arranges for Marina to be murdered, but Marina, unknown to Dionyza, is carried off by pirates to Mytilene (on the island of Lesbos, off western Turkey). There, Lysimachus, the governor, is attracted by her virtue. Meanwhile Dionyza, believing that Marina is dead, covers her "crime" by pretending that Marina has died of natural causes and that her body has been placed in a monument. Confronted with this empty monument, Pericles believes Marina to be truly dead. Overcome with grief, he eventually arrives off Mytilene, where he is reunited with Marina. The goddess Diana then sends Pericles to Ephesus, where he and Marina are reunited with Thaisa, Marina having been promised to Lysimachus.

Even so brief a summary makes clear that the stage stands for an array of locations and that a large passage of time is involved as well. To hold everything together, Shakespeare uses John Gower. Gower introduces and ends the play, introduces all the acts, and intervenes within the body of the play as well. Unlike the Chorus in *Henry V,* Gower is at one with the play he is in. There are no characters beyond his range of attention, and there is no undercurrent of criticism.

The real John Gower ([1330?]–1408) was born into the gentry and held the title "esquire of Kent." He may have practiced law, but, after 1377, he lived as a layman in semiretirement in St. Mary's Priory, Southwark, in London. Geoffrey Chaucer was one of his friends. The work by which he is best known today is his *Confessio Amantis* (*A Lover's Confession*), which was finished by 1393.[22] It is written in Middle English in octosyllabic couplets. Shakespeare drew heavily on the *Confessio Amantis* for *Pericles.* He also knew that Gower's monument was within walking distance of the Globe in what is now Southwark Cathedral. It showed, as it does today, Gower lying on his back with his head resting on three books, one of which is the *Confessio Amantis.*

In the prologue to *Pericles,* Shakespeare draws on the idea of an author revived from a distant past to establish the play's first important relationship with its audience (the Latin in the following quotation means "As for anything that is good, the older it is, the better"):

> GOWER: To sing a song that old was sung,
> From ashes ancient Gower is come,
> Assuming man's infirmities,
> To glad your ear and please your eyes.
> It hath been sung at festivals,
> On ember-eves and holy-ales;
> And lords and ladies in their lives
> Have read it for restoratives.
> The purchase is to make men glorious,
> *Et bonum quo antiquius, eo melius.*

If you, born in these latter times,
When wit's more ripe, accept my rhymes,
And that to hear an old man sing
May to your wishes pleasure bring,
I life would wish, and that I might
Waste it for you like taper light.

The great theme of love is a lasting one, a constant in the passage of years in contrast to man's evanescence, and the implication is that cultivated modernity needs someone like Gower to come back and remind it of such simplicities. Gower does not actually sing, of course, but by linking his tale to the harp and the lyre, he emphasizes its archetypal nature. As Shakespeare's Gower addresses the audience directly from the stage, he forms a nexus between the present of any given performance and the past he stands for, and this nexus is reinforced by his archaicizing echo of the original Gower's octosyllabic couplets. Primal simplicity is not a new idea in Shakespeare. In *Twelfth Night,* Orsino speaks of a song he wishes to rehear as "old and plain." It is "silly sooth," he says, "[a]nd dallies with the innocence of love, / Like the old age" (2.4; "silly" means "plain" or "simple").

In Shakespeare's Gower, authorship and authority go together. He controls time and space, thunder and shipwreck. When he opens act 2, he tells the audience to remain quiet and, when he opens act 4, scene 4, he humorously notes that (with the audience's permission), "we commit no crime / To use one language in each several clime / Where our scenes seems to live." That is to say, he makes English every country's language, as Shakespeare himself usually does; and he wants each scene, although it is only make-believe, to be experienced as if it were a living event.

As onstage teller, Gower appears to be in charge of the play. But is he *entirely* in charge? As stated above in the plot summary, after the death of Antiochus and his daughter, Pericles sets sail from Pentapolis for Tyre with Thaisa, who is pregnant. It is during this journey that the great storm breaks out, transforming the stage of the Globe into a heaving ship's deck, and Thaisa seems to die in childbirth (3.1). Gower concludes his introduction to the storm with the following lines ("appears" here means "enters"):

And what ensues in this fell storm
Shall for itself itself perform.
I nill relate, action may
Conveniently the rest convey,
Which might not what by me is told.

> In your imagination hold
> This stage the ship, upon whose deck
> The sea-toss'd Pericles appears to speak.

Narrative can achieve a lot, but drama makes its impact on the audience directly and therefore has a claim to validity *to which Gower explicitly defers.* The rightness of Gower's decision can be confirmed by contrasting any of his lines with the dramatic immediacy of lines from Pericles himself, like, "The seaman's whistle / Is as a whisper in the ears of death, / Unheard" or "O you gods! / Why do you make us love your goodly gifts / And snatch them straight away?" Moreover, in performance in the Globe, drama's impact would have been increased by loud imitation thunder and the deployment of firecrackers—it is this barrage of light, sound, and smell that prompts Pericles' "O, still / Thy deaf'ning, dreadful thunders, gently quench / Thy nimble, sulphurous flashes!" There is no way that Gower's narrative could compete with *that.*

The same functional distinction between narrative and drama is made elsewhere in the play, notably when Gower returns to the stage in act 4, scene 4, *"before the monument of Marina at Tharsus."* Thanks to a preparatory scene (4.3), the audience is fully mindful that the monument is empty. As Gower ushers in another dramatic high point in the play, he once more breaks off, this time deferring to the stylized, wordless action of a dumb show: *"Enter* PERICLES *at one door with all his* TRAIN; CLEON *and* DIONYZA *at the other. Cleon shows Pericles the tomb; whereat Pericles makes lamentation, puts on sackcloth, and in a mighty passion departs. Then exeunt Cleon and Dionyza."* The stage, the two flanking doors, and the central opening are all in use here. Although Pericles does not know that Cleon and Dionyza are deceiving him, the audience does, and it was standard practice for enemies to enter by separate doors. The monument would be shown by drawing back the arras; the stage would be largely filled by Pericles, his train, Cleon, and Dionyza; and Gower would remain onstage in his role as teller, but to one side, in order to allow Pericles' lamentation and his donning of sackcloth to have their full effect.

Gower's two lines preceding the dumb show are, as always, precisely chosen: "Like mótes and shádows sée them móve a whíle, / Your éars untó your éyes I'll réconcíle," and the key words "see" and "move"—emphasized by the iambic structure of the line they are in—are used not as a narrator would use them, but as a playwright would. That is to say, when Gower declares, "Like mótes and shádows sée them móve a whíle," he is effectively announcing a categorical shift from telling to performing. The implication of this shift is clear. Gower, the narrator, who has earlier described himself as "[standing] i' th' gaps to teach you, / The stages of our *story*" (4.4; italics added), can achieve a lot. But, when it comes to the play's big moments, only drama will do. By deploying Gower throughout the play, Shakespeare explores the limits as well as the abilities of narrative, and, in so doing, he vindicates his own art as a dramatist. Gower may open *Pericles* by speaking of his poetic song. But he concludes it by declaring, "Here our *play* has ending" (5.3; italics added).

Notes

CHAPTER I—FIRST STEPS

1. Throughout this book, "audience" is used undifferentiatedly. For a detailed analysis of Shakespeare's audiences, see Andrew Gurr, *Playgoing in Shakespeare's London,* 2nd ed. (Cambridge: Cambridge University Press, 1996; reprint, 1997).

2. *A Midsummer Night's Dream,* ed. Harold F. Brooks, The Arden Shakespeare (London: Methuen), 1979; reprint, Walton-on-Thames, UK: Thomas Nelson and Sons, 1997), xxiii.

3. *A Midsummer Night's Dream,* ed. Anne Barton, The Riverside Shakespeare, 2nd ed. (Boston: Houghton Mifflin, 1997), 259, note to 1.2.0 stage direction (hereafter "SD").

4. *A Midsummer Night's Dream,* ed. R. A. Foakes, The New Cambridge Shakespeare (Cambridge: Cambridge University Press, 1984; reprint, 1997), 57, note to 1.2.0 SD; and *A Midsummer Night's Dream,* ed. Barton, The Riverside Shakespeare, 259, 1.2. Location.

5. Andrew Gurr and Mariko Ichikawa, *Staging in Shakespeare's Theatres* (New York: Oxford University Press, 2000), 43.

6. Andrew Gurr, *The Shakespearean Stage, 1574–1642,* 3rd ed. (Cambridge: Cambridge University Press, 1992; reprint, 1999), 121–54 ("Early Amphitheatre Design" and "Later Amphitheatre Design").

7. Gurr and Ichikawa, *Staging in Shakespeare's Theatres,* 58 (beds) and 57 (the "chair of state"). The plinth Hermione stands on in act 5 of *The Winter's Tale* while she waits behind the arras to be brought to life again (discussed below) would not be moved out onto the stage, but, if the grand exit at the end of the play took place through the central opening, the plinth probably needed to be removed by stagehands (see Gurr and Ichikawa, *Staging in Shakespeare's Theatres,* 171, note 37).

8. For an analysis of act 4, scenes 3, 4, and 5, see *Romeo and Juliet,* ed. G. Blakemore Evans, The New Cambridge Shakespeare (Cambridge: Cambridge University Press, 1984; rev. 1997; reprint, 1998), 33. Discussions of *Romeo and Juliet* routinely assume the availability of a discovery space.

9. Ibid., 33.

10. Gurr, *Shakespearean Stage,* 147.

11. *Romeo and Juliet,* ed. Frank Kermode, The Riverside Shakespeare, 2nd ed. (Boston: Houghton Mifflin, 1997), 1127, note to 3.5.67 SD.

12. Cf. *King Richard II,* ed. Andrew Gurr, The New Cambridge Shakespeare (Cambridge: Cambridge University Press, 1984; reprint, 1996), 35: "It is likely that *Richard II* was written to be performed on a stage very like the Swan's, and may well actually have been performed there in the autumn of 1596. There is nothing in the play which could not have been accommodated at the Swan. It needs no more than an open platform with two substantial entry doors, and a balcony."

13. Cf. Andrew Gurr's notes to this scene in *King Henry V,* ed. Andrew Gurr, The New Cambridge Shakespeare (Cambridge: Cambridge University Press, 1992; reprint, 1995), 125–28. (This scene is given as 3. 4.)

14. *The Second Part of King Henry VI,* ed. Michael Hattaway, The New Cambridge Shakespeare (Cambridge: Cambridge University Press, 1991), 105, note to 1.4.21 SD.

15. Cf. Gurr and Ichikawa's reconstruction of 5.1 in *Staging in Shakespeare's Theatres,* 150–54 (this quotation 153). The comments of Gurr and Ichikawa make it necessary for Laertes' "I dare damnation" (4.5) to be taken literally.

16. Ibid., 27.

17. *Pericles,* ed. Doreen DelVecchio and Antony Hammond, The New Cambridge Shakespeare (Cambridge: Cambridge University Press, 1998), 196; *The Tempest,* ed. David Lindley, The New Cambridge Shakespeare (Cambridge: Cambridge University Press, 2002; reprint, 2003), 244–47; Gurr and Ichikawa, *Staging in Shakespeare's Theatres,* 60 and 109.

18. *Coriolanus,* ed. R. B. Parker, The Oxford Shakespeare (Oxford: Oxford University Press, 1994; reissued, 1998), 206, note to 1.11(*sic*).31. The story of the *Sea Adventure* is told in the introduction to *The Tempest,* ed. Hallett Smith, The Riverside Shakespeare, 2nd ed. (Boston: Houghton Mifflin, 1997), 1656–57. "*Sea Adventure*" is cited in other publications as "*Sea Venture.*"

19. Andrew Gurr, *William Shakespeare* (New York: HarperCollins, 1995), 100–103.

20. *Much Ado about Nothing,* ed. F. H. Mares, The New Cambridge Shakespeare (Cambridge: Cambridge University Press, 1988; reprint, 1991), 75, note to 2.1.191–92.

21. C. Walter Hodges, *Enter the Whole Army* (Cambridge: Cambridge University Press, 1999), 55–57; Andrew Gurr with John Orrell, *Rebuilding Shakespeare's Globe* (London: George Weidenfeld and Nicholson, 1989), 100–101 and 181. *Henry VI, Part One,* is usually ascribed to the Rose, but Hodges argues for an outside site at the Globe, too.

22. Sir Henry Wotton, quoted in The Riverside Shakespeare, 2nd ed., 1968. See also S. Schoenbaum, *William Shakespeare: A Compact Documentary Life* (New York: Oxford University Press, 1977; reprint, 1987), 276–77.

23. Gurr, *William Shakespeare,* 142.

24. For where musicians might be situated, see Gurr, *Shakespearean Stage,* 136, 148–49, and 176.

25. *The Two Gentlemen of Verona,* ed. Clifford Leech, The Arden Shakespeare (London: Methuen, 1969; reprint, Walton-on-Thames, UK: Thomas Nelson and Sons, 1998), p. xxvi (Launce); *Love's Labour's Lost,* ed. H. R. Woudhuysen, The Arden Shakespeare (Walton-on-Thames, UK: Thomas Nelson and Sons, 1998), 4 (Costard); Gurr, *Shakespearean Stage,* 89 (Peter, the original Dogberry; Armin as Feste and Lear's Fool); Gurr, *William Shakespeare,* 103 (Touchstone); Park Honan, *Shakespeare: A Life* (Oxford: Oxford University Press Paperback, 1999), 143 (Richard III); *Romeo and Juliet,* ed. Blakemore Evans, The New Cambridge Shakespeare, 28 (Romeo and Juliet); Gurr, *William Shakespeare,* 68 (Hamlet, Othello, Lear, and "all the other leading roles") and 69 (Falstaff); *A Midsummer Night's Dream,* ed. Foakes, The New Cambridge Shakespeare, 9 (Bottom and Quince, Dogberry and Verges).

26. *The Comedy of Errors,* ed. R. A. Foakes, The Arden Shakespeare (London: Methuen, 1962 and as a University Paperback, 1968; reprint, London: Routledge, 1988), 99, note to 5.1.238–42 (Pinch and Starveling); *The Taming of the Shrew,* ed. Brian Morris, The Arden Shakespeare (London: Methuen, 1981; reprint, Walton-on-Thames, UK: Thomas Nelson and Sons, 1997), 158, note to induction, 86 (Keeper in *Henry VI, Part Three;* Beadle in *Henry IV, Part Two;* Tailor in *The Taming of the Shrew;* Feeble in *Henry IV, Part Two;* Robert Faulconbridge in *King John;* and Apothecary in *Romeo and Juliet*); *King Henry IV, Part Two,* ed. A. R. Humphreys, The Arden Shakespeare (London: Methuen, 1966; reprint, Walton-on-Thames, UK: Thomas Nelson and Sons, 1999), 177, note to 5.4.0 SD (Beadle and Shadow).

27. The Riverside Shakespeare, 2nd ed., 1978.

28. Gurr, *William Shakespeare,* 80 ("tall" and "short" are inadvertently reversed). They may also have played Katherine and Alice in *Henry V.*

29. Gurr, *Playgoing in Shakespeare's London,* 107.

30. In his note to *Cymbeline,* 4.2.236, J. M. Nosworthy argues that their voices have already broken, but the text indicates that they are still breaking (*Cymbeline,* ed. J. M. Nosworthy, The Arden Shakespeare [London: Methuen, 1955; reprint, Walton-on-Thames, UK: Thomas Nelson and Sons, 1998], 131).

CHAPTER 2—ENTRANCES AND EARLY WORDS

1. Stage dimensions taken from a ground plan of the new Globe theater (Gurr and Ichikawa, *Staging in Shakespeare's Theatres,* 30). Stages varied in size (see Gurr, *Shakespearean Stage,* 115–71). For movement onstage, see Gurr and Ichikawa, *Staging in Shakespeare's Theatres,* 72–120; and J. L. Styan, *Shakespeare's Stagecraft* (Cambridge: Cambridge University Press, 1967), 65ff.

2. *Measure for Measure,* ed. J. W. Lever, The Arden Shakespeare (London: Methuen, 1965; reprint, Walton-on-Thames, UK: Thomas Nelson and Sons, 1998), 3, note to 1.1, SH: "[T]he Duke should enter 'dressed for travel,' taking leave 'in privacy'"; and *Measure for Measure,* ed. Brian Gibbons, The New Cambridge Shakespeare (Cambridge: Cambridge University Press, 1991), 80, note to 1.1.19: "The Duke literally transfers the dread power and the robes of the office of Duke, temporarily."

3. *Measure for Measure,* ed. Gibbons, The New Cambridge Shakespeare, 77. For convergences between *Measure for Measure* and Puritanism, see 1–7.

4. See *King Henry V,* ed. Gurr, The New Cambridge Shakespeare, 29; and Honan, *Shakespeare: A Life,* 49–50.

5. Gurr, *Playgoing in Shakespeare's London,* 115.

6. Gurr, *Shakespearean Stage,* 241. Gurr also links *Richard III* to the Globe, where the stage was always in the shade (Gurr with Orrell, *Rebuilding Shakespeare's Globe,* 22–24).

7. Styan, *Shakespeare's Stagecraft,* 71.

8. George Bernard Shaw, quoted in F. E. Halliday, *A Shakespeare Companion* (Harmondsworth, UK: Penguin Books, 1964; reprint, 1969), 29.

9. Remarks on tragedy in this section are indebted to Aristotle, *Poetics,* trans. and ed. Kenneth A. Telford (Chicago: Henry Regnery, 1961; reprint, 1968), "Analysis," 59–143.

CHAPTER 3—EXITS

1. Gurr and Ichikawa, *Staging in Shakespeare's Theatres,* 61.

2. B. L. Joseph, *Shakespeare's Eden: The Commonwealth of England, 1558–1629* (London: Blandford Press, 1971), 93–94.

3. C. Walter Hodges suggests special training, loose clothing, and a bank of rushes to cushion the landing. Hodges, *Enter the Whole Army,* 59–62.

4. Thomas Campbell, quoted in S. Schoenbaum, *Shakespeare's Lives* (Oxford: Oxford University Press, 1970), 314.

5. Gurr, *William Shakespeare,* 137 and 142. Stephen Orgel dates the composition between late 1610 and mid-1611. *The Tempest,* ed. Stephen Orgel, The Oxford Shakespeare (Oxford: Oxford University Press, 1987; reissued, 1998), 64.

6. "But to treat *The Tempest* as the grand finale to a writing life obscures the fact that in many respects this is as experimental a play as Shakespeare ever wrote." *The Tempest,* ed. Lindley, The New Cambridge Shakespeare, 3.

7. For a discussion of Prospero's epilogue, see *The Tempest,* ed. Lindley, The New Cambridge Shakespeare, 80–81.

CHAPTER 4—CHARACTERIZATION

1. Sir Philip Sidney, *A Defence of Poetry,* ed. J. A. Van Dorsten (London: Oxford University Press, 1966), 7, 12, and 33.

2. For a discussion of Sidney and Shakespeare, see chapter 2 of Pauline Kiernan's *Shakespeare's Theory of Drama* (Cambridge: Cambridge University Press, 1996). For a note on the unities, see Kenneth McLeish, *Aristotle* (London: Phoenix, 1998), 55–59.

3. *Samuel Johnson on Shakespeare,* ed. H. R. Woudhuysen, New Penguin Shakespeare Library (London: Penguin Books, 1989), 122.

4. Ibid.

5. Cf. a slightly inaccurate pen-and-ink sketch (1594–[1595?]) of a moment from act 1 of *Titus Andronicus* showing Aaron, with blacked face, hands, and legs, standing behind a kneeling Tamora, and reproduced in The Riverside Shakespeare, 2nd ed. (Boston: Houghton Mifflin, 1997), plate 9. Andrew Gurr and Mariko Ichikawa note the use of either lampblack or coal to darken the face (*Staging in Shakespeare's Theatres,* 55). For a sensitive discussion of *Othello* and race, see Leila Christenbury's "Problems with *Othello* in the High School Classroom," in *Teaching Shakespeare into the Twenty-First Century,* ed. Ronald E. Salomone and James E. Davis (Athens: Ohio University Press, 1997), 182–90.

6. *Measure for Measure,* ed. Anne Barton, The Riverside Shakespeare, 2nd ed. (Boston: Houghton Mifflin, 1997), 618, note to 5.1.496.

7. For a discussion of this exit, see *Troilus and Cressida,* ed. Anthony B. Dawson, The New Cambridge Shakespeare (Cambridge: Cambridge University Press, 2003), 188, note to 4.5.53 SD and 189, note to 4.5.63 SD.

8. Herschel Baker discusses the mixture of styles in *King John* in his introduction to the play in The Riverside Shakespeare, 2nd ed. (Boston: Houghton Mifflin, 1997), 806. In *Shakespeare's Language* (London: Penguin Books, 2001), Frank Kermode offers a comprehensive account of the ways Shakespeare's characters speak from his earliest to his latest plays.

9. Lytton Strachey, *Elizabeth and Essex* (Harmondsworth, UK: Penguin Books, 1971), 12.

10. G. B. Harrison, *Introducing Shakespeare,* 3rd ed. (Harmondsworth, UK: Penguin Books, 1966; reprint, 1968), 95.

11. These are collected and explained in Eric Partridge, *Shakespeare's Bawdy,* 3rd ed. (London: Routledge, 1968).

12. *Much Ado about Nothing,* ed. Anne Barton, The Riverside Shakespeare, 2nd ed. (Boston: Houghton Mifflin, 1997), 374, notes to 2.1.294 and 2.1.295. See also *Much Ado about Nothing,* ed. Mares, The New Cambridge Shakespeare, 76, note to 2.1.223.

13. *Much Ado about Nothing,* ed. Barton, The Riverside Shakespeare, 2nd ed., 384, note to 3.5.34.

CHAPTER 5—SCENES NOT SHOWN

1. *King Henry V,* ed. Gurr, The New Cambridge Shakespeare, 106, note to 2.3.14.

2. Gurr, *William Shakespeare,* 70ff.

3. *King Edward III,* ed. Giorgio Melchiori, The New Cambridge Shakespeare (Cambridge: Cambridge University Press, 1998), 9. Shakespeare's sole authorship of this play is disputed. For a discussion of its authorship, see Melchiori, 9–17. The lines quoted in this section are assumed to be by Shakespeare.

4. The title page of the First Quarto edition (1596) states, "As it hath bin sundrie times plaied about the Citie of London." Melchiori discusses the implications of this vague phrase in *King Edward III,* ed. Melchiori, The New Cambridge Shakespeare, 3–9.

5. *Much Ado about Nothing,* directed by Kenneth Branagh (Samuel Goldwyn Company and Renaissance Films, 1993).

6. *Macbeth,* directed by Roman Polanski (Columbia Pictures Industries, and Playboy Entertainment Group, 1971).

7. *Henry V,* directed by Laurence Olivier (Two Cities/Laurence Olivier Production, 1944).

8. Cf. *King Henry V,* ed. Gurr, The New Cambridge Shakespeare, 149, note to 4.0.50 and 171, note to 4.4.0 SD.

9. Johann Joachim Winckelmann, *On the Imitation of the Painting and Sculpture of the Greeks* (1755). Winckelmann's original phrase is *eine edle Einfalt, und eine stille Größe.*

CHAPTER 6—CONTROLLING THE AUDIENCE'S RESPONSES (I)

1. McLeish, *Aristotle,* 15. See also chapter 5 of Kiernan's *Shakespeare's Theory of Drama.*

2. *Macbeth,* ed. A. R. Braunmuller, The New Cambridge Shakespeare (Cambridge: Cambridge University Press, 1997; reprint, 1999), 128, note to 1.6.0 SD.

3. BANQUO: If there were truth from them—
    As upon thee, Macbeth, their speeches shine—
    Why, by the verities on thee made good,
    May they not be my oracles as well,
    And set me up in hope? . . .

                                                                    (3.1)

4. *King Richard III,* ed. Janis Lull, The New Cambridge Shakespeare (Cambridge: Cambridge University Press, 1999), 198, note to 5.3.183.

5. *Troilus and Cressida,* ed. Kenneth Palmer, The Arden Shakespeare (London: Methuen, 1982; reprint, Walton-on Thames, UK: Thomas Nelson and Sons, 1997), 298, note to 5.8.18.

6. The standard study is François Laroque, *Shakespeare's Festive World* (Cambridge: Cambridge University Press, 1991).

7. *The First Part of King Henry IV,* ed. Herbert Weil and Judith Weil, The New Cambridge Shakespeare (Cambridge: Cambridge University Press, 1997), 80, note to 1.2.128, and 111, note to 2.4.46; *Romeo and Juliet,* ed. Blakemore Evans, The New Cambridge Shakespeare, 70, note to 1.3.16; *The Merry Wives of Windsor,* ed. Anne Barton, The Riverside Shakespeare, 2nd ed. (Boston: Houghton Mifflin, 1997), 326, note to 1.1.204–5; *The Second Part of King Henry IV,* ed. Giorgio Melchiori, The New Cambridge Shakespeare (Cambridge: Cambridge University Press, 1989), 93, note to 2.2.78.

8. *"The Sonnets" and "A Lover's Complaint,"* ed. John Kerrigan, The New Penguin Shakespeare (London: Penguin Books, 1986), 34–35.

9. *The Second Part of King Henry IV,* ed. Melchiori, The New Cambridge Shakespeare, 121, note to 3.2.30–31. Melchiori explains that Stamford was an important market town in Lincolnshire but unfortunately confuses Ecclesiastes and Ecclesiasticus.

CHAPTER 7—CONTROLLING THE AUDIENCE'S RESPONSES (II)

1. That this is a trick is made clear by a verbal link. "Vlouting-stog" (meaning "laughing-stock") is used in act 3, scene 1, by Evans when he has revenge in mind; and he uses "vlouting-stocks" in act 4, scene 5, when things start to look bad for the Host of the Garter Inn. Cf. *The Merry Wives of Windsor,* ed. David Crane, The New Cambridge Shakespeare (Cambridge: Cambridge University Press, 1997), 131, note to 4.5.64: "We are perhaps to remember the last time Evans used this word [vlouting-stocks] . . . as he and Caius resolved to revenge

themselves upon the Host. They have clearly arranged the whole incident of the horse-stealing 'Germans.'"

2. Peter Levi, *The Life and Times of William Shakespeare* (London: Papermac, 1989; reprint, 1991), 136.

3. Edmund Spenser, *Poetical Works*, ed. J. C. Smith and E. de Selincourt (Oxford: Oxford University Press, 1970; reprint, 1990), 583.

4. Robert Graves, *The White Goddess* (London: Faber and Faber, 1948; reprint, 1962), 396.

5. *Henry IV, Part One*, ed. Herschel Baker, The Riverside Shakespeare, 2nd ed. (Boston: Houghton Mifflin, 1997), 890, note to 1.1.53.

6. In act 3, scene 1, Brutus again overrules Cassius's uneasiness about Mark Antony. "I will myself into the pulpit first," he says, "[a]nd show the reason of our Caesar's death. / What Antony shall speak, I will protest / He speaks by leave and by permission."

7. S. T. Bindoff, *Tudor England* (Harmondsworth, UK: Penguin Books, 1950; reprint, 1966), 28.

8. *Samuel Johnson on Shakespeare*, 218.

9. Arguably less well managed than the scenes discussed above is the denunciation of Hero in act 4, scene 1, of *Much Ado about Nothing*. In a tongue-in-cheek letter of March 20, 1883, to Ellen Terry, who was playing Beatrice at the time, Lewis Carroll (author of *Alice's Adventures in Wonderland*) asked, "Why in the world did not Hero (or at any rate Beatrice when speaking on her behalf) prove an 'alibi,' in answer to the charge?" It is a good question. In performance, however, what comes across is not a shaky forensic situation but—very powerfully—Hero's victimization and the foolishness of Don Pedro, Claudio, and Leonato. (Carroll's letter is quoted in *Much Ado about Nothing*, ed. Mares, The New Cambridge Shakespeare, 157–58.)

10. *Julius Caesar*, ed. David Daniell, The Arden Shakespeare (Walton-on-Thames, UK: Thomas Nelson and Sons, 1998), 3.

CHAPTER 8—UNTRUTHFUL BEHAVIOR

1. Harrison, *Introducing Shakespeare*, 95. Cf. *The Tempest*, ed. Lindley, The New Cambridge Shakespeare, 162, note to 3.1.91–92, where Lindley generalizes the contract between Ferdinand and Miranda: "Strenuous efforts were being made during the sixteenth and seventeenth centuries to enforce the celebration of marriages in church and to require parental consent, but though they might be disapproved of, contracts such as these were still regarded as binding."

2. Levi, *Life and Times*, 212.

3. *The Merry Wives of Windsor*, ed. T. W. Craik, The Oxford Shakespeare (Oxford: Oxford University Press, 1990), 168, note to 3.4.49.

4. *Hamlet*, ed. Harold Jenkins, The Arden Shakespeare (London: Methuen, 1982; reprint, Walton-on-Thames, UK: Thomas Nelson and Sons, 1997), 187, note to 1.2.132; and *Cymbeline*, ed. Nosworthy, The Arden Shakespeare, 92–93, note to 3.4.77–79.

5. *The Tragedy of King Lear*, ed. Jay L. Halio, The New Cambridge Shakespeare (Cambridge: Cambridge University Press, 1992; reprint, 1997), 3.

6. Ibid., 217, note to 4.5(*sic*).27. Halio writes, "Having been pulled along, wearily climbing the 'hill' . . . , Gloucester is in a crouching position." Possibly, however, the blind Gloucester, having been positioned "within a foot / of th' extreme verge" and still holding Edgar's hand, is instinctively stooping or crouching to feel for the cliff's edge, and Edgar is gently raising him to prevent him from discovering that there is none. Once Edgar releases Gloucester's hand and steps away, Gloucester kneels, confident of where he is and ready to plunge forward.

CHAPTER 9—STAGING DECISIVE MOMENTS

1. *Twelfth Night,* ed. Elizabeth Story Donno, The New Cambridge Shakespeare (Cambridge: Cambridge University Press, 1998), 78, note to 2.3.100, SD. Feste is taken to exit after saying, "Yes, by St. Anne, and ginger shall be hot i' th' mouth too." (Ginger was considered to be an aphrodisiac.)

2. Gurr, *Shakespearean Stage,* 242; and Gurr, *William Shakespeare,* 182.

3. Anthony Arlidge, *Shakespeare and the Prince of Love* (London: Giles de la Mare, 2000), 26. This book provides information on John Manningham, a fourth-year student at the Middle Temple, who recorded the February 2, 1602, performance in his diary; on Christmas revels at the Middle Temple; and on the connection between the Middle Temple and London's theatrical life in Shakespeare's day.

4. Hodges, *Enter the Whole Army,* 142–43. For hall screens and tiring-house facades, see Gurr, *Shakespearean Stage,* 23.

5. Arlidge, *Shakespeare,* 118–21.

6. Ibid., 118.

7. Ibid., 119.

8. *Twelfth Night,* ed. Story Donno, The New Cambridge Shakespeare, 80, note to 2.3.157, and 90, notes to 2.5.72–73.

9. Ibid., 92, note to 2.5.107–8.

10. *Troilus and Cressida,* ed. Dawson, The New Cambridge Shakespeare, 6–9.

11. For a sensitive study of Cressida, see *Troilus and Cressida,* ed. Dawson, The New Cambridge Shakespeare, 27–32.

12. Reproduced in full in *Troilus and Cressida,* ed. Dawson, The New Cambridge Shakespeare, 73–74.

13. Useful notes to Troilus's thoughts are to be found in *Troilus and Cressida,* ed. Dawson, The New Cambridge Shakespeare, 212–13; *Troilus and Cressida,* ed. Palmer, The Arden Shakespeare, 276–79; and *Troilus and Cressida,* ed. Anne Barton, The Riverside Shakespeare, 2nd ed. (Boston: Houghton Mifflin, 1997), 520.

14. *Troilus and Cressida,* ed. Dawson, The New Cambridge Shakespeare, 231, note to 5.11(sic).21–22, and 232, note to 5.11(sic).30–31.

15. The Riverside Shakespeare, 2nd ed., p. 1967. Forman's notes on *Macbeth, Cymbeline,* and *The Winter's Tale* are reproduced in full 1966–68.

CHAPTER 10—PROLOGUES AND CHORUSES

1. *The Two Noble Kinsmen,* ed. Hallett Smith, The Riverside Shakespeare, 2nd ed. (Boston: Houghton Mifflin, 1997), 1690.

2. *King Henry VIII,* ed. John Margeson, The New Cambridge Shakespeare (Cambridge: Cambridge University Press, 1990), 4–14.

3. Thomas Heywood, *The Foure Prentises of London,* vol. 2, *The Dramatic Works of Thomas Heywood* (New York: Russell and Russell, 1964), 165. Date of publication from Gurr, *Shakespearean Stage,* 236. In *Staging in Shakespeare's Theatres,* Gurr and Ichikawa write of three knocks to announce the Prologue or the arrival of the first actors onstage (6).

4. Heywood, *The Foure Prentises of London,* 165.

5. Thomas Dekker, *The Guls Horn-Booke,* vol. 2, *The Non-Dramatic Works of Thomas Dekker,* ed. Alexander B. Grosart (New York: Russell and Russell, 1963), 250.

6. *The Second Part of King Henry IV,* ed. Melchiori, The New Cambridge Shakespeare, 59, note to induction, 0 SD.

7. Ibid., 3 and 33–36.

8. *Romeo and Juliet,* ed. Blakemore Evans, The New Cambridge Shakespeare, 28; and Gurr, *Shakespearean Stage,* 182.

9. *Romeo and Juliet,* ed. Blakemore Evans, The New Cambridge Shakespeare, 88, note to 1.5.144–57.

10. *Samuel Johnson on Shakespeare,* 236.

11. *Romeo and Juliet,* ed. Jill L. Levenson, The Oxford Shakespeare (Oxford: Oxford University Press, 2000), 202, note to 2.0.14. For Levenson's consideration of Juliet's "defection" and its consequences, see 38–41.

12. *King Henry V,* ed. Gurr, The New Cambridge Shakespeare, 1–6. Gurr writes, "We are unlikely ever to know for sure whether *Henry V*'s Prologue was written either to celebrate the opening [of the Globe] or to lament the older venue" (6).

13. Cf. ibid., 72, notes to 1.0.32–33 and 1.0.33.

14. For a detailed discussion of the Chorus, see *King Henry V,* ed. Gurr, The New Cambridge Shakespeare, 6–16.

15. Ibid., 90, note to 2.0.9–11.

16. Ibid., 91, note to 2.0.30, and 92, note to 2.0.41. The conjectural emendation is attributed to Peter Blayney.

17. *Pericles,* ed. DelVecchio and Hammond, The New Cambridge Shakespeare, 1 and 16–17.

18. Levi, *Life and Times,* 296.

19. *Pericles,* ed. DelVecchio and Hammond, The New Cambridge Shakespeare, 196, supplementary note on 5.1.231 SD 2 ("DIANA *descends from the heavens*").

20. Levi, *Life and Times,* 296. For a discussion of the play's authorship, see *Pericles,* ed. DelVecchio and Hammond, The New Cambridge Shakespeare, 8–15.

21. A map is provided in *Pericles,* ed. DelVecchio and Hammond, The New Cambridge Shakespeare, xiv. Correctly, it does not locate Pentapolis in North Africa.

22. *English Verse, 1300–1500,* ed. John Burrow (London: Longman Group, 1977), 234–35. For Shakespeare's sources, see *Pericles,* ed. DelVecchio and Hammond, The New Cambridge Shakespeare, 1–8.

Bibliography

SHAKESPEARE PLAYS

The Arden Shakespeare

All's Well That Ends Well. Ed. G. K. Hunter. The Arden Shakespeare. London: Methuen, 1959. Reprint, Walton-on-Thames, UK: Thomas Nelson and Sons, 1998.

As You Like It. Ed. Agnes Latham. The Arden Shakespeare. London: Methuen, 1975. Reprint, Walton-on-Thames, UK: Thomas Nelson and Sons, 1997.

The Comedy of Errors. Ed. R. A. Foakes. The Arden Shakespeare. London: Methuen, 1962, and as a University Paperback, 1968. Reprint, London: Routledge, 1988.

Coriolanus. Ed. Philip Brockbank. The Arden Shakespeare. London: Methuen, 1976. Reprint, London: Routledge, 1996.

Cymbeline. Ed. J. M. Nosworthy. The Arden Shakespeare. London: Methuen, 1955. Reprint, Walton-on-Thames, UK: Thomas Nelson and Sons, 1998.

Hamlet. Ed. Harold Jenkins. The Arden Shakespeare. London: Methuen, 1982. Reprint, Walton-on-Thames, UK: Thomas Nelson and Sons, 1997.

Julius Caesar. Ed. David Daniell. The Arden Shakespeare. Walton-on-Thames, UK: Thomas Nelson and Sons, 1998.

King Henry IV, Part One. Ed. A. R. Humphreys. The Arden Shakespeare. London: Methuen, 1960. Reprint, Walton-on-Thames, UK: Thomas Nelson and Sons, 1997.

King Henry IV, Part Two. Ed. A. R. Humphreys. The Arden Shakespeare. London: Methuen, 1966. Reprint, Walton-on-Thames, UK: Thomas Nelson and Sons, 1999.

King Henry V. Ed. T. W. Craik. The Arden Shakespeare. London: Routledge, 1995. Reprint, Walton-on-Thames, UK: Thomas Nelson and Sons, 1998.

King Henry VIII. Ed. R. A. Foakes. The Arden Shakespeare. London: Methuen, 1957. Reprint, Walton-on-Thames, UK: Thomas Nelson and Sons, 1997.

King John. Ed. E. A. J. Honigmann. The Arden Shakespeare. London: Methuen, 1954. Reprint, Walton-on-Thames, UK: Thomas Nelson and Sons, 1998.

King Lear. Ed. R. A. Foakes. The Arden Shakespeare. Walton-on-Thames, UK: Thomas Nelson and Sons, 1997.

King Richard II. Ed. Peter Ure. The Arden Shakespeare. London: Methuen. Reprint, Walton-on-Thames, UK: Thomas Nelson and Sons, 1956.

King Richard III. Ed. Antony Hammond. The Arden Shakespeare. London: Methuen, 1981. Reprint, Walton-on-Thames, UK: Thomas Nelson and Sons, 1997.

Love's Labour's Lost. Ed. H. R. Woudhuysen. The Arden Shakespeare. Walton-on-Thames, UK: Thomas Nelson and Sons, 1998.

Macbeth. Ed. Kenneth Muir. The Arden Shakespeare. London: Methuen, 1951. Reprint, Walton-on-Thames, UK: Thomas Nelson and Sons, 1999.

Measure for Measure. Ed. J. W. Lever. The Arden Shakespeare. London: Methuen, 1965. Reprint, Walton-on-Thames, UK: Thomas Nelson and Sons, 1998.

The Merchant of Venice. Ed. John Russell Brown. The Arden Shakespeare. London: Methuen, 1955. Reprint, Walton-on-Thames, UK: Thomas Nelson and Sons, 1997.

A Midsummer Night's Dream. Ed. Harold F. Brooks. The Arden Shakespeare. London: Methuen, 1979. Reprint, Walton-on-Thames, UK: Thomas Nelson and Sons, 1997.

Pericles. Ed. F. D. Hoeniger. The Arden Shakespeare. London: Methuen, 1963. Reprint, Walton-on-Thames, UK: Thomas Nelson and Sons, 1998.

The Taming of the Shrew. Ed. Brian Morris. The Arden Shakespeare. London: Methuen, 1981. Reprint, Walton-on-Thames, UK: Thomas Nelson and Sons, 1997.

Timon of Athens. Ed. H. J. Oliver. The Arden Shakespeare. London: Methuen, 1959. Reprint, Walton-on-Thames, UK: Thomas Nelson and Sons, 1997.

Troilus and Cressida. Ed. Kenneth Palmer. The Arden Shakespeare. London: Methuen, 1982. Reprint, Walton-on-Thames, UK: Thomas Nelson and Sons, 1997.

Twelfth Night. Ed. J. M. Lothian and T. W. Craik. The Arden Shakespeare. London: Methuen, 1975. Reprint, Walton-on-Thames, UK: Thomas Nelson and Sons, 1997.

The Two Gentlemen of Verona. Ed. Clifford Leech. The Arden Shakespeare. London: Methuen, 1969. Reprint, Walton-on-Thames, UK: Thomas Nelson and Sons, 1998.

The Two Noble Kinsmen. Ed. Lois Potter. The Arden Shakespeare. Walton-on-Thames, UK: Thomas Nelson and Sons, 1997.

The Winter's Tale. Ed. J. H. P. Pafford. The Arden Shakespeare. London: Methuen, 1963, and as a University Paperback, 1966. Reprint, London: Routledge, 1996.

The New Cambridge Shakespeare

All's Well That Ends Well. Ed. Russell Fraser. The New Cambridge Shakespeare. Cambridge: Cambridge University Press, 1985. Reprint, 1989.

Antony and Cleopatra. Ed. David Bevington. The New Cambridge Shakespeare. Cambridge: Cambridge University Press, 1990. Reprint, 1995.

As You Like It. Ed. Michael Hattaway. The New Cambridge Shakespeare. Cambridge: Cambridge University Press, 2000.

The Comedy of Errors. Ed. T. S. Dorsch. The New Cambridge Shakespeare. Cambridge: Cambridge University Press, 1988. Reprint, 1994.

Coriolanus. Ed. Lee Bliss. The New Cambridge Shakespeare. Cambridge: Cambridge University Press, 2000.

The First Part of King Henry IV. Ed. Herbert Weil and Judith Weil. The New Cambridge Shakespeare. Cambridge: Cambridge University Press, 1997.

The First Part of King Henry VI. Ed. Michael Hattaway. The New Cambridge Shakespeare. Cambridge: Cambridge University Press, 1990.

Hamlet. Ed. Philip Edwards. The New Cambridge Shakespeare. Cambridge: Cambridge University Press, 1985. Reprint, 1998.

Julius Caesar. Ed. Marvin Spevack. The New Cambridge Shakespeare. Cambridge: Cambridge University Press, 1988. Reprint, 1989.

King Edward III. Ed. Giorgio Melchiori. The New Cambridge Shakespeare. Cambridge: Cambridge University Press, 1998.

King Henry V. Ed. Andrew Gurr. The New Cambridge Shakespeare. Cambridge: Cambridge University Press, 1992. Reprint, 1995.

King Henry VIII. Ed. John Margeson. The New Cambridge Shakespeare. Cambridge: Cambridge University Press, 1990.

King John. Ed. L. A. Beaurline. The New Cambridge Shakespeare. Cambridge: Cambridge University Press, 1990.

King Richard II. Ed. Andrew Gurr. The New Cambridge Shakespeare. Cambridge: Cambridge University Press, 1984. Reprint, 1996.

King Richard III. Ed. Janis Lull. The New Cambridge Shakespeare. Cambridge: Cambridge University Press, 1999.

Macbeth. Ed. A. R. Braunmuller. The New Cambridge Shakespeare. Cambridge: Cambridge University Press, 1997. Reprint, 1999.

Measure for Measure. Ed. Brian Gibbons. The New Cambridge Shakespeare. Cambridge: Cambridge University Press, 1991.

The Merchant of Venice. Ed. M. M. Mahood. The New Cambridge Shakespeare. Cambridge: Cambridge University Press, 1987. Reprint, 1998.

The Merry Wives of Windsor. Ed. David Crane. The New Cambridge Shakespeare. Cambridge: Cambridge University Press, 1997.

A Midsummer Night's Dream. Ed. R. A. Foakes. The New Cambridge Shakespeare. Cambridge: Cambridge University Press, 1984. Reprint, 1997.

Much Ado about Nothing. Ed. F. H. Mares. The New Cambridge Shakespeare. Cambridge: Cambridge University Press, 1988. Reprint, 1991.

Othello. Ed. Norman Sanders. The New Cambridge Shakespeare. Cambridge: Cambridge University Press, 1984. Reprint, 1998.

Pericles. Ed. Doreen DelVecchio and Antony Hammond. The New Cambridge Shakespeare. Cambridge: Cambridge University Press, 1998.

Romeo and Juliet. Ed. G. Blakemore Evans. The New Cambridge Shakespeare. Cambridge: Cambridge University Press, 1984; revised 1997. Reprint, 1998.

The Second Part of King Henry IV. Ed. Giorgio Melchiori. The New Cambridge Shakespeare. Cambridge: Cambridge University Press, 1989.

The Second Part of King Henry VI. Ed. Michael Hattaway. The New Cambridge Shakespeare. Cambridge: Cambridge University Press, 1991.

The Taming of the Shrew. Ed. Ann Thompson. The New Cambridge Shakespeare. Cambridge: Cambridge University Press, 1984. Reprint, 1988.

The Tempest. Ed. David Lindley. The New Cambridge Shakespeare. Cambridge: Cambridge University Press, 2002. Reprint, 2003.

The Third Part of King Henry VI. Ed. Michael Hattaway. The New Cambridge Shakespeare. Cambridge: Cambridge University Press, 1993.

Timon of Athens. Ed. Karl Klein. The New Cambridge Shakespeare. Cambridge: Cambridge University Press, 2001.

Titus Andronicus. Ed. Alan Hughes. The New Cambridge Shakespeare. Cambridge: Cambridge University Press, 1994.

The Tragedy of King Lear. Ed. Jay L. Halio. The New Cambridge Shakespeare. Cambridge: Cambridge University Press, 1992. Reprint, 1997.

Troilus and Cressida. Ed. Anthony B. Dawson. The New Cambridge Shakespeare. Cambridge: Cambridge University Press, 2003.

Twelfth Night. Ed. Elizabeth Story Donno. The New Cambridge Shakespeare. Cambridge: Cambridge University Press, 1985; revised 1998.

The Two Gentlemen of Verona. Ed. Kurt Schlueter. The New Cambridge Shakespeare. Cambridge: Cambridge University Press, 1990.

The Oxford Shakespeare

Coriolanus. Ed. R. B. Parker. The Oxford Shakespeare. Oxford: Oxford University Press, 1994. Reissued, 1998.

King Richard III. Ed. John Jowett. The Oxford Shakespeare. Oxford: Oxford University Press, 2000.

Measure for Measure. Ed. N. W. Bawcutt. The Oxford Shakespeare. Oxford: Oxford University Press, 1991.

The Merry Wives of Windsor. Ed. T. W. Craik. The Oxford Shakespeare. Oxford: Oxford University Press, 1990.

Romeo and Juliet. Ed. Jill L. Levenson. The Oxford Shakespeare. Oxford: Oxford University Press, 2000.

The Tempest. Ed. Stephen Orgel. The Oxford Shakespeare. Oxford: Oxford University Press, 1987. Reissued, 1998.

Troilus and Cressida. Ed. Kenneth Muir. The Oxford Shakespeare. Oxford: Oxford University Press, 1982.

The Winter's Tale. Ed. Stephen Orgel. The Oxford Shakespeare. Oxford: Oxford University Press, 1996.

Other Shakespeare Works

Mr. William Shakespeares Comedies, Histories, & Tragedies. Facsimile of the First Folio edition. Prepared by Helge Koekeritz and Charles Tyler Prouty. New Haven: Yale University Press, 1954. Reprint, 1955.

The Riverside Shakespeare. 2nd ed. Ed. G. Blakemore Evans (general editor), J. J. M. Tobin (assistant general editor), and Herschel Baker, Anne Barton, Frank Kermode, Harry Levin, Hallett Smith, and Marie Edel. Essays by Heather Dubrow, William T. Liston, and Charles H. Shattuck. Boston: Houghton Mifflin, 1997.

"The Sonnets" and "A Lover's Complaint." Ed. John Kerrigan. The New Penguin Shakespeare. London: Penguin Books, 1986.

OTHER WORKS

Aristotle. *Poetics.* Trans. and ed. Kenneth A. Telford. Chicago: Henry Regnery, 1961. Reprint, 1968.

Arlidge, Anthony. *Shakespeare and the Prince of Love.* London: Giles de la Mare, 2000.

Bate, Jonathan. *The Genius of Shakespeare.* London: Picador, 1997.

Bindoff, S. T. *Tudor England.* Harmondsworth, UK: Penguin Books, 1950. Reprint, 1966.

Blayney, Peter W. M. *The First Folio of Shakespeare.* Washington, DC: Folger Library Publications, 1991.

Burrow, John, ed. *English Verse, 1300–1500.* London: Longman Group, 1977.

Christenbury, Leila. "Problems with *Othello* in the High School Classroom." In *Teaching Shakespeare into the Twenty-First Century,* ed. Ronald E. Salomone and James E. Davis, 182–90. Athens: Ohio University Press, 1997.

Crystal, David, and Ben Crystal. *Shakespeare's Words.* London: Penguin Books, 2002.

Dekker, Thomas. *The Non-Dramatic Works of Thomas Dekker.* Vol. 2, ed. Alexander B. Grosart. New York: Russell and Russell, 1963.

Dessen, Alan C., and Thomson, Leslie. *A Dictionary of Stage Directions in English Drama, 1580–1642.* Cambridge: Cambridge University Press, 1999.

The Geneva Bible. Madison: The University of Wisconsin Press, 1969.

Graves, Robert. *The White Goddess.* London: Faber and Faber, 1948. Reprint, 1962.

Gurr, Andrew. *Playgoing in Shakespeare's London.* 2nd ed. Cambridge: Cambridge University Press, 1996. Reprint, 1997.

———. *The Shakespearean Stage, 1574–1642.* 3rd ed. Cambridge: Cambridge University Press, 1992. Reprint, 1999.

———. *William Shakespeare.* New York: HarperCollins, 1995.

Gurr, Andrew, and Mariko Ichikawa. *Staging in Shakespeare's Theatres.* New York: Oxford University Press, 2000.

Gurr, Andrew, with John Orrell. *Rebuilding Shakespeare's Globe.* London: George Weidenfeld and Nicholson, 1989.

Halliday, F. E. *A Shakespeare Companion.* Harmondsworth, UK: Penguin Books, 1964. Reprint, 1969.

Harrison, G. B. *Introducing Shakespeare.* 3rd ed. Harmondsworth, UK: Penguin Books, 1966. Reprint, 1968.

Heywood, T. *The Dramatic Works of Thomas Heywood.* Vol. 2. New York: Russell and Russell, 1964.

Hodges, C. Walter. *Enter the Whole Army.* Cambridge: Cambridge University Press, 1999.

Holden, Anthony. *William Shakespeare: His Life and Work.* London: Little, Brown, 1999.

Honan, Park. *Shakespeare: A Life.* Oxford: Oxford University Press Paperback, 1999.

Johnson, Samuel. *Samuel Johnson on Shakespeare.* Ed. H. R. Woudhuysen. New Penguin Shakespeare Library. London: Penguin Books, 1989.

Joseph, B. L. *Shakespeare's Eden: The Commonwealth of England, 1558–1629.* London: Blandford Press, 1971.

Kastan, David Scott. *Shakespeare and the Book.* Cambridge: Cambridge University Press, 2001.

Kermode, Frank. *Shakespeare's Language.* London: Penguin Books, 2001.

Kiernan, Pauline. *Shakespeare's Theory of Drama.* Cambridge: Cambridge University Press, 1996.

Laroque, François. *Shakespeare's Festive World.* Cambridge: Cambridge University Press, 1991.

Levi, Peter. *The Life and Times of William Shakespeare.* London: Papermac, 1989. Reprint, 1991.

McLeish, Kenneth. *Aristotle.* London: Phoenix, 1998.

Onions, C. T. *A Shakespeare Glossary.* Rev. Robert D. Eagleson. Oxford: Oxford University Press, 1986. Reprint, 1991.

Partridge, Eric. *Shakespeare's Bawdy.* 3rd ed. London: Routledge, 1968.

Schmidt, Alexander. *Shakespeare Lexicon and Quotation Dictionary.* 3rd ed., vols. 1 and 2. Rev. George Sarrazin. New York: Dover Publications, 1971.

Schoenbaum, S. *Shakespeare's Lives.* Oxford: Oxford University Press, 1970.

———. *William Shakespeare: A Compact Documentary Life.* New York: Oxford University Press, 1977. Reprint, 1987.

Sidney, Sir Philip. *A Defence of Poetry.* Ed. J. A. Van Dorsten. London: Oxford University Press, 1966.

Spenser, Edmund. *Poetical Works.* Ed. J. C. Smith and E. de Selincourt. Oxford: Oxford University Press, 1970. Reprint, 1990.

Strachey, Lytton. *Elizabeth and Essex.* Harmondsworth, UK: Penguin Books, 1971.

Styan, J. L. *Shakespeare's Stagecraft.* Cambridge: Cambridge University Press, 1967.

FILM VERSIONS

Branagh, Kenneth, director. *Much Ado about Nothing.* Samuel Goldwyn Company and Renaissance Films, 1993.

Olivier, Laurence, director. *Henry V.* Two Cities/Laurence Olivier Production, 1944.

Polanski, Roman, director. *Macbeth.* Columbia Pictures Industries, and Playboy Entertainment Group, 1971.

Index

(Titles of Shakespeare's plays vary from publication to publication. For simplicity's sake, plays are referred to in the index and in the main part of this book by titles they have come to be known by in practice, e.g., *Henry IV, Part One*.)

Abraham, 85
"actors at work," 2–3
advance preparation of important events, 115–20
Agamemnon, 61, 88
Ajax, 61
alienation, 141
All's Well That Ends Well, 26, 27, 32, 33–35, 36–38, 52, 69, 77, 121, 131, 132, 135, 136, 137
  Bertram, Count of Rossillion, 32, 34, 36, 37–38, 52, 77, 121, 137; Countess of Rossillion, 27, 34–35; France, King of, 26, 37–38; Helena, 33–34, 37–38, 52, 77, 121, 136, 137; Lafew, 37; Widow, 135, 136
analogy, 102, 105, 106, 151–52
Antony and Cleopatra, 10, 17, 21, 28, 75–76, 91–92, 112
  Alexas, 76; Antony, Mark, 10, 28, 63, 75, 76, 91–92; Caesar, Octavius, 91, 112; Charmian, 10, 76; Cleopatra, Queen of Egypt, 10, 21, 75–76, 91–92; Domitius, 91–92; Enobarbus, Iras, 10; Octavia, 75, 76; Philo, 28
Aristotle, 38, 99
Arlidge, Anthony, 149, 150
Armin, Robert, 19
arras, viii, 5–7, 8, 11–12, 13, 181
Arthur (malapropism for Abraham), 84, 85
As You Like It, 15, 16, 18, 19, 21, 27, 40, 78, 110, 111, 141
  Adam, 18, 19, 27, 40; Celia, 21; Hymen, 15; Jaques, 16, 78; Orlando, 18, 27, 141; Rosalind, 21, 111, 141; Senior, Duke, 18; Touchstone, 19
aside(s), 5, 14, 127, 159, 160, 163, 167
ass(es), 7, 32, 65, 78, 81, 118, 148, 152; assified, 48. *See also* folly
association(s), 49, 51, 78, 98, 99, 100, 105–7, 108, 111, 112, 176. *See also* time(s)
attention, taking risks with the audience's, 121, 122–27, 188ch7n9
authority, parental and marital, 120–22, 188ch8n1
avenging. *See* revenge; vengeance; vengefulness

Bacon, Sir Edmund, 17
balconies and balcony, 4, 5, 9–12, 15, 53
bell, 46, 53, 103, 159
Bible(s), 25, 98, 113, 114; Bishops', 25; Geneva, 25, 113–14, 135; Ecclesiasticus, 113; Exodus, 137, 138; Gospel, St. Matthew's, 25, 114; Proverbs, 113–14, 135; Psalms, 113; Revelations, 135
Bindoff, T., 121–22
Blackfriars, The, 18, 56, 168
Blakemore Evans, G., 171
bookkeeper, 1, 3–4
boy actors, 10, 16, 19, 20–23, 30, 34, 53, 94, 102, 136, 160, 163
Branagh, Kenneth, 93
Brooke, Arthur, 47
Burbage, Richard, 19, 29

Cain, 13
Campbell, Thomas, 55

cannon(s), 15, 16–18, 88, 176; cannoneer, 14, 16

canopy, viii, 5, 13, 14–15, 16; also known as "heavens," 5, 12, 15, 16, 17, 177. *See also* Globe, The

Carroll, Lewis, 188ch7n9

central opening, viii, 5, 11–12, 15, 177-78, 181

characteristic(s), 5, 29, 35, 62, 63, 74, 79, 84, 106, 119, 124, 140, 155

characterization, 60–80; complementary, 63, 65; evildoer(s), 63, 64–67; issues, in relation to, 63; "just representations of general nature," 63, 77; names, 25, 26, 62, 67, 78, 109, 113, 116, 178; personalizing abstractions, 61–62, 64; plays on words, 78–79; in scenes not shown, 82–83; self-discovery, 67–73; self-knowing characters, 63–64; small details, 77; ways of speaking, 73–76, 79–80. *See also* entrances: rank, character, and situation

chorus(es), 88, 94, 129, 166–82

clock(s), 31, 98, 100–101, 102–3, 109, 110, 111, 112, 161

Comedy of Errors, The, 20, 27, 111
Egeon of Syracusa, 27; Ephesus, Duke of, 27; Pinch, Dr., 20

"cool reason," 60–61, 105–6, 141

Coriolanus, 2, 15–16, 28, 33, 56, 63, 91, 116
Aufidius, Tullus, 15–16, 63; Citizen, Third, 33; Coriolanus, Caius Martius, 2, 28, 33, 63, 71, 91; Coriolanus's mother (Volumnia), 91; Menenius, 2, 33; tribunes, 63 (Brutus, Junius, 33; Velutus, Sicinius, 33)

Cowley, Richard, 19

Cox, Paul, 17

Craik, T. W., 133

Curtain, The, 168, 169, 172–73, 175

Cymbeline, 9, 15, 18, 20, 23, 27, 62, 83, 112, 131, 132, 135, 136, 138, 142, 143, 144, 178
Arviragus (Cadwal), 23; Belarius, 20; Cloten, 18; Gentleman, First, 27; Gentleman, Second, 27; Guiderius (Polydore), 23, 62; Imogen, 9, 18, 20, 112, 135, 138, 143 (Fidele, 23); Jachimo, 9, 112; Jupiter,

15, 83; Pisanio, 135, 136, 142, 143, 144, 145, 146; Posthumus's father (Leonatus, Sicilius), 83

damnation, 13

darkening: of face, 186ch4n5; of sun, 108; of woes, 46

darkness, 4, 12, 36, 98, 99, 100, 107, 112, 137 and *passim;* bed tricks, 137; bringing light to, 106; Cassius's recruitment of Casca, 128–29; choric authority, 174; Duncan's murder, 93; onstage, 128; and uncertain time, 101–3. *See also* evil: *Macbeth;* night: midnight; time: associations

death(s), 21, 29, 66, 70, 77, 93, 114, 120 and *passim;* an enigma, 112–13; apparent, 43, 58, 67, 135, 136, 179, 180; Constance's praise of, 74–75; of Falstaff and Ophelia, 84–85; Hector's, at sunset, 107–9, 159; imagery of, 47; imitated in *The Winter's Tale,* 6; intended for Desdemona, 38; intended for Polixenes, 159; a living dead man, 20; murder, 64; natural, 39, 40–41; news of Hotspur's, 168–9; Ophelia's grave, 13; outstanding, 53–54; in *Pericles,* 178, 180, 181; Polonius's, 47–48; premature, 39; in *Romeo and Juliet,* 169–70; staging of, 137–42; of Suffolk and York, 94–95; in *Twelfth Night,* 18 and 28; variety of, 53. *See also* sun: sunset(s)

deathbed, 85, 171, 172

Dekker, Thomas, 167

Devereux, Robert, second Earl of Essex, 77

devil(s), 15, 31, 38, 39, 60, 66, 114; "devilish," 176

de Witt, Johannes, viii, ix

dialogue instead of onstage action, 96

dialogue instead of props or special lighting, 4

discovery space, 4, 5, 6–9

disguise(d), 20, 21, 47, 92, 93, 131, 137, 143

dividing the playing area: letter scene in *Twelfth Night,* 147–52; observation scene in *Troilus and Cressida,* 152–59 door(s), flanking, viii, 1, 11, 14, 15, 34, 49, 128, 149, 160, 177, 181; doorways, flanking, 2, 5

Drury Lane theater, 63

Edward III, 88–89
    Boheme, King of, 88; Edward III, King, 88; Edward, Prince of Wales, 88, 89; John II, King of France, 88; Mariner, 88, 89

Elizabeth I, Queen, 77, 85

entrances, 1–2, 24–41 and *passim;* naming of characters, 26, 124–25; naming of places, 26–27; of new characters late in a play, 32, 124–25; rank, character, and situation, 24–26, 27–32, 124–25; returns of known characters, 32–41, 125–27

evil, 69, 112, 116; in *Macbeth,* 83–84, 99–100, 127; Mark Antony, 120; perpetrators and victims, 64–65; predominance of, 43–44; repentance, 66–67; and self-knowledge, 63–64; and trapdoor, 12, 13. *See also* characterization: evildoers; darkness

exits, 2, 42–59; aborted, 57–58; commands, 48–51; dialogue, implied by, 42; and emotions, 51–52; having more to them than is apparent at first sight, 43–44; masterly, 43; outstanding, 51, 53–54; perfunctory, 42–43, 58; Prospero's from *The Tempest,* 55–57; royal, 50; serving practicalities of staging, 44–46; serving practicalities of the plot, 43–44, 46–48, 125; wide range of, 51–52, 53, 58–59

facade, tiring-house, viii, 2, 5, 8, 14, 34, 49, 118, 149, 160

firecrackers, 18, 83, 181

flag, viii, 5, 12, 16. *See also* Globe, The

Fletcher, John, 166, 167

folly, 39, 154

fool(s), 32, 36, 65, 79, 80, 107, 112, 119, 154, 155; foolishness, 30, 39, 65, 79, 80, 151. *See also* ass; folly

Forman, Dr. Simon, 159–60

Globe, The, 55–56, 168, 175; burning down, 17–18; central opening, 15;

Chorus in *Henry V,* 172ff; first protracted storm, 127–28; letter scene in *Twelfth Night,* 149ff; Leontes' denunciation of Hermione to Camillo, 159ff; newly opened, 16; observation scene in *Troilus and Cressida,* 152ff; and *Pericles,* 177ff. *See also* canopy; flag; jealousy: Leontes

Goffe, Robert, 19

Gower, John, 179, 180

Graves, Robert, 117

Gurr, Andrew, 13, 15, 18, 29, 149

Halio, Jay L., 138

Hamlet, 6, 13, 14–15, 16, 17, 26, 46, 47–48, 57, 62, 85, 89, 98, 100–101, 112, 113, 138, 140, 141, 167
    Barnardo, 100; Claudius, King of Denmark, 6, 13, 14–15, 16, 17, 26, 47–48, 62, 73, 89; Gertrude, Queen of Denmark, 6, 13, 48, 85; Ghost, 13, 17, 89, 101; Hamlet, Prince of Denmark, 6, 13, 14, 15, 16, 17, 19, 22, 23, 48, 56, 57, 73, 77, 89–90, 100–101, 112, 113, 138, 167; Hamlet's father, 13, 16, 89, 100; Horatio, 13–14, 17, 100–101; Laertes, 13, 14, 46, 47–48; Marcellus, 17, 100–101; Ophelia, 13–14, 46, 47, 48, 85, 138, 167; Players, 22, 167; Polonius, 6, 46, 47, 73; Prologue, 167; Yorick, 13, 113

Harrison, G. B., 77, 132

Hattaway, Michael, 12

"heavens." *See* canopy

hell, 12, 13, 45, 53, 60, 65, 84, 100, 114, 144

Henry IV, Part One, 6, 9, 11, 30–32, 36, 45, 49–50, 51, 53, 57, 62, 77, 79, 85, 87, 104, 109, 110, 115, 118–19, 133, 168
    Blunt, Sir Walter, 50; Falstaff, Sir John, 6, 19, 30–31, 32, 36, 53, 62, 77, 85, 87, 109, 110, 118; Francis, 109; Glendower, Owen, 9, 119; Hal, Prince (Henry, Prince of Wales and Crown Prince), 6, 30–32, 36, 53, 62, 77, 79, 118–19, 133; Henry IV, King, 45, 49–50, 53, 57, 104; Hostess, 21, 36, 85; Hotspur (Percy,

Henry IV, Part One (continued)
Henry), 50, 53, 54, 57, 110, 115,
118–19; Mortimer, Edmund, Earl of
March, 9; Mortimer, Lady, 9;
Northumberland, Earl of, 57, 119;
Percy, Lady, 119; Peto, 36, 77; Poins,
87; Sheriff, 6; Westmerland, Earl of,
49; Worcester, Earl of, 49–50, 57,
119
Henry IV, Part Two, 9, 11, 18, 20, 31–32, 36,
85, 101, 109, 112–13, 166, 168, 169,
172–73
Bardolph, Lord, 169; Beadle, 20;
Falstaff, Sir John, 18, 19, 20, 31–32,
36, 62, 85, 101, 109, 112; Hal, Prince
(Henry, afterwards King Henry V),
31–32, 36, 169; Henry IV, King
(Harry), 168–69; Justice, Lord
Chief, 112; Northumberland, Earl
of, 168, 169; Poins, 109; Rumor
(Presenter), 166, 168–69, 172;
Rushes, Strewers of, 9; Shadow, 20;
Shallow, 101, 112–13; Silence,
112–13; Tearsheet, Doll, 20
Henry V, 11–12, 31, 32, 36, 52, 73, 84–85,
88, 92, 94–97, 110, 156, 166, 167,
172–77, 17
Ambassador, French, 110; Bar-
dolph, 172, 177; Bates, 94; Bedford,
Duke of, 96; Boy, 94; Burgundy,
Duke of, 176; Charles VI, King of
France, 175; Chorus, 12, 95, 166,
172–77, 179; Citizens, 11–12; Ex-
eter, Duke of, 12, 94–95; Falstaff,
Sir John, 19, 32, 36, 62, 84–85;
Fluellen, 32, 36, 94, 95; France,
Constable of, 94, 96; Gower, 95;
Grandpré, 96–97; Hal, Prince
(Monmouth, Harry), 32, 36;
Harfleur, Governor of, 12; Henry
V, King, 11–12, 52, 94–96, 97,
174–75, 176, 177; Henry VI, King,
175; Hostess, 21, 84–85; Katherine,
175–76; Montjoy, 94, 95; Nym,
172, 177; Orleance, Duke of, 96;
Pistol, 94, 156, 177; Salisbury, Earl
of, 96; Suffolk, Earl of, 94–95;
Williams, 94; York, Duke of, 94–95

Henry VI, Part One, 12, 17, 175
Talbot, 17
Henry VI, Part Three, 12, 20, 29, 175
Keeper, First, 20; Richard (after-
ward Gloucester, Duke of), 29
Henry VI, Part Two, 4, 12, 127, 175
Henry VIII, 17–18, 56, 122, 166–67
Henry VIII, King, 17–18; Katherine,
Queen, 122; Wolsey, Cardinal, 17–18
Hercules (Heracles), 16
Heywood, Thomas, 167
Hodges, C. Walter, 17, 149–50
hut, viii, 5

Ichikawa, Mariko, 13, 15

jealousy: Bianca, 127; Claudio (*Much Ado
about Nothing*), 65, 78, 93; Cleopatra,
76; defective judgement, 49; Dionyza,
178; Ford, 65; Leontes, 54, 62, 159ff;
Othello, 38, 62, 65, 90; sexual, 29. *See
also* Globe, The: Leontes' denunciation
Johnson, Samuel, 63, 77, 122, 171–72
Jonson, Ben, 177
Julius Caesar, 3, 27, 47, 51, 53, 101–2, 110,
115, 127–29, 141
Antony, Mark, 54, 119, 120; Brutus,
Decius, 120; Brutus, Marcus, 47,
54, 101–2, 115, 119–20; Caesar,
Julius, 53, 54, 71, 101–2, 110, 119,
120, 128, 129; Casca, 127–29; Cassius, 47, 101–2, 119–120, 128–29;
Cicero, 128, 129; Flavius, 27; Lu-
cius, 47, 101; Murellus, 3

Kemp(e), Will, 2, 19, 23
King John, 20, 53, 74–75, 111
Arthur, Duke of Britain, 53; Constance, 74–75; Elinor, Queen, 75;
Faulconbridge, Robert, 20
King Lear, 19, 39–41, 49–50, 64, 66, 73–74,
77, 91, 112, 127, 131, 132, 137–42
Cordelia, 39, 40–41, 66, 74; Cornwall, Duke of, 138; Edgar, 41, 66,
137–42; Edmund, 64, 65, 66, 67;
Fool, 19; Gentleman, 40; Goneril,
73–74; Gloucester, Earl of, 66, 77,
137–42; Kent, Earl of, 40–41, 112;

Lear, King of Britain, 19, 38, 39–41, 49–50, 73–74, 112, 141; Man, Old, 138; Oswald, 49–50; Regan, 74, 112, 138

ladder, rope 10, 47
leading, verbal 47
Levenson, Jill L., 47, 172
Levi, Peter, 116, 132–33, 178
light(s), viii, 4, 10, 103, 106–7, 129, 139, 174, 181; candlelight, 4, 12, 149; daylight, viii, 4, 99; fading, 105, 107; failing, 107; lightening, 46; moonlight, 4, 5, 103, 117, 141, 142; starlight, 103; taper light, 180; thickening, 106–7
lighting, 4–5
lightning, 15, 128. *See also* storm(s) and thunder
likelihood, 38, 39
literalism, 1, 4, 118
lords' rooms, viii, 5, 10
Love's Labor's Lost, 19, 27, 112
Berowne, 27; Costard, 19; Dumaine, 27; Longaville, 27; Navarre, King of, 27

Macbeth, 6, 12–13, 15, 25, 45–46, 50–51, 52–53, 63, 82, 83–84, 87, 89, 91, 92, 93–94, 98–100, 102–3, 105, 107, 110, 112, 127, 167
Angus, 25, 98; Apparition, Third, 12; Banquo, 50, 63, 64, 82, 87, 98, 99, 102–3, 106; Doctor (Scots), 63; Donalbain, 82, 83, 98; Duncan, King of Scotland, 45, 51, 52–53, 64, 83–84, 92, 93, 98–100, 103; Fleance, 64, 87, 102–3, 106; Lennox, 50, 83, 98; Macbeth (later king), 12–13, 25, 45–46, 50–51, 52–53, 64, 71, 82, 83–84, 89, 93–94, 98, 99, 100, 102–3, 106–7, 110, 112; Macbeth, Lady (later queen), 45–46, 50–51, 53, 62, 63, 84, 93, 99, 100, 138; Macduff, 12–13, 45–46, 63, 64, 82, 89, 98; Malcolm, 82, 83, 98; Porter, 45–46; Rosse, 25, 50, 82–83, 98; Sergeant, 82–83; Sisters, Weïrd, 12, 63, 102 (Witches, 12, 83)

make-believe, 135, 137, 139, 140, 180
marriage, 121–22; forced, 122, 132–33
McLeish, Kenneth, 99, 106, 107
Measure for Measure, 15, 24–26, 27–28, 64, 67, 68–71, 78, 112, 114, 131, 132, 135, 136–37, 143
Angelo (deputy), 24–26, 27–28, 64, 67, 68–71, 114, 135, 136, 137; Claudio, 137; Escalus, 24–26, 69, 70, 78, 79; Isabella, 68–69, 70, 114, 135, 136, 137, 143; Mariana, 69, 136, 137; Pompey, 70; Provost, 70; Thomas, Friar, 136; Vincentio, Duke, 24–26, 69, 70, 135, 136–37, 143, 146
Menelaus, 61
Merchant of Venice, The, 52, 57, 133, 156
Portia, 57, 133; Lorenzo, 156; Shylock, 52, 57
Merry Wives of Windsor, The, 2, 6, 21, 30, 36–37, 48–49, 62, 65, 84, 109, 115–16, 122, 131–35, 167
Caius, Dr., 49, 115, 131, 133, 134; Evans, Sir Hugh, 30, 49, 115; Falstaff, Sir John, 2, 6, 19, 49, 62, 84, 167; Fenton, 65, 115–16, 122, 131–32, 133–34; Ford, Master Francis, 36, 37, 48, 49, 65, 134; Ford, Mistress Alice, 2, 48, 49, 167; Host, 115–16, 131–32; John, 48–49; Nym, 65; Page, Master George, 30, 49, 65, 116, 122, 132, 133, 134; Page, Mistress Anne, 30, 115–16, 122, 131, 132, 133, 134, 137; Page, Mistress Margaret, 2, 6, 49, 84, 116, 133, 134; Pistol, 65; Quickly, Mistress, 115; Robert, 48–49; Robin, 2, 49; Shallow, Robert, 133; Simple, Peter, 109, 115; Slender, Abraham, 21, 30, 62, 115, 131, 133, 134
Midsummer Night's Dream, A, 1–5, 7, 9, 13, 19–20, 21, 22, 26, 27, 42–43, 44, 48, 56, 57, 60–62, 68, 73, 78, 81–82, 104, 105–6, 115, 116–18, 120, 121, 122–23, 124, 135, 136, 140, 141–42, 147, 167
Bottom, 1, 2, 3, 4, 7, 9, 19–20, 42, 44, 45, 48, 56, 81, 104, 115, 117–18, 136, 142, 147 (Pyramus, 3, 4, 5, 20, 42, 56, 81, 118); Demetrius, 13, 26,

Midsummer Night's Dream, A (continued)
27, 43, 44, 121, 122, 123; Egeus, 26,
27, 43, 44, 122, 135; Flute, 1, 22, 78
(Thisby, 4, 5, 22, 42, 44, 118); Helena, 2, 13, 20, 21, 26, 43, 44, 121,
122–23; Hermia, 20, 21, 26, 27, 43,
44, 121, 122, 123; Hippolyta,
Queen of the Amazons, 4, 44, 60,
61, 117; Lysander, 21, 26, 27, 43, 44,
68, 122–23; Nedar, 121; Oberon,
King of the Fairies, 9, 13, 48, 57,
68, 81, 117, 118, 122; Philostrate,
Master of the Revels, 44, 73, 167;
Puck, 2, 7, 116–17, 118 (Goodfellow, Robin, 116–17, 118; Pouke,
116); Quince, 1, 2, 3, 4, 9, 19, 22,
26, 42, 56, 117, 118, 136, 147, 167
(Prologue, 19–20, 167); Snout, 1, 4
(Wall, 1, 4, 42); Snug, 1, 3, 4, 26, 82,
104, 118 (Lion, 3, 104, 118); Starveling, 1, 4, 5, 20 (Moonshine, 1, 4–5,
142); Theseus, Duke of Athens, 4,
26, 27, 43, 44, 60–61, 62, 73, 81, 82,
105–6, 117, 122, 135, 140, 167; Titania, Queen of the Fairies, 4, 9, 48,
57, 81, 115, 117, 118, 122
mimesis, 98, 99, 106
Mowbray, Sir Thomas, 85
Much Ado about Nothing, 6, 8, 13–14, 16,
19, 21–22, 27, 29–30, 32, 36–37, 43–44,
44–45, 57–58, 64, 66–67, 77, 78–79,
92–93, 104–5, 111, 116, 121, 122, 126,
131, 132, 135–36, 142, 143, 178
Antonio, 58, 93; Beatrice, 13–14,
16, 21–22, 58, 78, 121, 122; Benedick, 13, 14, 16, 19, 21–22, 43, 58,
79, 93, 122; Borachio, 6, 14, 32, 44,
58, 65, 66, 67, 79, 93, 116; Claudio,
6, 13, 32, 36, 37, 43, 44, 58, 64, 65,
66, 67, 77, 78, 79, 92, 93, 111, 116,
126, 136, 178; Conrade, 14, 58, 66,
67, 79, 116; Dogberry, 14, 19, 32,
44, 45, 58, 66, 78, 79; Francis, Friar,
32, 43, 135–36, 137, 142, 143, 144,
145, 146; Hero, 8, 14, 20, 21–22, 32,
43–45, 57, 67, 78, 79, 92, 93, 111,
116, 121, 122; Innogen, 121; John,
Don, 32, 43, 44, 64, 65, 66, 67, 93;

Leonato, Governor of Messina, 19,
22, 27, 30, 32, 43, 44–45, 57–58, 77,
78, 79, 93, 121, 122; Margaret, 93;
Pedro, Don, Prince of Arragon, 6,
13, 16, 27, 29–30, 32, 43, 44, 58, 65,
66, 67, 78, 79, 92, 93, 104, 116, 126,
136; Sexton, 58, 67; Ursula, 13, 14,
44; Verges, 14, 19, 44, 45, 79; Watch,
14, 32, 58, 66, 79, 116; Watchman,
Second, 14
music, 1, 15, 16, 18–19, 55, 110, 111, 177

narrative and drama, 177, 180–82
necessity, 38, 39, 40, 65
night(s), 27, 30, 35, 64, 74, 93, 98, 110, 147
and *passim;* dangerous and haunted,
101; dead of, 102; dead waste and middle of, 100; hell and, 65; seeling, 106;
the stocking of Kent, 112; thick, 100;
ugly, 108
nightcap, 169
nightgown, 45, 46

Olivier, Laurence, 94, 96, 97
Omphale, Queen of Lydia, 16
Othello, 5, 21, 32, 38–39, 64–65, 66, 83, 91,
120, 121, 122, 124–27, 136–37, 167
Bianca, 124–27, 137; Brabantio, 39,
90, 122; Cassio, 124–27, 137, 167;
Desdemona, 21, 38–39, 90–91, 121,
122, 124, 125, 126, 127; Emilia, 38,
127; Iago, 38–39, 64, 65, 66, 67, 90,
124–27, 136, 167; Gratiano, 39;
Montano, Governor of Cyprus,
167; Othello, 19, 38–39, 62, 64–65,
67, 90–91, 124–27, 137

parents, 121, 132, 134, 169–70, 171,
188ch8n1; parental authority, 121–22,
134
Penthesilea, 21
performance, writing for, 1–2
Pericles, 5, 15, 18–19, 32, 127, 166, 167,
177–82
Antiochus, Daughter of, 178, 180;
Antiochus, King of Antioch, 178,
180; Cerimon, 18, 178; Cleon,
Governor of Tharsus, 178, 181;

Diana, 15, 177–78, 179; Dionyza, 178–79, 181; Gower (Chorus), 177, 178, 179–82; Lysimachus, Governor of Mytilene, 179; Marina, 178–79, 181; Pericles, Prince of Tyre, 178–79, 180–81; Simonides, King of Pentapolis, 178; Thaisa, 18–19, 178, 179, 180

Phoebus, 104, 175, 176; Phibbus, 104

pig's blood, 45

place as a dramatic concept, 3

platform stage, viii, 5, 24, 29, 159, 160, 169

plot lines: convergence, 117–18; long, 115–16, 117–20, 121

Polanski, Roman, 93, 94

Pope, Thomas, 19

pride, 21, 22, 33, 58, 65, 79, 81; proud, 4, 32, 37, 40, 63, 75, 86, 87, 88

prologue(s), 19–20, 166–82; used instead of dialogue, 168

prop(s), 1, 3–4, 5, 13, 89, 136, 149, 150

purgatory, 13

"purpose of playing, the," 1, 19, 23, 57

revenge, 13, 35, 48, 89, 115, 147, 148, 152, 156, 157, 158, 159. See also vengeance; vengefulness

Richard II, 11, 31, 85–87, 133, 141
Aumerle, Duke of, 11; Bullingbrook, Henry, Duke of Herford and of Lancaster (afterward King Henry IV), 11, 31, 85–87; Carlisle, Bishop of, 11; Hal, Prince of Wales ("my unthrifty son"), 31, 133; Langley, Edmund of, Duke of York, 85–87; Northumberland, Earl of, 11; Richard II, King, 11, 50, 85–87; Salisbury, Earl of, 11; Scroop, Sir Stephen, 11

Richard III, 11, 28–29, 53, 87, 103–4
Bishops, 11; Brakenbury, Sir Robert, 29; Buckingham, Duke of, 11; Citizens, 11; Clarence, George Duke of, 29, 53; Gloucester, Richard Duke of (afterward King Richard III), 11, 19, 28–29, 64, 87, 103–4; Lord Mayor, 11

Romeo and Juliet, 4, 5, 8, 9, 10, 19, 20, 46–47, 68, 103, 104, 109, 111, 113–14, 121, 122, 131, 132, 142–43, 166, 167, 169–72, 173
Apothecary, 20; Benvolio, 172; Capulet(s), 8, 103, 132, 170, 172; Capulet, Lady, 10, 132, 172; Chorus, 166, 167, 169–72, 173; Escalus, Prince of Verona, 104, 143, 170; Gregory, 171; John, Friar, 143; Juliet, 8, 10, 19, 20, 46–47, 109, 121, 132, 138, 143, 170, 171–72; Lawrence, Friar, 47, 113, 132, 137, 142, 143, 144, 145, 146; Mercutio, 172; Montague(s), 170, 172; Nurse, 8, 10, 109, 132; Paris, 8, 132, 172; Peter, 19; Romeo, 10, 19, 20, 46–47, 48, 63, 68, 114, 138, 143, 170–72; Sampson, 171; Tybalt, 46, 143

Rose, The, viii

rushes, 5, 9

Sackerson, 62

scenes not shown, 81–97; changes made by film versions, 93, 94, 96, 97; choosing what to show and what not to show, 81–82; controlling audience responses, 92–97; with horses, 87–88; large-scale settings, 88–89; recalled from the past, 89–92; teller(s) of, 84–89, 90–91, 179–82

Schoenbaum, S., 55

Sea Adventure (more usually, Sea Venture), 15

Shaw, George Bernard, 35

Sidney, Sir Philip, 61

Sincler (or Sincklo), John, 20

soliloquizing, 31

soliloquy (soliloquies), 5, 29, 44, 45, 53, 66, 153, 155, 157, 164

Spenser, Edmund, 116

stage: clearing, 44, 163; platform, viii, 5, 24, 29, 159, 160, 169. See also stage post(s)

stage directions, embedded, 6, 7, 48, 72, 132, 148, 154, 160

stage post(s), viii, 5, 12, 13–14, 149, 150, 160

storm(s), 83, 115, 127–30, 178, 180–81; tempest(s), 128. *See also* lightning and thunder

Strachey, Lytton, 76, 77

Styan, J. L., 34

suicide, 3, 138, 139–40, 143

sun, 10, 28, 29, 31, 37, 65, 82, 96, 103, 104; absence of sunlight, 103; dark'ning (*see* dark); obscured, 104; refuses to shine, 103; rising, 103, 104, 105; setting, 105, 108; sunrise, 104–5, 109; sunset(s), 105, 108, 109

Swan, The, viii, 13

swordfight, 14, 87

Taming of the Shrew, The, 9, 20–21, 23, 26–27, 73, 87–88, 122, 134
Bartholomew, 20, 21; Biondello, 87; Grumio, 87; Katherina, 122; Lord, 20, 23, 73; Lucentio, 26; Petruchio, 87, 134; Player, First, 23; Tailor, 20; Tranio, 26

Tempest, The, 6, 7–8, 10, 15, 27, 55–57, 111–12, 127, 129–30, 162
Alonso, King of Naples, 7–8, 57, 111; Ariel, 55, 56, 111; Boatswain, 27, 111; Ferdinand, 7–8, 111, 162; Juno, 15; Master of a Ship, 27; Miranda, 7–8, 112; Prospero, Duke of Milan, 7–8, 10, 55–57, 111–12, 127, 129–30

Temple, Middle, 149–50

Terry, Ellen, 188ch7n9

Theatre, The, 29, 168, 169, 172

Theobald, Lewis, 85

theophanies, 15

thunder, 1, 15, 83, 128, 180, 181; thunderbolt, 15, 83. *See also* lightning; storm(s)

time(s), 11, 23, 38, 61, 98, 109, 174, 180 and *passim;* associations, 112; compression of, 173; of the clock, 110ff; control over, 89, 180; of day, 30–31; large passage of, 179; needed offstage, 44–46; not definite, 100–101; objective and subjective, 111; real, 111–12; right deadly, 153; slipping away, 103; strange-disposed, 129; uncertain, 101–3. *See also* association(s); unities

Timon of Athens, 52, 91, 105

Apemantus, 105; Timon of Athens, 52, 105

tiring-house, viii, 4, 5, 6, 10, 24, 33, 44

Titus Andronicus, 51–52, 64
Aaron, 64, 66, 67; Andronicus, Titus, 51–52; Chiron, 51–52; Demetrius, 51–52; Lavinia, 51–52; Tamora, Queen of the Goths, 51–52

torch(es) and torch bearer(s), 98, 99, 102, 104, 153, 154; torch-staves, 97

"Totus mundus agit histrionem," 16

trapdoor, viii, 4, 5, 9, 12–13, 15

trapeze, 178

Troilus and Cressida, 67, 71, 105, 107, 110, 121, 141, 147, 152–59, 166
Achilles, 107–9, 110–11, 159; Agamemnon, 72; Andromache, 107; Calchas, 72, 153, 154; Cassandra, 107, 109; Cressida, 67, 71–73, 121, 152–59; Diomedes, 71, 72–73, 152–59; Hector, 72, 107–9, 158–59; Nestor, 72; Pandarus, 153, 159; Paris, 72; Patroclus, 108; Priam, King of Troy, 109; Prologue, 166; Thersites, 152–56; Troilus, 71, 72–73, 107, 109, 152–59; Ulysses, 72–73, 110–11, 152–59

Twelfth Night, 7, 15, 18, 19, 21, 22, 26, 27, 28, 32, 35–36, 51, 52, 79–80, 82, 110, 111, 116, 120, 123–24, 137, 141, 147–52, 156, 180
Aguecheek, Sir Andrew, 35, 51, 80, 147–51; Belch, Sir Toby, 18, 21, 28, 35, 51, 80, 147–51; Captain, Sea, 26–27, 116; Fabian, 148–52; Feste, 18, 19, 35, 137, 148, 156; Malvolio, 21, 22, 32, 35–36, 52, 80, 82, 123–24, 147–52; Maria, 21, 35, 36, 51, 82, 123, 147–52; Olivia, 7, 21, 22, 35–36, 51, 110, 123–24, 141, 147, 148, 149, 150–51, 156; Orsino, Duke of Illyria, 18, 22, 111, 116, 141, 148, 180; Sebastian, 26, 51; Viola, 7, 21, 22, 26, 110, 111, 116, 141, 148, 156 (Cesario, 7, 22, 51, 124, 156)

Two Gentlemen of Verona, The, 10–11, 19, 46, 67–68, 69
Julia, 46, 48, 67, 68; Launce, 19; Proteus, 10, 11, 46, 67, 68, 69; Sil-

via, 10, 11, 67, 68; Valentine, 46, 48, 68
Two Noble Kinsmen, The, 56, 166
    Prologue, 166

unities, 38, 61, 173. *See also* time(s)
untruthful behavior, 131–46; and minor characters (Friar Lawrence, Friar Francis, Pisanio, Camillo, Paulina), 32, 135–36, 142–46; bed tricks, 135, 136, 137; exculpation, 131–35, 136–37, 138

van Buchell, Arand, viii
vanity, 82, 148
vengeance, 149, 150, 152, 159. *See also* revenge; vengefulness
vengefulness, 52, 54, 82. *See also* revenge; vengeance

winding gear, 5, 15
Winter's Tale, The, 6–7, 18, 19, 32, 35, 36–37, 51, 53, 54, 62, 82, 111, 112, 122, 129, 131, 132, 135, 136, 142, 143–46, 147, 159–65, 166, 178

Antigonus, 53, 54, 55, 62, 145; Archidamus, 160, 163; Autolycus, 144–45; Bear, 51, 54, 62; Camillo, 35, 54, 135, 136, 142, 143–44, 145, 146, 147, 159, 160, 163–65; Cleomines, 145; Florizel, Prince of Bohemia, 135, 136, 143, 144, 162; Gentlemen, 82; Hermione, queen to Leontes, 6–7, 19, 35, 82, 112, 122, 145–46, 147, 159–65; ladies, 160; Lady, Second, 160; Leontes, King of Sicilia, 6, 7, 35, 36–37, 54, 62, 112, 122, 144–46, 147, 159–65; Mamillius, Prince of Sicilia, 35, 160, 162, 163–64; Paulina, 6–7, 19, 54, 142, 145–46; Perdita, 54, 135, 146; Polixenes, King of Bohemia, 112, 146, 159, 160–65; Shepherd, Old, 54, 162; Son of Old Shepherd, 54; Time as Chorus, 166
Wotton, Sir Henry, 17–18
Wriothesley, Henry, third Earl of Southampton, 77